JAN 1 3 2004

THE POWER OF
ANCIENT FOODS

Dr. Gene S
Rowena Hubbard, RD

Contributions and Foreword by
John W. Farquhar, MD

Book Publishing Company
Summertown, Tennessee

Cover design: Warren Jefferson

Published in the United States by
Book Publishing Company
P.O. Box 99
Summertown, TN 38483
1-888-260-8458

Printed in the United States

ISBN 1-57067-140-0

08 07 06 05 04 03   6 5 4 3 2 1

Spiller, Gene A.
  The power of ancient foods / by Gene Spiller and Rowena Hubbard ;
contributions and foreword by John W. Farquhar.
      p. cm.
Includes bibliographical references and index.
  ISBN 1-57067-140-0
  1. Nutrition. 2. Food--History. 3. Natural foods. I. Hubbard,
Rowena. II. Title.

RA784.S6565 2003
641.3'009--dc21

                          2002155263

Khoshaf (Dried Fruit Salad) and Ful Medames (Egyptian Brown Beans) recipes
from *Mediterranean Cookery* by Claudia Roden. Copyright © 1987 by Claudia
Roden. Reprinted with permission of the author and Alfred A. Knopf, Inc.

The Traditional Healthy Mediterranean Diet Pyramid used with permission of
Oldways Preservation & Exchange Trust, Boston, MA ©1994

"Grapes, An Ancient Gift of Nature to Mankind" and "Precious Compounds in
Grapes" reprinted by permission of Sphera Foundation.

Seek real, whole foods, the foods of ancient peoples, the foods that have sustained and provided vitality to humanity for millennia.

In these foods find joy, health, and strength and discover how easy and enjoyable it is to keep fit and well.

To these ancient peoples, this book is dedicated.

TABLE OF CONTENTS

≈ PREFACE ≈

This book tells us how centuries ago the native peoples of the Americas, Europe, Asia, and Africa sought out foods packed with basic nutrients and protective factors, long before modern science gave a sophisticated chemical name to these compounds and studied their biochemical mechanisms of action. Together, we'll travel the world: It will be an exciting journey full of history, lore, science, and recipes that will change the way you look at foods and plan your meals forever. The foods chosen and the suggestions for their use combine the best knowledge of modern science and medicine with the best wisdom of ancient civilizations.

Many of the foods we'll encounter on our journey can be found in every good food store in North America; sometimes a food more difficult to find on a store shelf will be introduced for the reader who is willing to search it out or grow it. The foods and recipes in this book will help you not only make major steps in staying fit, controlling body weight, and preventing chronic diseases, but will bring joy to your meals—for without joy no dietary suggestion will be followed for long.

≈ FOREWORD ≈

Through tribal wisdom, human beings took millennia to discover the benefits of certain patterns of eating and certain foods. Folk wisdom, acquired by natural experiments, evolved into food choices that were adapted by ancient peoples for their survival. The selection process was a very gradual one. Food choices that produced disease or lack of energy in a large portion of the population would quickly fall into disfavor. We cannot go back 2,000 years or more to re-create the way of life that existed then, nor would we want to. What we can do now to achieve optimum health, longevity, and disease prevention—and to cultivate food with the least damage to our environment—is to apply the scientific knowledge of ancient foods to our benefit, with the confidence that this knowledge is supported by centuries of consumption of these foods.

Consider how wise it is to eat the whole, unrefined foods that sustained ancient peoples. Every day we learn more fascinating facts about the protective value of certain food compounds such as the antioxidant phenolic compounds of grapes, raisins, and other fruits and vegetables. These are present in whole, unrefined plant foods, many of which were only yesterday important merely as flavors or colors. And these whole, unrefined ancient grains, beans, nuts, seeds, fresh fruits and vegetables, and other foods were the foundation of the diet of farming societies for millennia.

In the last century, technology has changed many of these foods. The milling and refining of grain has gone so far now that the white flour we eat is "whiter" than ever before. In the process, all the wheat germ and similar constituents of the grains are removed, right along with their vitamin E, other vitamins and minerals, fiber and plant sterols—important in cholesterol lowering—and many other precious compounds. It is crucial that these refined foods not be the foundation of our diet.

If people instead make the foundation of their diet the whole, unrefined plant foods that have been used for millennia, they will have made a giant step toward chronic disease prevention.

John W. Farquhar, M.D.

THE POWER OF ANCIENT FOODS

≈ ACKNOWLEDGEMENTS ≈

This book would not have been possible without the talent of so many contributors in medicine and food preparation. John W. Farquhar, M.D., is professor emeritus of medicine at Stanford University School of Medicine and the founder of the Center for Research in Disease Prevention, also at Stanford University. The author of many scientific publications on disease prevention, he is also a pioneer in this field, especially with relation to heart disease. He is the coauthor of various international declarations on disease prevention, such as the Victoria Declaration (Canada) of 1993 and the Catalonia Declaration (Spain) of 1995.

Letters to one of the authors (Dr. Spiller) from the late Denis Burkitt, M.D., and the late Hugh Trowell, M.D., the two cofounders of the fiber era in nutrition, brought the insight of these two great physicians-epidemiologists regarding the problems of Western refined diets to this book. This material is precious and we are extremely grateful for their posthumous contributions.

Cornelia Carlson has a degree in food research and a Ph.D. in molecular biology. For many years, she owned the renowned Spice House store in Palo Alto, California. She has studied spices and herbs extensively, is the author of *A Practically Meatless Gourmet*, and is currently working on a major book on spices and herbs while writing articles about them for popular magazines. She has contributed her in-depth knowledge of every aspect of herbs.

Many cookbook authors and chefs have added their touch to the recipes. A dear friend, Deborah Madison, who contributed great recipes to our previous book, *The Superpyramid Eating*

Program, is widely recognized for her books *The Greens Cook Book* (a best-seller) and *The Savory Way*. She was the founding chef of the Greens Restaurant in San Francisco, teaches cooking classes across the United States and elsewhere, and has won prizes for her work.

Lorna Sass, Ph.D., is a cookbook author and food historian who contributes articles to many major magazines in the United States and is the author of *Cooking Under Pressure, Recipes from an Ecological Kitchen*, and *Complete Vegetarian Kitchen*. Her contribution focused on preparing fast ancient food meals using modern pressure cooking.

Claudia Roden is the author of many well-known cookbooks on Mediterranean cuisine, including *A Book of Middle Eastern Food, The Good Foods of Italy*, and *Mediterranean Cookery*. She is the host of the BBC-TV series "Mediterranean Cookery." She has contributed two very special recipes from Egypt and the Middle East.

Aglaia Kremezi lives in Athens, Greece, and is a renowned author of books on Greek cuisine, including the beautifully illustrated and filled with fabulous recipes *The Foods of Greece*.

Jesse Cool is the owner and chef of the Flea Street Cafe near Stanford University and the author of *Tomatoes—A Country Garden Cookbook* and of the forthcoming *Onions—A Country Garden Cookbook*. She specializes in using whole, natural foods in traditional ethnic recipes. Jesse also writes a produce column for the *San Jose Mercury News*.

Monica Spiller has worked with and studied ancient, natural leavenings for whole grain breads and ancient wheats. She is the author of the section "The Superpyramid Bakery," in Gene Spiller's *The Superpyramid Eating Program*, and the author of *The Barm Bakers' Book*. She has taught professional baking classes at Mission College in California, is actively engaged in developing recipes using ancient barm leavening, and is a consultant to bakers on leavening whole grain breads using ancient barms. She has been a consistent and inspiring supporter of the concept of ancient breads.

Tsukiko Hattori is an expert in the ancient culinary traditions of both Japan and China and is chairman of the Hattori Nutrition College and the Institute of Hattori Cooking in Tokyo. Widely renowned in her own country for her in-depth knowledge of both modern and ancient styles of Japanese and Chinese cooking, Tsukiko has been the chef for important traditional imperial ceremonies in Japan.

Leslie Cerier has done extensive work with teff, the Ethiopian grain. She is the author of a forthcoming cookbook, *The Quick and Easy Organic Gourmet*, with over 200 whole food recipes and is a consultant on recipe development to U.S. teff farmers.

Jody Main was the author of many Asian and American recipes for *The Superpyramid Eating Program*. She has contributed recipes to other books and writes newsletters and recipes for San Francisco Bay Area whole food stores and for Silicon Valley food services.

The late Hazel Gibson of Los Altos and Wai Tu of Alameda contributed their fine drawings to this book. Hazel's drawings remind us of her great talent, which is missed. Wai Tu has contributed his fine artwork and graphic designs to many food companies and other clients nationwide.

Our friends Sara Baer-Sinnott, Dun Gifford, and Greg Drescher of the Oldways Preservation & Exchange Trust in Boston have helped us to increase our awareness of traditional, ancient, and real foods. Scott Hubbard has shared his knowledge of ancient Roman foods and brought to our attention the use of grains on one of the very earliest coins in existence, the ancient Mesopotamian silver stater.

Rosemary Schmele assisted in all phases of the manuscript's development.

Many books and publications have been the source of the facts and stories that are the foundation of this book. They are listed in the References, but *Indian Givers* by Jack Weatherford and *America's First Cuisines* by Sophie Coe deserve a special mention. It was *Indian Givers* that inspired us to start this book with the Americas. Also extremely valuable was *The Complete Book of Fruits and Vegetables* by Francesco Bianchini and his coauthors.

1 ≋

ANCIENT FOOD WISDOM

Once upon a time, people from every continent discovered and grew great foods for joy, health, and strength. Highly sophisticated agricultural practices evolved that made possible a constant supply of these precious foods from the land. Beautiful fields of crops covered mountain slopes, valleys, and plains. Without our modern laboratories, computer-driven statistics, and national organizations to tell them what or what not to eat to prevent disease and live a long life, these ancient people knew many of the answers in the quest for healthful, nourishing foods.

Ancient foods were the staples upon which the native populations relied to build energy and prevent disease. The inhabitants of many regions of the earth long ago discovered that certain foods from the land would give them strength and keep them healthy throughout their life span—that's why these foods became the foundation of many ancient diets. Over the centuries, people would see other men and women in good health with no major illnesses or—on the opposite side—people sick with chronic diseases that led to death or to a life of disability and pain. Health and disease became linked to the food people ate (or didn't eat) and their way of life. Had ancient farmers not known how to find the best possible food, there would be no human beings alive today!

In our modern fervor to research what's good for us, we are finding out that keeping healthy can be very simple, but we are finding this out at great cost. In order to choose a more healthful way to eat we expect formal statements by major research or government organizations—all this while the peasants of Crete and the Incas of Peru knew ages ago all we need to know about healthful foods.

The stories in this book will remind us that eating should be a gentle, beautiful experience, free from the painful thought that we need to count each little item we eat and that healthful eating is equivalent to suffering. Don't look for calorie-counting or grams of fat in the recipes in this book. Trust us: Nothing in this book is high in undesirable fats or low in the good stuff of life.

NUTRITION OF THE ANCIENTS

When we look at the foods that ancient peoples ate and add up all their nutrients, we find that a combination of those unrefined foods supplied a perfect balance of life-giving, health-protective compounds. Combine, like the ancient South American Incas, whole grains, beans, peppers, avocados, and tomatoes, add some amaranth leaves grown in virgin soils rich in minerals, and you have a marvelous dish that is super-rich in protective nutrients: the B vitamins and vitamin E of the whole grains with their good carbohydrates; the great protein combination of grains and beans consumed at the same meal, the vitamin C, the beta-carotene (which becomes vitamin A in the body) and other carotenes of the peppers, tomatoes, and amaranth leaves; and the minerals present in all these unrefined foods. Add the good unsaturated fats of the avocado and of the germ of grains and you have a well-balanced diet. The same holds true for the native foods of the ancient peoples of all the regions of the world, or none of these people would have survived.

These people would occasionally stray from a good diet, as most humans do, but then the real food of the land would again become the foundation of their meals. Sadly enough, other factors destroyed some of the great civilizations of the past. The Inca Empire, for instance, was destroyed by infectious diseases brought by the Spanish conquerors.

It's hard for sophisticated researchers at the dawn of the twenty-first century to admit that, most likely, we already know all we need to know to stay healthy. But let the scientists not feel anxious, distressed, or troubled: We still need research to reassure our modern minds that we are indeed on the right track and to rediscover that a grain such as amaranth—worshipped by the Aztecs as sacred—is a great grain!

THE DEGENERATION OF ANCIENT EATING PATTERNS

Traditional food patterns can lead to delightful, joyful meals and allow us to enjoy an amazing variety of menus. For many complex reasons, these traditional patterns have been changing and degenerating with the influx of misused technology, over-refining of whole grains, more and more preparation of meals at home from processed foods, and increased use of meats and related products. As civilization moves in, or as people move to industrialized countries, the pace of life becomes so fast and intense that prepared or fast foods become the normal way of life, rather than the occasional meal they should be.

The problem is not fast foods in their proper role as part of an occasional meal or as a snack between meals. The problem is fast or prepared foods as the staples of life. Jack, for instance, is single, sixty-five, and lives in a suburban town just south of San Francisco. His life is easy; he retired early and has an income from a small business that takes only a few hours of his time each day. You'd think that Jack would have the time to prepare most of his meals at home. Wrong: *He eats mostly frozen dinners and other prepared foods.* He took a nutrition course and analyzed the nutrients in these prepared dinners as part of a class project; they were often low in many vital components and usually contained refined ingredients such as white flour or sugar. It would have been as easy for him to cook some brown rice or beans, prepare a few fresh vegetables, and maybe add a bowl of yogurt. Instead, his diet was far from the traditional, whole ancient foods that could have done so much for him.

THE COMPLEXITY OF UNREFINED, WHOLE FOODS

A few years ago we thought we knew everything about what we needed in foods for good health: certain vitamins and minerals, certain
types of proteins, some carbohydrates. These were the early days of
nutritional science, and the discoveries of the early nutritionists made
possible a knowledge of foods unequaled in history. But as soon as we
thought we knew all about nutrition, how much we needed of this or
that vitamin or what kind of protein was best for us, researchers slowly unveiled a totally different aspect of food and health. The focus
became the prevention of "killer diseases," such as cancer and heart
disease, or diseases of aging, such as afflictions of the colon, which if
not "killers," were quite unpleasant and potentially dangerous or
painful.

Researchers began with the understanding that an excess of animal fats could be harmful and that fiber deficiency could lead to heart
disease or certain types of cancer. Plant sterols were found to lower
blood cholesterol. Later scientists discovered new aspects of vitamins
and minerals related to their antioxidant properties. Beta-carotene,
vitamin C, vitamin E, and selenium were discussed as protective
against cancer, heart disease, and cataracts. Soon compounds with
powerful protective properties, which were neither vitamins nor minerals, and which were found in whole foods, often in minute quantities, became a major focus of medical and food research. Today the
list of these protective compounds is so long that a whole book could
be written just about them. The list includes phenolics, phytoestrogens, isoflavonoids and bioflavonoids, carotenes such as lutein,
lycopene, and many other compounds.

In the chapters that follow we travel around the world in search
of the great foods of ancient peoples. We'll encounter foods rich in
many of these compounds and learn more about some of their newly
discovered protective effects.

Here in the third millennium, refined foods, such as polished
grains, white flours, and sugar, appear to be even more deficient than
previously thought. We have begun to understand that adding back
just a few vitamins and minerals is not enough, and that a host of

protective compounds may have been removed and lost through refinement. It now appears almost naive that "enriched" bread should have just a few added vitamins and minerals. Why not leave the entire beauty and benefit of the kernel with its germ and bran "whole" in the first place?

Prepare part of your meal from fresh foods often. Get back in touch with what food really is and you'll have made a major step in understanding what health-giving foods should be.

THE REFINING OF FLOUR AND WESTERN DISEASES

"I came back to England after many years as a medical missionary in Africa to find the kind of diseases that I had not seen in the natives of Uganda, but had seen often in British people living there," Dr. Denis Burkitt, a famous British physician, wrote to us a few years ago. "I began to research all this with my dear friend [Dr.] Hugh [Trowell], and the hypothesis of unrefined food was born, a hypothesis that led to our books *Dietary Fiber, Fiber Depleted Foods and Disease,* and *Western Diseases: Their Emergence and Prevention.*"

This concept—that when refined flour becomes the only type of flour used (there is a place for occasional use of these flours), the body suffers—is not new. In the nineteenth century other medical pioneers had written about this subject, but most of the scientific and medical community looked down on them as extremists. Today there is no doubt that problems develop when refined grains and their products become the only type used, but habits are difficult to change. Many people have grown up—consciously or not—with the idea that white bread equals affluence and dark bread equals poverty.

REFINED DRINKS

Even drinks that are refined are very popular today. We drink cola or other soft drinks instead of ancient beverages such as tea, which contains many compounds that have positive physiological effects, such as the phenolic compounds of green teas (page 259). Cola drinks contain caffeine (if not decaffeinated) and pure sugar (or an artificial sweetener). Distilled alcoholic beverages, such as vodka, whisky, and gin, contain very little other than the alcohol itself and should be considered "refined" foods. Wine and beer, on the other hand, are rich sources of many other compounds. Red wine, for example, is a treasure chest of antioxidants. Should you choose to drink alcohol, wine and beer are your most healthful choices.

 Dr. Farquhar on refining

When we refine foods such as flours we know some of the things we have lost, for example, vitamin E from the wheat germ. But what else have we lost? We don't yet know, and don't know whether these other lost substances may have benefits and may work together with other known nutrients to maintain health. This is the difficulty of the reductionist approach, where we take a lot of things away and then give back a few of them, cross our fingers, and hope that we've restored all of the potential health benefits of the still unidentified substances that were removed.

ADDING UP THE "REFINED" FOODS IN INDUSTRIALIZED SOCIETIES

The question is not whether it's "bad" to put a cube of white sugar in your tea or eat a cookie that is made with white flour. The real question is how often we do it, and—just as important—what other foods we eat that day or that week. It's all right to eat some refined foods as long as the foundation of your diet is made up of unrefined grains, beans, vegetables, fruits, and other whole foods. But if your regular diet is based on white bread (remember that hamburger on a white bun you had for lunch?), high intake of foods such as meat and white sugar–rich foods, and if your regular beverage is a sugar–based soft drink, the picture changes. It is not the amount of all the precious nutrients in a single food that is going to make a difference in your life; it is the sum of all the foods you eat. There is a place, in the fast pace of our modern life, for prepared foods, for some refined foods, and for an occasional white sugar–sweetened food. Some properly formulated foods are in fact high in nutrition and may be just the right supplement to your diet. But we must make the staples of our diet ancient, unrefined foods.

THE FOOD INDUSTRY CAN HELP

Food technology has done—and can continue to do—much to help us, but it should be used properly to make available to us whole foods in their unrefined state or prepared foods with their wholeness and integrity preserved. But even properly designed and prepared whole foods should never entirely replace home preparation of a meal from scratch. People become too removed from real foods if their daily routine is opening a package of precooked, preflavored food to be microwaved as a complete dinner day after day. Convenience foods have a place, but they should not become our daily staples. Let's prepare our food at home more often. And let's demand the right foods from fast-food outlets, based on ancient, unrefined ingredients. If we must eat fast foods because of our busy schedule, let's search for prepared foods that are based on whole, ancient ingredients.

FORGOTTEN ANCIENT CROPS OR BIOTECH FOODS?

Some ancient crops that have been the staples of many civilizations for centuries are now on the verge of being lost to us forever or relegated to a very small role in feeding the world and in keeping us healthy. We spend millions of dollars to develop new, bioengineered food crops, while investments in reviving forgotten ancient crops are very modest. Why not look again to growing the great ancient foods that have been tested by centuries of use, many of which have tremendous built-in resistance to diseases or pests? Why not balance our agricultural budgets and efforts by placing at least as much emphasis on growing ancient foods as in developing new ones?

One of the great books of the 1990s—little known outside scientific circles—is *Lost Crops of the Incas,* compiled by a distinguished panel of scientists and published under the auspices of the National Research Council in Washington, a highly respected organization.

This book offers many examples of the ancient foods of the Incas, some very much in use today, but many others forgotten or just slowly making a comeback. *Kiwicha,* now known as amaranth, one of the great grains of the ancient Americas, is coming back into use. Others, such as a potato with a natural resistance to a mite that is a major potato pest, are practically unknown and could one day be extinct. Some agricultural groups, such as Seeds of Change in New Mexico, are working on the preservation of these species, which are usually high in nutritional value and selected for resistance to various pests or weather conditions and which could be reestablished as important crops with just a little effort.

 Dr. Farquhar on bioengineered foods

Bioengineered foods are a phenomenon of the last decade of the twentieth century, something that has never happened before. We are modifying the very genetic core of the plant cell by human technologies not available until just a few years ago. Sometimes animal and plant genes are crossed. If a new tomato keeps so well, or if a new strawberry is so resistant to frost, something must be different in its composition. We need to know more about all this before these foods become a major part of our diet.

WEIGHT CONTROL

A 1994 government report—widely reported by the press—finds that while Americans eat less fat than in the 1970s, the percentage of obese and overweight people is higher now than ever, about 35 percent of the population. The problem is quite simple: We are basing our diets on meat and related products combined with too many refined foods, such as white flour.

Weight loss and weight control—a major concern for people of all ages—should be based on a diet high in unrefined, ancient foods from plants. This diet will let people enjoy great meals with no fear of weight gain. No one will feel starved on the real, whole foods found in this book. Weight control for a healthy person should not mean suffering, but just following a few simple rules.

Dr. Farquhar on weight loss

There is no doubt that weight problems are caused not only by lack of physical activity but by the consumption of mass-produced convenience foods with high caloric density (calories per ounce) and with large amounts of fat, often saturated, that are hidden from the consumer. These foods are always available and reasonably low-priced for any time that you might feel any twinge of hunger. It is different for lower caloric density ancient foods with their own fiber still present, foods that take a longer time to chew and digest. For weight loss, these foods—whole grains, beans, and fruits and vegetables—must be the foundation of the diet. For weight maintenance, some natural higher-fat foods—such as nuts and olive oil—bring a proper balance of good fats and add flavor that makes you feel satisfied. These fats from nuts and certain oils, such as the oil of the olive or sesame, will not cause blood cholesterol problems.

Be careful with lowfat or nonfat foods. Most people think, "They're fat-free, I can eat all I want!" But we all know this is not true. All foods supply calories and if you eat too much of them you will gain weight!

FATS: THE RIGHT KIND AND THE RIGHT AMOUNT

The choice of how much fat and what kind of fat is easy when we choose real, natural fats from plants in the form either of oils or of fat-rich foods such as nuts, avocados, olives, and sunflower or pumpkin seeds. When these fats are part of the diet we need not fear that some new research is going to tell us that we are way off track and that something else would be better. Here are the facts:

1. Keep fats from land animals low. This means fats from meat, poultry, and milk products, including butter. Keep to a minimum artificial fats, such as hydrogenated fats.

2. Fats from fish are much better than other animal fats.

3. Use unrefined oils from plants for cooking and dressing food.

4. Feel free to use, in moderation, fat-containing foods such as avocados, nuts (and their nonhydrogenated butters), sunflower and sesame seeds, olives, and other seeds or fruits.

5. When using oils prefer the ones with a reasonable percentage of monounsaturated fats. Excellent choices are the ancient Mediterranean oils of the olive or sesame. We need some polyunsaturated fats and these should come from whole foods or unrefined oils rich in protective antioxidants.

Remember that fats in the body do not live a life of their own; the other foods that we eat have a major impact on how much or little fat we should have.

HERBS AND SPICES: THE KEY TO EXCITING DISHES

Herbs and spices are much more than wonderful flavors. Each day science discovers some new component that is protective against disease. Rosemary is a good example of an herb rich in antioxidants, which, added to the many other antioxidants in other foods from plants, can play a role in the health–disease balance in our lives. Sharp peppers contain capsaicin, used as a painkiller, and pungent herbs such as horseradish help to stimulate digestive secretions.

Many times people relate the flavor of an herb to the basic food of a well-liked dish. J. B. and his wife are in their early forties and somewhat overweight. Their diet is high in meats with a considerable amount of fat. One evening they went to dinner at the home of Janet and David. They knew, and were willing to accept, that there would be no meat that evening. When they arrived, a wonderful aroma filled the house. They were sure that Janet, a great cook, had prepared a meat dish and yet they could not quite believe it. Soon they discovered that the aroma was from rosemary and thyme, herbs often used in roasting beef and pork. This story reminds us that often the flavor we enjoy is not the main ingredient itself, but the herb or spice used in preparing the dish. Herbs and spices play a key role in making a meal enjoyable.

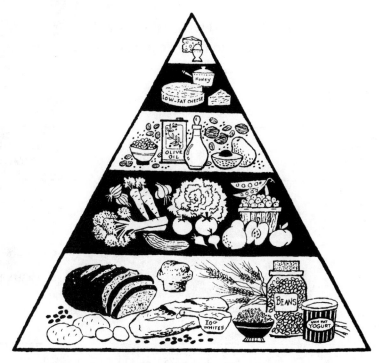

The Superpyramid

ANCIENT FOODS ON "FOOD PYRAMIDS"

To help us balance our meal of ancient foods, food pyramids are a great tool. Quite a few food pyramids have been suggested by researchers, organizations, and government agencies in recent years to guide people in their choice of healthful foods. One of the first dates back to the early 1970s and was suggested by a Swedish nutritionist. The various pyramids differ in some aspects in their ranking of foods, but they all agree on two key points: (1) that grains should be one of the foundations of the diet and one of the major sources of energy, and (2) that vegetables and fruits are the great protective foods that should regularly complement the foods of tier one.

Grains are always on the first tier of all these food pyramids, and fruits and vegetables are on the second tier. In all these pyramids, beans and lowfat dairy products play a key role in balancing the nutrients of the other foods. Beans should be on the first tier of all pyramids, but the low emphasis on beans in industrialized society, or perhaps their aura of being "the food of the poor," has moved them

FOOD GUIDE PYRAMID
A Guide to Daily Food Choices

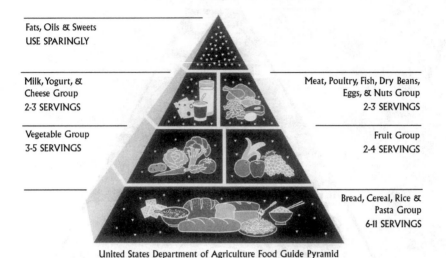

Fats, Oils & Sweets
USE SPARINGLY

Milk, Yogurt, &
Cheese Group
2-3 SERVINGS

Meat, Poultry, Fish, Dry Beans,
Eggs, & Nuts Group
2-3 SERVINGS

Vegetable Group
3-5 SERVINGS

Fruit Group
2-4 SERVINGS

Bread, Cereal, Rice &
Pasta Group
6-11 SERVINGS

United States Department of Agriculture Food Guide Pyramid

> We find some differences in the ways oils and nuts are used, and
> the low emphasis on these foods is another flaw of the USDA food
> pyramid of 1992. Olive oil, for instance, is a great, healthful oil and
> should not be confused with animal or hydrogenated fats.

THE TRADITIONAL HEALTHY MEDITERRANEAN DIET PYRAMID

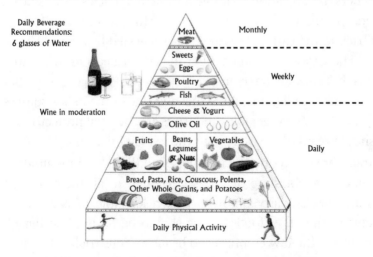

Daily Beverage
Recommendations:
6 glasses of Water

Meat   Monthly

Sweets

Eggs

Poultry   Weekly

Fish

Wine in moderation   Cheese & Yogurt

Olive Oil

Fruits   Beans,   Vegetables
          Legumes   Daily
          & Nuts

Bread, Pasta, Rice, Couscous, Polenta,
Other Whole Grains, and Potatoes

Daily Physical Activity

Mediterranean Diet Pyramid of Oldways Preservation & Exchange Trust

up to the third tier of the United States Department of Agriculture (USDA) pyramid, one of its major flaws. Other pyramids place them on either the first or second tier, where they belong. Similarly, the USDA pyramid fails to separate lowfat dairy products from high-fat ones, placing them all together.

The Superpyramid we developed with other researchers in the mid-1980s (found in *The Superpyramid Eating Program* by Gene Spiller) divides dairy products according to their fat content and places them on higher or lower tiers accordingly.

While no vegetable oil should be used in excess, we just can't put it together with saturated fats. Both the Mediterranean pyramid and our own Superpyramid place more emphasis on proper oils and nuts than does the USDA pyramid, while de-emphasizing meats, poultry, and related foods.

The flaws of some food pyramids notwithstanding, they all emphasize the kind of diet that was typical of ancient people. Did we have to come to the dawn of a new millennium to find out that we really knew the best foods for good health centuries ago?

Laurel Walks the Ancient Food Path

Laurel, a business administrator, decided to participate in a recent study at our center in the San Francisco Bay Area about the effect of whole, real, ancient, unrefined foods on people with high blood cholesterol.

"When I first began the study diet in July," says Laurel, "I had no idea what I was getting into! My doctor had told me that I had high blood cholesterol, so I answered an ad in the paper for this study. Keeping the food record for the first three days was no problem. As a veteran of many diets, I was accustomed to writing down all that I ate. Until the study began, my eating habits were of the most recent (I thought) theory of very lowfat eating. I would try to eat as little fat as possible. Of course, this did not stop me from indulging in all the new fat-free goodies on the market!

"At one time I had attended a class on controlling cholesterol at a local hospital and found it of little help. I figured having researchers and nutritionists working with me might make a difference. I expected the study to be the typical fat-reduced diet. The Mediterranean diet that was presented to me at our initial meeting was a bit of a surprise: It was a diet moderate but not too low in fat, and all the foods were real, whole, unrefined foods. I could not believe it!

"After reviewing all the required food I was shocked to find out the quantity of fats I was to consume: olive oil, nuts, nut butters—even avocados! This seemed to be contrary to all the books I had read up to that time. Add to this the raisins, the sunflower seeds, the special whole-grain breads, and the beans to be eaten and I felt overwhelmed, even a bit of panic. I didn't want to gain weight either!

"I had no problem eliminating all meat products and processed foods; I seldom ate them anyway. And I had no problem eating all the bread, raisins, beans, rice, and all the other whole unrefined foods we were supposed to eat.

"But after a few days on this diet, I was feeling very bloated. My digestive system was not accustomed to the high-fiber diet. This also wreaked havoc with my problem of chronic constipation. I was all backed up! But about halfway into the second week, something amazing happened: I realized that my constipation was a thing of the past. I was actually regular on a daily basis! I no longer felt bloated and was thinking of how to prepare the foods required in the study in ways that my family might also enjoy. I started to peruse my extensive library of cookbooks and recipes, thinking of ways to use the ingredients the study required. This was what inspired me to create what turned out to be some of my family's favorite dishes. And at the end of the fourth week my blood cholesterol was down."

LEARNING FROM LAUREL

There is an important message in Laurel's story: When we begin to eat natural, unrefined plant foods, when whole grains replace white flours and polished rice, when we eat more beans, fruits, and vegetables, and all the other great plant foods that should be the foundation of a good diet, some time is required for adaptation. A digestive system accustomed to a low-fiber, meat-based diet needs time to change.

Usually, depending on our previous eating habits, a couple of weeks should be enough. The "gas" and bloating experienced in the first few days disappears and you feel great and light.

Dr. Farquhar sums up key points on food and chronic diseases

Research has exploded in the last forty years in defining the relationship of different types of foods or combinations of foods to coronary artery disease and the process of atherosclerosis (clogging of the blood vessels), to stroke, to osteoporosis, and to various cancers—especially breast, rectal, and prostate cancers. Increasing your consumption of whole grains, beans, fruits, and vegetables, and making plant foods such as nuts and olive oil your sources of fat, are major steps in disease prevention.

BEYOND ANCIENT FOODS FOR TOTAL HEALTH

The ancient peasants of the Inca empire, of ancient Greece and Rome, or of anywhere else in the world had something else in common: the necessity for much more intense physical activity than in our time. Over the centuries, as more and more of what we call "civilization" evolved, the rich and powerful began to consider physical activity as equivalent to peasant's labor. Similarly, intellectuals shunned physical activity as something inferior to them, something we find true even today, although fortunately to a much lesser extent. Bellini, for example, one of the great Italian composers of the nineteenth century, was frail and sitting at the piano day after day did not help him: No one in those days would have thought to suggest to him some kind of physical activity. The exceptions were few and far between and did not apply to the majority of the rich and powerful; a few of them were physically active hunting, horseback riding, and mountain climbing, but the majority were sedentary. Military people were one of the exceptions, as they had to be and look fit. Not to have to engage in physical activity was considered a privilege. The fat, powerful people with rounded faces we find in some Renaissance and baroque paintings tell us how true this is. Tennis, skiing, and similar sports became acceptable in recent times, but a man or woman of means jogging in the streets was unheard of until recently and in some countries a jogger in the streets is still a strange sight.

No diet can assure the best possible health, given our inherited strengths and weaknesses, unless it goes together with some of each of the three basic kinds of physical activity: aerobics (as in jogging), stretching (as in yoga), and weight-bearing activity (as in lifting weights). If you have time to go to a stadium to watch a ball game, why not try playing it yourself instead? The human body was made to be physically active.

That tobacco smoking is harmful over time and that illegal drugs do damage is well known. But too often the dangers of self-medication with over-the-counter drugs and careless or improper use of prescription medications are ignored. Television ads lead us to use painkillers and other medications as though they were something that we can use daily with no side effects. Remember, any powerful drug has side effects and should be used with great care and proper professional advice.

And now we are off on a trip around the world, in search of the great foods that kept ancient peoples strong and healthy… and we'll find easy-to-prepare and gourmet recipes to please everyone.

2 ≈

SEARCHING THE WORLD
FOR THE FOODS OF
ANCIENT PEOPLES

BEYOND CHANGE

The ancient foods you'll read about in this book have such a long history of use that we can feel confident that medical and scientific progress won't tell us someday that they were not as good as we thought they were or that they might be bad for us. These foods have been tested in the laboratory of life for hundreds of life spans, the kind of test no one can repeat even in a few decades or the lifetime of any medical researcher.

THE GIFTS OF ANCIENT AMERICANS TO THE WORLD

Our journey starts in South and Central America, Mexico, and the Southwestern United States, the lands of the Incas, Aztecs, Mayas, Anasazi, and many other ancient Indian cultures. Where else could it start? These American regions have given the world more great foods than any other continent. There is something almost magic in these native American foods, foods that have changed the way of eating of so many regions of the world and that, like the potato, have saved many people from starvation in past centuries. Many common, great foods we use every day have their origins in the Americas. Potatoes, tomatoes, squashes, corn, pinto beans, and avocados—these are the great gifts of ancient native Americans to the world.

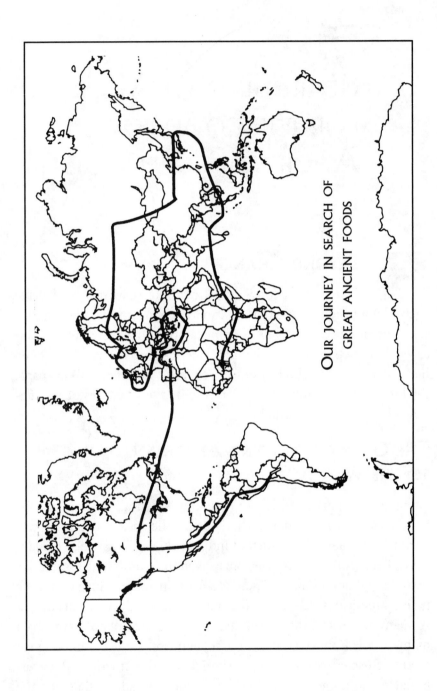

Our journey in search of great ancient foods

And the Americas gave us lesser-known foods that deserve to become more popular again, such as amaranth, quinoa, and the purple potato. In this book we have divided the Americas into three great regions: the foods of the Incas and other South Americans, the foods of the Aztecs, Mayas, and Anasazi, who lived in temperate or warm regions, and the foods of the Ojibwa, who lived in the cold central northern plains of North America.

It is sad that the foods of these ancient Americans are so often forgotten or relegated to a very minor role in some otherwise great books about these peoples. It is as though their ceramics, buildings, and textiles were the only heritage they left. Perhaps we should blame the way history is taught: It's primarily a history of wars, of heads of states, of political upheavals, freedom, and slavery. Just as important is the history of foods and crops, for it is because of these crops that we are alive today!

Anthropologist Jack Weatherford, in his book *Indian Givers*, says it so well: "American foods brought about the miracle of centuries of prayer, what work and medicine have been unable to do: they cured Europe of the episodic famines that had been one of the major restraints on the population for millennia." And he reminds us that, "The protein supply of the Old World also increased with the great variety of beans brought in from the Americas."

We'll find some wonderful grains (yellow, white, and blue corn), all kinds of potatoes (including the lesser-known purple potato), pinto and other American beans, leeks, tomatoes, squashes, peppers (sharp and sweet), pecans, and avocados. And we'll find cocoa, a food that contains one of the few saturated fats that does not raise your blood cholesterol. Most of these foods have traveled far and wide. Less well-traveled, but beginning to make their wonders known, are quinoa and amaranth—two fabulous grains we'll encounter on our trek—the latter making fast inroads in both Europe and the United States. We'll also find chia seeds and cactus paddles. As we move to the northern central plains of the U.S. Midwest and southern Canada, we'll encounter the wild rice of the Ojibwa Indians. Sunchokes and cranberries will round out the gifts of the Americas to our present-day life.

THE GIFTS OF ANCIENT EUROPE AND NORTH AFRICA

In the Mediterranean countries—Italy, Greece, Provence, North African countries, the Middle East—the foods of the Mediterranean Triad (page 110) are at the top of the list. The grains are wheat and barley consumed as breads and pastas, the Old World beans (lentils and chickpeas), grapes and their products (raisins and wine), and olives and their oils. Other great native foods include cultured milk products (of which yogurt is the best known), sesame seeds and their butter (tahini), almonds, hazelnuts, and walnuts.

In northern Europe, in Scotland, and in the Scandinavian countries, the colder climates limited the kind of foods that could be grown. Here we find kale and other greens, barley and oats, sea vegetation, rye breads and crackers, cultured milks, and dried fruits.

In Russia and surrounding regions such as the Ukraine, the climate ranges from very cold in the extreme north to mild and temperate in the south. Typical foods include buckwheat, beets and other root vegetables, cabbage, mushrooms, pomegranates, and cultured milks.

THE GIFTS OF ANCIENT ASIA AND EQUATORIAL AFRICA

In China, Japan, Southeast Asia, and India, rice, soybean products (tofu, tempeh, miso) and other beans, sea plants, starchy roots, and garlic, combined with other native vegetables and fruits, have been the foundation of the diet for centuries. The soybean has become a major crop in North America today and its products—from oils to tofu, tempeh, miso, soy beverages, and concentrated proteins—supply one of the great proteins of the plant kingdom. Garlic, even though widely used in ancient times in Mediterranean countries, probably originated in central Asia. For centuries, garlic has been considered a "healing" food for its antibiotic properties, and today we know that it beneficially affects blood coagulation and blood cholesterol levels.

In equatorial Africa, teff is the ancient staple grain in Ethiopia, while in Ghana and Uganda underground vegetables are basic sources of energy. Teff is a small grain that deserves a better place in Western kitchens, for it is one of the nutritionally rich "small" grains, like amaranth and quinoa.

Spices and Herbs

Many of these foods need the added "life" of herbs and spices to make them into delicious and appealing dishes that we can eat day after day. On our various stops during our journey around the world, we'll search for spices and herbs indigenous to the various regions. Many of them have traveled to other continents. The health-protective properties of flavoring herbs and spices are often overlooked today, yet many of them were considered medicinal in past centuries. Mixtures of herbs and spices, as used by the native populations, will add to our understanding of the ways of each region of the world.

"Fast" Ancient Food Recipes or Gourmet Choices

In each chapter, following the history, science, and lore of the ancient foods of that region, you'll find many great recipes. You'll have a choice of complex, homemade gourmet dishes for special occasions; moderately difficult recipes; and many simple and quick-to-prepare recipes, truly the "fast" ancient foods. Each recipe is followed by icons to help you identify the difficulty level of the dish. Keep the following key in mind:

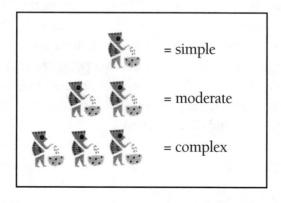

3 ≋

SOUTH AMERICA

A VALLEY IN THE PERUVIAN ANDES

There is mystery in the air as we make our way up the mountain first by train and then by bus to the village of Machu Picchu in the Peruvian Andes, not far from the equator. As we look at the surrounding mountains from the ruins of this ancient Inca village, now a tourist mecca, we realize how advanced farming was in this region before the Spanish conquest. The ancient Incas terraced mountain slopes, developed a sophisticated irrigation system, and constructed immense storehouses for grains and other dried foods that could feed millions of people for years. More than fifteen million people were fed by the Incas' agricultural system, in an empire that stretched from what is now the southern frontier of Colombia to over 4,000 kilometers south.

After the Spanish conquest, neither Pizzaro nor the Church cared very much for this native agricultural system. They wanted silver and to teach their religion to the natives. In suppressing the Incas' traditions the conquerors destroyed their agriculture as well. They wanted the natives to grow Old World foods such as wheat and broad beans. Although a few native foods became popular and were taken over by the Old World—such as peppers, potatoes, and many of the American beans and tomatoes—others survived only in remote regions of the Andes and distant plains.

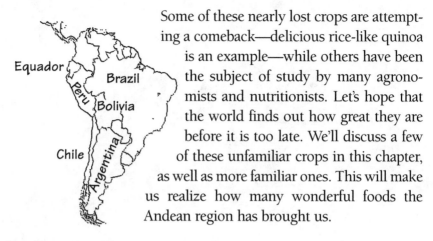

Some of these nearly lost crops are attempting a comeback—delicious rice-like quinoa is an example—while others have been the subject of study by many agronomists and nutritionists. Let's hope that the world finds out how great they are before it is too late. We'll discuss a few of these unfamiliar crops in this chapter, as well as more familiar ones. This will make us realize how many wonderful foods the Andean region has brought us.

PEPPERS AS FOODS AND SPICES

Of all the foods that the world has inherited from South America, peppers deserve to be discussed first. Peppers have found a special niche in just about every country and cuisine of the world and they are a great storehouse of protective nutrients. They are one of the great fruits, the kind that has made Dr. John Potter, head of the cancer prevention research program at the Hutchinson Cancer Research Center in Seattle, place fruits and vegetables at the top of his list of foods that protect against cancer. And the pungent varieties contain a powerful medicinal substance that reminds us how spices are often more than just wonderful flavors.

This food is useful both as a spice and as a fruit. As a spice, it is usually known as chilies or chiles, which range from mildly hot to extremely fiery. As fruits of all shapes and colors, peppers can be consumed raw or cooked in a variety of ways. And peppers are an extremely rich source of many biologically active compounds that are used not only as foods, but as the active ingredient in ointments and even in sprays used now in self-defense! Their extraordinarily high content of vitamin C—one of the highest in common foods—might have been one of the reasons peppers were found to be such a health-giving food by the ancient Incas.

PEPPERS AS SPICES: CHILES, CHILIS, CHILIES, CHILLIES . . .

by Cornelia Carlson

Only three of the major spices came from the New World: vanilla, allspice, and chiles. But what this hemisphere lacked in variety, it made up for in volume. Chiles are now the most widely used spice, both in tonnage terms and in the numbers of people who eat them. At least one-quarter of the world's peoples enjoy peppers every day. Just imagine what phantoms the world's cuisines would be if all the chiles disappeared: Hungarian goulash without paprika, Indian curries minus their searing peppers, East African dishes without piri-piri sauce, Szechwan stir-fries without hontaka flecks, Morocco's couscous without its *harissa* sidekick, Italy's antipasto plate without pickled pepperoncini, or Mexican moles with no chile medley.

Exactly when and where people began eating chiles and other peppers isn't clear. Fossilized remains found in northern Peru indicate their presence there by about 2500 B.C. Although experts have documented an even earlier presence in southeastern Mexico, perhaps about 7000 B.C., most ethnobotanists agree that chiles originated farther south. Not surprisingly for a spice that stirs the passions, the precise origination point is a matter of hot dispute among academics. Some believe chiles developed in central Bolivia, others favor southern Brazil.

What is certain is that by the time Columbus arrived, chiles had saturated much of the Western Hemisphere, including the Caribbean islands where Columbus made his first stop. Columbus found the local Indians eager to share these healthful fruits. He in turn was receptive to their power, writing "The land was found to produce much aji, which is the pepper of the inhabitants, and more valuable than the common sort." His patrons weren't impressed.

However, the Spaniards' next-door neighbors (and competitors), the Portuguese, immediately recognized chiles' potential. Within a few years of Columbus' discovery, they began disseminating the spice and inexorably changed many of the world's cuisines. The precise sequence of chiles' transmission isn't clear, but it is assumed to have begun with Caribbean or Brazilian peppers, which were taken first to Spain and Portugal, or their Atlantic island or West African settlements. From there, chiles traveled to East Africa and Goa, then on to Malaysia, Indonesia, China, Japan, and the Philippines. In this latter country, the Spaniards reentered the scene and brought them home to Acapulco on their Manila galleons. In less than 75 years chiles had insinuated themselves into cuisines circling the globe.

Chiles swept eastward around the tropics making converts among Asians and Africans, but were less popular with northern peoples. Initially, only the Hungarians embraced the peppers to which their Turkish conquerors introduced them in the sixteenth century. The Hungarians took to chiles wholeheartedly, bred them to perfection, and even guarded their industry so well that no one has yet matched their paprikas.

In later centuries, the memsahibs who acquired a taste for the hot and spicy pepper in their colonial postings might carry this penchant back home. Otherwise, the Europeans only slowly incorporated the milder varieties of peppers into their cuisines and mostly shunned the best, a practice they maintained in their migration to what became the United States.

Now, however, Americans can't get enough of these hot and luscious fruits. Chile festivals spring up everywhere, bookstores' racks bulge with chile cookbooks, and each day some new chile product appears on grocers' shelves. One magazine is even devoted to nothing but chile recipes and lore. Some call it a chile mania. The United States has finally caught on to what most of the world has long known: Chiles are just great stuff.

PUNGENT PROPERTIES AND THE MAGIC OF CAPSAICIN

Chiles, chilis, chilies, chillies ... There is no definitive spelling for this spice, which you can also call red pepper, hot pepper, capsicum, pimiento, aji, and plenty of other names. But would a chile by any other name taste any less exciting?

Whatever you call them, the chiles represent a huge group of plants belonging to the *Capsicum* genus, which includes the familiar mild bell pepper, the warm and fragrant paprikas, the hot cayennes and jalapeños, and believe it or not, far hotter varieties. All begin their lives an emerald green, then ripen into gem-colored fruits ranging from brilliant yellows to crimson and aubergine. In size, they range from the tiny pequins, smaller than a pencil eraser, to the giant pimientos. And best of all, their flavors vary from sweet to smoky to slightly nutty to almost fruity. Together they're a feast for the eyes as well as the tongue.

Most of us get to know the bland bell pepper before any others, but it's the hot varieties that are driving us wild. Chiles' heat comes from a group of closely related molecules, collectively known as capsaicinoids, and named after the major member, capsaicin. These compounds don't act in an identical way. Some target the back of the mouth and throat, while others inflict their pain farther forward in the mouth and on the tongue. This may explain the devious ways some chiles skip-bomb your mouth: just as the fire subsides in one place, a fresh explosion blasts a new site.

In the chiles themselves the capsaicinoids are concentrated in discrete locations. Most are in the chile's placenta (the pepper's "core"), in its septa (which are like ribs radiating out from the placenta), and, to a lesser extent, in its seeds. By selectively removing these hot structures, you can—to some extent—regulate the heat of your chile preparations.

Just how hot is a chile? For almost a century the pungency of chiles was measured by the Scoville Organoleptic Test, a taste-test named after its creator, Wilber Scoville. In this test the capsaicinoids are extracted from the chile with alcohol. The liquid is diluted, then applied to volunteers' tongues. If they can feel the heat, the solution is diluted more, until no one can detect its pungency. This final dilution point represents the chile's heat potential. The amount of dilution is therefore used as a unit of measure: the chile's Scoville HU (heat unit) value. These range from 0 for bell peppers with no pungency to 350,000 for habanero chiles, probably the hottest in the world. Modern analytical procedures have largely supplanted this method, but you may still see "HU" designations on packaged chiles.

Why the passion for a spice that sears tongue and throat, bringing on tears, sweat, and a runny nose, and keeps us happily choking, gasping for water, beer, anything to quench the fire? Answers are varied. Some researchers believe that capsaicin irritates the tongue in ways that make it more responsive to other flavors, and therefore makes food, especially bland grains, more palatable. Others suggest that chiles appeal to those who live in the tropics because they make them sweat and thus cool off. Still others maintain that it is the chile high that keeps people coming back for more. Perhaps all theories are true.

Until recent decades no one paid much attention to the chile high. It was just accepted as a curious, individual quirk. Now we know that capsaicin really does create a euphoria, perhaps even an "addictive" one. Evidently capsaicin stimulates the pain receptors in one's tongue and throat. The receptors use a small protein messenger, called *substance P*, to alert the brain to the painful threat. In response, the brain releases beta endorphin, its self-made painkiller. Thus the pleasure found in chiles' heat.

CHILES IN THE KITCHEN

There are five species of cultivated chiles. Three (*Capsicum chinense, C. baccatum var pendulum,* and *C. pubescens*) are grown almost exclusively in Latin America. A fourth (*C. frutescens*) provides us with our favorite pepper sauce, Tabasco. And the fifth species (*C. annuum var annuum*) furnishes virtually all the chiles that come to market in the United States. Yet within this one species, you'll find an enormous number of varieties to enjoy. In practical terms, you're limited only by what local markets carry or what your garden can produce.

The most common varieties of fresh chiles found in supermarkets include the Anaheim and poblano (mild to medium-hot), and the serrano and jalapeño (hot). For dried chiles you're likely to find the California chile (the mildest), New Mexican (medium-hot), and hontaka (very hot). Markets with a significant ethnic clientele usually carry others. Those with Asian customers may carry incendiary Thai chiles; those with Hispanic customers should stock the medium-hot pasilla and ancho, each with their distinctive earthy/sweet flavors, guajillo (large and hot), arbol (semisweet but hot as a hontaka), and the tiny blasting caps, tepin and pequin. If you can collect a range of these chiles you'll be prepared for any cuisine. Even if you're not "into" chiles, keep a selection of ground chiles on hand. The luscious qualities of Hungarian paprika or ancho (which may be labeled pasilla) powder can lift prosaic foods like steamed vegetables or omelets into stunning dishes.

There are lots of chile-powered recipes in this book. When you've prepared them all, try some others in chile cookbooks listed in the References. Some, believe it or not, feature recipes for chile-flavored brownies and ice cream. They are good! Try them when you want a rare, high-fat indulgence.

Be extra cautious when you work with hot chiles. A diluted bleach solution, or else vinegar, is said to reduce capsaicin's sting, so keep a bowl on the counter into which you can dip your hands. Better yet, wear form-fitting rubber gloves and make sure they don't have holes, even tiny ones. Never touch your face, particularly your lips or eyes. Those areas are unbearably sensitive and you can't use bleach on them.

Use the same degree of caution when eating chiles. Take small bites until you can judge the dish's heat and your own tolerance. Capsaicin isn't soluble in water, so you can't quench the fire with water or iced tea. It is soluble in diluted alcohol, and it binds to casein. Your best bet is to drink beer or milk, or serve a bowl of raita (page 288) alongside your chile-spiked foods. Add a heap of fresh peppermint, as many Indians do. The herb's menthol will help cool your mouth while the yogurt mops up the heat.

If you're really into chiles, you'll want to grow your own. Many have stringent requirements, and those that grow well in San Diego might not survive a month in Maine. But you can grow some variety of chile in virtually every corner of the United States. Check with your local nursery or seed catalog for those that do well in your locale. The Sources section at the end of this book lists several seed houses that carry common and even some rare types.

PEPPERS AS SWEET FRUITS: A STOREHOUSE OF PRECIOUS PROTECTIVE NUTRIENTS

The history of sweet peppers runs on a parallel track to that of the spicy peppers. The difference is that we can eat even larger amounts of this sweet fruit, making it a greater source of protective nutrients. Both ounce for ounce and calorically, sweet peppers contain more antioxidants and vitamins than just about any other of the common vegetables and fruits.

Few people realize that peppers are one of the richest sources of vitamin C. There are close to 100 milligrams in 3 ounces of a red, mature pepper, compared to about 53 milligrams in a medium-size orange. A 100-calorie serving of red pepper contains about 700 milligrams of vitamin C versus 120 milligrams in a 100-calorie serving of oranges or unsweetened orange juice. Green peppers contain slightly less vitamin C, about half that of mature red peppers. All red, yellow, purple, and other non-green peppers are, from a botanical point of view, ripe peppers, and while not all of them have been analyzed for vitamins, you may assume that they are richer in vitamin C than green peppers. They also taste better. The Italians and Greeks often grill or broil ripe peppers as a sophisticated dinner course. In cooking, some vitamin loss will occur, but you will still have a great vitamin C food. What a terrific food for weight control! The vitamin C content of ripe peppers is so high that, before the era of synthetic vitamins, vitamin C was often extracted from peppers.

Beyond vitamin C, peppers are rich in beta-carotene—which is not only an antioxidant, but changes to vitamin A in the body as needed—and other carotenes. Peppers offer about 5,700 units of beta-carotene in 3 ounces, which translates to 400 units per calorie, while an orange of the same weight supplies only 470 units of beta-carotene total. And peppers contain phenolics (page 112), another family of antioxidants. Why not then, we suggest, call peppers the "superantioxidants"?

TOMATOES: THE PERUVIAN APPLE THAT BECAME THE GOLDEN LOVE APPLE

Tomatoes originated in South America, most likely in Peru. They belong to the same family as the New World potato and the Old World eggplant—the *Solanaceae.* In sixteenth-century Europe, the first tomatoes that arrived became known as Peruvian apples. The original tomatoes were tiny, currant-like fruits, similar to some modern varieties like the "Sweet 100," known to many gardeners.

Although we are placing tomatoes in this South American section to do justice to their ancestry, tomatoes were much more important

for the Aztecs of Mexico than for
the Incas of Peru. In fact, the
name "tomato" originated
from the Aztec *tomatl*
(from the Nahuatl lan-
guage), which meant
plump fruit. The English
noun *tomate* was first used
in 1604 and later became
tomato, most likely because the word
"potato," which sounds similar to tomato, had been given to another
food also imported from the Americas and because, like potato, it had
a Spanish sound that related it to the Spaniards who had brought it
to Europe. In the sixteenth century the tomato entered Italy in Naples
(what could be more appropriate than the probable birthplace of
pizza and focaccia), which at that time was under Spanish rule. The
Neapolitans, with their love for romance, called it *pomodoro*, which
means golden apple. From Naples the tomato traveled to Provence in
southern France, where it was called *pomme d'amour*, the love apple,
then it spread to other parts of Europe.

Other types of tomatoes belonging to different botanical families
originated in Mexico, but it appears that the modern, most common
tomatoes come from Peru. No matter what the ancestry of the tomato, it is an American fruit that changed the way Europeans ate forever. A fascinating and often overlooked bit of history is that tomatoes
and other American foods were reintroduced to the Americas from
Europe as an intrinsic part of the diet of European immigrants.

POTASSIUM WITH GENTLE FIBER AND FEW CALORIES

In nutrition, good flavor can be just as important as nutrients.
Tomatoes give us lots of flavor, fiber, potassium, and a reasonable
amount of vitamins and minerals as well as being low in calories and
sodium. The Europeans of the 1600s discovered how many otherwise bland dishes could be brought to life by the "Peruvian apple"
and how this fruit could be used in a wide variety of ways. Tomatoes

increase the food value of many dishes without adding calories. Even though the 25 milligrams of vitamin C in a raw, medium tomato does not compare to peppers, it is still almost half of our daily requirement, and the fact that most of us can eat many more tomatoes than peppers makes this amount an important contribution to our diet.

Tomatoes contain good insoluble as well as soluble fiber, which complement each other's health benefits, increasing the fiber content of some modern low-fiber white-flour foods such as commercial pizzas. A medium tomato has about 9 or 10 milligrams of potassium per 1 milligram of sodium, and that can help us keep our potassium intake high in relation to our sodium intake. While other fruits have similar ratios, many of them also are higher in calories (a medium tomato has only 25 calories) and are not as flexible as the tomato in cooking. In the kitchen we can use the tomato's magic in many ways, from salads to Italian sauces to Mexican cuisine.

PROTECTIVE LYCOPENE

When we think "tomato" we should think lycopene, a powerful antioxidant. At the biochemical level, lycopene has been found to be extremely effective in rendering harmless a certain type of cell-damaging oxygen (here it works along with beta-carotene and other antioxidants) and in protecting blood cholesterol (pages 38-39) from oxidation. Several studies showed what appears to be a lower occurrence of pancreas and bladder cancer for people with high levels of lycopene in their blood.

Let's learn how foods balance each other: Tomatoes are high in lycopene and low in beta-carotene. Carrots, spinach, and sweet potatoes have no lycopene but are high in beta-carotene. Let's always eat a variety of protective vegetables, fruits, and other whole plant foods!

QUINOA: SACRED MOTHER GRAIN OF THE INCAS

Quinoa (pronounced keen-wa or keen-nooha) grew over a wide area of South America under the Inca Empire, from Colombia to southern Chile. Its cultivation dates back to about 5,000 years ago in the

Peruvian, Bolivian, and equatorial Andes. It was grown on terraced mountain slopes and in fertile valleys.

Quinoa had many advantages over corn (maize) for the Incas and their predecessors, because it grows well at high altitudes and is one of the best sources of proteins in the vegetable kingdom—something that ancient people discovered by a process of trial and error. When hard-working peasants did well on certain foods, when women bore healthy children that grew better on certain foods than on others, and when people looked healthy, that food was then accepted as a key part of the diet. Thus quinoa become the sacred grain of the Incas and was called "the mother grain." Today quinoa is successfully used to improve the nutritional value of foods for Peruvian children.

Quinoa has been called "the small rice of the Incas," because the seeds are white, similar to rice, and often cooked in the same manner as rice. Quinoa was also toasted, ground, and made into breads. The Indians in their wisdom ate both the seeds and the tender leaves of the quinoa plant. Here we have the perfect combination that we'll find over and over again in ancient diets: a grain (energy and proteins) from the first tier of a food pyramid (Chapter 1) and a leaf (a vegetable, rich in protective factors) from the second tier. Beans complete the triad of key health-giving South American foods, for a good reason that we'll discover soon as we meet the South American pulses.

Quinoa is beginning to make its appearance in North American specialty stores and is one staple that we believe deserves to become much more popular.

POTATOES

If a choice has to be made on the basis of economic value as to which American native food has been the greatest gift to the world, the potato wins hands down. The common potato added a basic staple to the grain-based diets of the Old World and saved many people from starvation in past centuries, when grain crops failed. It became so closely associated with saving Ireland in times of famine that some people think of the potato as an ancient Irish crop. But the potato probably came from Peru, and in that region we can trace potatoes back to the year 8000 B.C. They were first used in the highlands and then in coastal regions. The ancient Peruvians knew many more than just the few varieties of common potatoes we buy in supermarkets today.

Cuzco, the ancient capital of the Inca Empire, is probably where the first potatoes that traveled to the Old World originated. The introduction of the potato into Europe during the sixteenth century has often been called "the potato revolution" because it changed the eating habits of millions of people—more so than any other New World crop, including corn. Potatoes were easy to grow in cold climates and soon became staples in cold northern and central European countries, often replacing ancient grains as the main source of energy. In addition to their carbohydrates and some protein, potatoes eaten with the skin have some good fibers, vitamins (including vitamin C, which is absent from grains), and minerals. Grains, on the other hand, have vitamin E and related compounds and some good oils in the germ. These differences between the vitamin content of potatoes and grains is another reminder that a diet that supplies a variety of foods is always the best choice. The vitamin C in potatoes became exceptionally important in past centuries in Nordic countries, where fresh produce was scarce in the cold winter months.

Please note that vitamin C is a powerful antioxidant, which is quickly destroyed by exposure to the air when food is finely ground. This means that mashed potatoes left sitting for awhile probably have little or no vitamin C left. (This is something to be remembered also for foods such as juices, purées, and jams.)

Plant breeders have developed potato varieties that produce large yields but that are often fairly bland in taste and are practically colorless. The Incas and their predecessors in the Andes had potatoes with exciting flavors and often brilliant colors and unusual shapes. Purple and other unusual Andean potatoes are now found in some North American farmers' markets.

But ancient potatoes, still growing wild in the Andes, can bring another gift to humanity: natural resistance to some of the most destructive potato pests. R. W. Gibson, a British researcher, has discovered that some varieties of wild potatoes are extremely resistant to an aphid that has been called "the potato's worst enemy." The leaves of these wild Bolivian potatoes secrete a sticky substance that is released when pests walk on the leaves, and the enemy dies since it cannot escape. This catches not only the aphid, but potato mites, the Colorado beetle, and other damaging insects as well. While these wild potatoes are not desirable as food, they are being bred with other edible varieties to combine the sticky leaves with good flavor and texture.

SWEET POTATOES

Not a relative of the common potato, the sweet potato appears to have been used for food first in the coastal regions of Peru. Most historians agree that it originated in South America. It found its way to Polynesia about 1,000 years ago, long before the Europeans came to the Americas. Columbus himself brought sweet potatoes back to the Old World. It was brought to China in 1593 when the Chinese were looking for new plants to save the population from famine, and today sweet potatoes are more important in Asia than in Europe or North America. The sweet potato is more productive and easier to grow than rice, the Chinese staple, and one of the richest sources of beta-carotene, with about 15 milligrams in 3 ounces, much richer than carrots, which contain about 5 milligrams in 3 ounces. Today sweet potatoes are an important source of energy for many Asian populations. Do not confuse sweet potatoes with yams, which belong to a different family and are a very poor source of carotenes. To avoid confusion when shopping, don't pay attention to the names on the signs. Instead, look at the tubers themselves. Sweet potatoes have a deep mahogany skin and bright orange flesh, while true yams have white flesh with a rough brown skin.

LEGUMES, PODS, AND PULSES

A large group of plants was found in ancient times on many continents, the legumes or *Leguminosa*. These plants bear pods (think of green peas in a pod) with seeds attached to one half of the inside of the pod. Over millennia, wild leguminous plants developed in different ways in various regions and adapted to various climates. They became part of the crops grown by developing agricultural civilizations.

The seeds, or edible pods, of the legume family became known as *pulses*; these are what we now know as peas, beans, lentils, and related types of food. Pulses were held in high esteem by many ancient civilizations. To the ancient Mediterranean people, pulse meant chickpeas (garbanzos), lentils, and fava beans (Chapter 7). To the ancient Asians, beans meant adzuki, mung beans, broad beans, and soybeans, this last a "bean" that is quite different from any other common bean (Chapter 10).

THE BEANS OF THE AMERICAS

Pintos; Anasazis; kidney and similar red, pink, or red-and-white striped beans; lima beans; black-eyed peas; and related varieties are the pulses that originated in the Americas. To many people these are the typical beans in a culinary sense. Beans were a key source of protein for the Incas and other ancient Americans. For the Incas, the lima bean was an important pulse. The lima bean was encountered by European invaders for the first time near what is now Lima, Peru. The red-and-white-speckled Anasazi beans, named after the Anasazi of the southwestern United States, are not as well known as pinto or kidney beans but are a good way to learn to enjoy beans. They are somewhat lighter, cook faster than other red beans, and have a very delicate flavor.

These American beans belong to a part of the legume family called *Phaseolus vulgaris.* We know that, since prehistoric times, these plants have grown in their wild state on the slopes of the South American Andes and in Mexico. Sophie Coe, in her wonderful book *America's First Cuisines,* tells us that these beans were domesticated by humans from Mexico to South America millennia ago and that early dates for this domestication range from 5000 B.C. in Tehuacan in Mexico, and about 5600 B.C. in the highlands of Peru, to 2550 B.C. on the Peruvian coast.

FORGOTTEN YET PRECIOUS BEANS OF THE INCAS

> While you'll have a hard time finding some of these foods in a supermarket, it's important to begin to think about the value of little-known ancient crops and realize how many plants are available, overlooked in our anxiety to "create" new things by biotechnology.

Many beans, like limas or pintos, grow better at low or moderate elevations and do not do well at higher elevations. In our search for ancient foods, we discovered two beans, practically unknown outside of South America, which not only grow well at high elevations, but are extremely high in basic nutrients: the *tarwi* (pronounced tar-wee) and the *Nuñas* (pronounced noon-yas).

The diet of the Indians living in the highlands of Peru is often based on quinoa, corn, potatoes, and tarwi beans. In the ancient Inca capital of Cuzco you often see these beans in the markets. The tarwi is part of the lupine family and is extremely high in proteins rich in lysine, the amino acid that is lacking in grains. The shelled bean contains about 50 percent protein. Tarwis are the equivalent of the Asian soybean, another legume high in good proteins.

Nuñas were useful to the inhabitants of the high mountainous regions, where the boiling temperature of the water is too low for proper cooking of typical beans. Nuñas can be popped like popcorn: They explode, double their size, and shed their shell. And Nuñas can be grown at altitudes of about 7,500 feet. These popped beans taste great and cook in two or three minutes, making them very energy-efficient while containing about 22 percent protein.

A SECRET CODE THAT ANCIENT PEOPLES BROKE

A diet based solely on the grains corn, amaranth, or quinoa did not quite work for the hardworking American Indians. We may never know how the ancient Incas, Aztecs, Mayas, and Anasazi broke the secret code of the nutritional value of beans. Most likely they saw that when grains were fed as the only staple, children did not grow well and working people did not have enough stamina and strength. Soon they discovered that when beans and grains were combined, things were different; children grew well, the working person was strong and vital. It was not until the twentieth century that scientists discovered the reason: The proteins of beans and grains in combination provide us with the right balance of amino acids, the body-building blocks of proteins.

Mexican beans-and-corn dishes are a great example of how these people used a wisdom that is unsurpassed today. The only difference is that today we know why: The bean-grain combination is a key feature of good ancient diets from the Americas to the Mediterranean region to Asia.

Ancient farmers also discovered that grains and legumes love to work together in the soil as well. Leguminous plants, such as beans, fix nitrogen from the air in little nodules on their roots. If the farmer planted a grain—be it quinoa, corn, or amaranth in the Americas, or barley or wheat in Europe—the grain grew better and stronger after rotation with bean plants. Thus crop rotation was discovered and made for healthier and larger crops for centuries. It seems that nature meant for the grains and legumes to be good friends, working together from the land to the dinner table.

The Seeds of Pulses: The Ultimate Cholesterol-Control Food?

Beans are one of the great sources of fiber, and just as their proteins balance the proteins of grains, so their type of fiber is different in its effects on the human body from the fiber of common grains such as rice and wheat. One of the effects of the fiber of beans is to lower elevated blood cholesterol, as now shown by many clinical studies. When we reach China and Japan in Chapter 10, we'll find tofu, the concentrated protein of the soybean, low in fiber but highly beneficial for people with high cholesterol because of its *phytoestrogens* (pages 253-54), and because when plant proteins replace animal proteins blood cholesterol often drops. One major health-giving step for anyone with high blood cholesterol is to eat whole cooked beans and bean products regularly.

THE AMERICAN BEAN GOES TO EUROPE

American beans made their long journey to Europe and joined their relatives of the Mediterranean region in the sixteenth century. In about 1528, Pope Clement VII gave some of these kidney-shaped beans from the West Indies to Canon Pietro Valeriano. The good Canon planted them and found out how prolific they were. French writers tell us that the people of Provence in southern France were the first to eat these American beans. They later became known in France as haricot beans and were added to the list of ancient Mediterranean relatives from the legume family.

PEANUTS: THE UNDERGROUND "NUT"

It's appropriate for peanuts to follow beans, since just like beans, they are part of the *Leguminosae* family and are of South American origin. Peanuts are unusual plants in that the flower goes underground on a bent branch to yield its fruit.

There are no wild peanut species found anywhere outside South America, according to Sophie Coe in *America's First Cuisines*. Bolivia appears to have been the site of these original peanuts. From Bolivia they spread to other countries in the Americas and later to the world. Some ancient Peruvian peanut shells tell us that peanuts were roasted in the shell, just as we do today. The Portuguese brought the peanut to Europe in the 1500s, and today peanuts are an important crop in many countries because they have good proteins (25 percent), as do most members of the legume family, as well as a good oil (50 percent) that is well balanced, rich in good monounsaturated fats, and contains a reasonable amount of polyunsaturated fats. As in most oils of plant origin, its saturated fats are very low. As roasted peanuts, as peanut butter—still the most popular of all butters made from seeds—and as peanut oil, the peanut has truly conquered the world. Peanuts are now a part of many diverse diets in Africa, India, and China.

GOLDEN SUNFLOWERS

Our path is crossed for the first time by a highly polyunsaturated oil-rich seed, the sunflower. Its oil has become very popular, and even in the land of the olive—the Mediterranean region—the summer tourist often drives past large fields of sunflowers with their beautiful yellow blossoms, and, more important to the farmer, their precious oil-bearing seeds. Together with the oil, we find good proteins and fiber.

An oil that is highly polyunsaturated needs "protection" from oxygen (page 9), which means that it should be rich in friendly antioxidants. In the case of most seeds and nuts, these are the tocopherols (the vitamin E family).

The whole sunflower seed is rich in three key tocopherols—alpha, gamma, and delta—that complement each other and protect the oil both in the seed and after extraction. If you use the oil, be sure it is unrefined so that it still contains all of its original tocopherols. Avoid polyunsaturated oils that have been so highly refined as to have their tocopherols reduced to extremely low levels. Let's refer to this as the "golden sunflower rule" from now on in this book.

SQUASHES AND PUMPKINS

We can't say that squashes are a gift of the Incas or of the Americas, because squashes and their relatives are widely distributed throughout the world. There are about 760 species of squashes, and they come from just about every continent and climate. Some squashes are native to the Old World. Others, such as winter squash and pumpkins, are of South American origin. Still others come from other parts of the Americas: Crooknecks appear to have originated in Mexico and Central America. Some squashes may have been domesticated in the United States, where they can be traced back to 2700 B.C. In ancient America, squashes were used as containers and carved into drinking "cups," often in a very sophisticated manner, for the upper classes.

Bees have pollinated squash plants and crossed many varieties through the centuries, giving us the wide array of shapes and flavors we find today, from the very bland pumpkins (a pumpkin pie

without sweetening and spices would never have become popular!) to the richly flavored butternut and Kabocha squashes, which can be baked and eaten as they are when ripe and properly grown.

Squashes are so universally used today that it is hard to place them in this book: We have Brazilian pumpkins, Ohio squashes, Chioggia and Naples squashes, and hundreds of others, usually part of the prolific family the *Cucurbitaceae*, which likes its children in all sizes and shapes. Some of them have become so closely linked to a country that they are known by a local name, like zucchini (Italian for small squash), which is an unripe type of squash.

The Latin name for squashes, *Cucurbita,* comes from the squashes consumed in ancient Rome, which were considered rather dull. It seems their squashes were not the delicious types we have today. As these tasty squashes are apparently of South American origin, we put their recipes in this chapter. To some sophisticated palates, these "American" squashes are the only ones worth eating!

The Pulp, the Seeds, and the Flowers

Most people think of the pulp of the squash as the edible part. The seeds usually end up in the garbage can or the compost pile, and the flowers are left at the farm. Not true for ancient Americans. The shelled seeds were just as important or even more so, since, like any seed, they are a storehouse of protein and precious oils. Today we can buy pumpkin seeds and oils in specialty stores and they deserve to play more of a role in our diet. In Mediterranean countries pumpkin seeds are roasted in the oven, shelled, and salted, and the beautiful yellow flowers and young shoots are eaten as a vegetable. Think of this terrific combination of the nutrients of seeds, pulp, flower, and even young shoots. At farmers' markets we may find zucchini with their flower left on. Try them, since many Mediterranean countries use them regularly.

The pulp of squashes is a good source of gentle fibers and as with most orange vegetables, squashes are excellent sources of antioxidant carotenes.

The seeds are a balanced source of good proteins and unsaturated oils with good antioxidants present. Let's remember our golden sunflower rule: When the entire seed is consumed, the tocopherols are all there. Everyone should learn to roast their squash and pumpkin seeds (page 51). When properly roasted, they are easy to shell and make a delicious snack.

Flowers and young shoots supply protective factors (when you see bright colors, think phenolics) and their nutrients complement those of seeds and fruits.

In our modern ways, we often waste precious foods. Squash seeds are an example. The pulp and the seeds make such a good nutritional combination that these friendly seeds of our squashes and pumpkins deserve a better fate than complete oblivion.

Every fall for thousands of years, Americans have harvested the native summer crops of corn, beans, and squash to be eaten fresh and then dried for use all year. These sustaining crops, called by Native Americans "the three sisters of life," are planted together each spring on mounds over buried fish and become "the magic triangle." The corn acts as poles for the beans to climb, the beans add nitrogen to the soil and help shade the squash from the midday sun, and the squashes mulch the ground to keep the weeds out and the moisture in.

THE AMERICAN WALNUT— ON THE BRINK OF EXTINCTION

Of the hundreds of foods from South America, some are still used locally but practically unknown elsewhere, and others are almost lost. On the verge of being lost, but still available in markets in the highlands of western Venezuela, Colombia, Ecuador, and northern Peru, is what has been called the Andean Walnut, an evergreen tree. Unfortunately, because it produces a very valuable wood, it is logged extensively and the number of trees is rapidly declining. Even though it's an equatorial tree, it grows well at elevations above 7,000 feet where frost is present, making it adaptable to other regions. The South American walnut deserves a better fate.

Most walnuts on the market are Old World walnuts (sometimes called English walnuts). American walnuts have a thick shell and are larger than regular walnuts.

THE JOY OF SOUTH AMERICAN FOODS IN MODERN CUISINE

As we travel from region to region, exciting recipes will always follow the history, lore, and science of the healthful ancient foods we have just encountered. Let's now enjoy these great foods for our South American-inspired meals by beginning with some grain-based dishes.

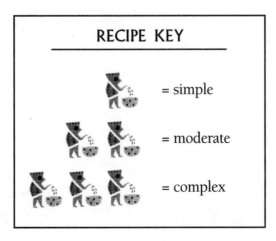

RECIPE KEY

= simple

= moderate

= complex

Basic Quinoa

by Jody Main

Makes 3 cups

Quinoa is fluffy in texture with a light delicate crunch. Quinoa makes a perfect quick-cooking bed for steamed vegetables or beans. It is also delicious as a filling for winter squash, peppers, and tomatoes and is well suited for grain salads.

>   1 cup quinoa
>   2 cups water

Bring quinoa and water to a boil. Turn down heat, cover, and simmer very gently for about 15 minutes until water is absorbed. Fluff with fork and serve.

OPTION: WASHING QUINOA

Many recipes suggest washing quinoa before cooking to remove the saponins—somewhat bitter soapy substances—that coat the seed. Usually the quinoa sold in the U.S. is pre-washed and can be used without further washing.

If you want to wash quinoa, swirl it in a bowl of water and drain 4 to 5 minutes until water is clear, or run water through the quinoa in a sieve while stirring with the fingertips for about 30 seconds until water is clear.

Quinoa Drink

by Rowena Hubbard

Makes about 1½ quarts

Still used today in the Andes as a nutritious drink for breakfast, this simple recipe can be made and kept chilled in the refrigerator for a refreshing snack just as it is. Blended with fresh fruit, it makes a quick, easy, and delicious breakfast drink or provides a tasty energy boost any time of day.

> ½ cup quinoa
> 1 quart water
> Pinch of salt (optional)
> 2 to 3 tablespoons honey
> 2 large ripe bananas or 2 cups fresh berries

Combine quinoa, water, and salt in a medium saucepan, and bring to a boil. Turn heat down to a strong simmer, and cook, uncovered, about 30 minutes until quinoa is very soft. Remove from heat, stir in honey and cool. Turn mixture into a blender jar with optional fruit if using, and blend until smooth. Serve at once, or cover and refrigerate.

Cusco Quinoa

by Rowena Hubbard

Serves 6

A typical use of quinoa in the high Andes is to cook it simply, add a few available vegetables, and serve it as a meal. This is a savory way to enjoy the soft taste and great nutrition.

> 1 cup quinoa
> 2 cups water
> Salt
> 1 tablespoon sunflower or olive oil
> 1 medium onion, chopped
> 1 small clove garlic, minced
> 1 cup chopped ripe tomatoes and their juice
> ⅛ teaspoon dried crushed chili peppers
> 2 tablespoons chopped parsley

Combine quinoa, water, and salt to taste in a medium saucepan. Bring to a boil; turn heat down, cover, and cook about 12 minutes until all water is absorbed. Meanwhile, heat the oil in a medium skillet. Sauté onion and garlic until lightly browned. Stir in tomatoes and juice and chili peppers. Stir in cooked quinoa. Simmer 5 minutes longer for flavors to blend. Fold in parsley just before serving.

Golden Baked Quinoa

by Jody Main

Serves 8

A delightful main course or side dish that is easy to prepare in advance. The hot savory quinoa is excellent served as a fluffy bed for braised squash and peppers. To complete the menu add a simple salad of tossed baby greens.

> 2 cups water
> 1 cup quinoa
> 1 onion, coarsely chopped
> ½ pound mushrooms, coarsely chopped
> 1 tablespoon sunflower oil
> 6 fresh or dried chiles (mild to hot depending on your preference), cleaned and chopped

Preheat oven to 350 degrees. Bring water to a boil, add quinoa, cover, lower heat, and gently simmer for 15 minutes or until tender. In a food processor with the metal blade in place, whirl the onion and mushrooms for a few seconds until minced. Heat the oil in a medium skillet. Sauté the chiles in the oil 2 to 3 minutes. Add the onion and mushrooms and sauté a few minutes longer. Toss with quinoa and spoon into a lightly oiled 6-cup casserole. Bake, uncovered, about 30 minutes until hot and fragrant.

Pumpkin Seed Quinoa

by Jody Main

Serves 6

This crunchy grain dish combines richly flavored toasted pumpkin seeds with soft, mild, tender quinoa. Try it as a bed for Lima Beans in Sorrel Garlic Sauce (page 85).

> 1 cup quinoa
> 2 cups water
> 1 cup raw, hulled pumpkin seeds
> ¼ teaspoon ground red pepper (sweet or hot)
> Salt

Combine quinoa and water in a medium saucepan. Bring to a boil; reduce heat, cover, and simmer gently 15 minutes until all water is absorbed. While quinoa is cooking, toast the pumpkin seeds in a dry medium-hot skillet, stirring often to prevent burning, for about 5 minutes or until they become plump, golden, and fragrant. Toss pumpkin seeds with hot quinoa. Lightly add red pepper and salt to taste. Serve at once while the seeds are crunchy.

Quinoa Pepper Salad

by Jody Main

Serves 8 to 10

This makes a delicious picnic meal or potluck dish, and is perfect served over baby greens. It refrigerates well overnight, but bring it to room temperature before serving. This will soften the grain and bring out the vegetable flavors.

> 4 cups water
> 2 cups quinoa
> 1 medium summer squash
> 1 yellow or red pepper, seeds removed
> 1 chile (Anaheim or similar), seeds removed
> 1 medium onion
> 3 cloves garlic, crushed
> ¼ cup unsweetened pineapple juice
> 1 tablespoon sunflower oil
> ½ cup minced roasted sweet peppers
> ½ cup toasted pumpkin seeds (page 51)

Bring water to a boil, add quinoa, cover, and reduce heat to low. Simmer gently for about 15 minutes or until all water is absorbed. Remove from heat and fluff with fork. Cool. Finely chop squash, pepper, and chile. Peel and finely chop onion and garlic. Fold vegetables into quinoa. Combine the pineapple juice, oil, and roasted peppers. Toss lightly with quinoa and vegetables. Sprinkle with pumpkin seeds just before serving.

Sunflower Quinoa Salad

by Jody Main

Serves 6 to 8

A refreshing, light, and crunchy salad, which is wonderful served with warmed cornbread for lunch or a simple dinner.

> 2 cups water
> 1 cup quinoa
> 2 small summer squash, finely chopped
> 2 sweet peppers, finely chopped
> 2 tablespoons minced (or grated) fresh onion
> 1 cup raw, hulled sunflower seeds
> 1 avocado
> Crisp lettuce leaves

Bring water to a boil. Add quinoa, cover, lower heat, and simmer gently for about 15 minutes or until tender. Add squash, peppers, and onion and toss gently. Cover and refrigerate several hours for flavors to blend. Remove and bring to room temperature about 30 minutes before serving. Gently fold in sunflower seeds. Peel, seed, and chop avocado and gently fold into salad. Spoon onto lettuce leaves to serve.

Basic Winter Squash

by Jody Main

Grown in the summer months, winter squash are so named because their hard shell enables them to store well through the long winter. Fall harvest would not be the same without the seemingly endless array of brilliant winter squash.

Choose squash with a hard consistent shell, such as buttercup or Kabocha. Wash and bake one of several ways:

- Preheat oven to 350 degrees. Pierce a few holes in the squash to release steam while baking and set on a baking sheet. For larger squash, bake about 1 hour or until tender when a knife is inserted. Smaller squash take about 45 minutes. Remove from oven, slice in half, and remove seeds and fibers. Serve plain, with sunflower butter or maple syrup, or fill with grain stuffing.

- Preheat oven to 350 degrees. Wash squash and cut in half. Clean out seeds and fibers. Rub cut end with a little oil and lay face down on a baking sheet. Bake for 30 to 45 minutes or until tender when knife is inserted.

- Wash squash and cut in half. Clean out seeds and fibers. Peel and cut into cubes. Simmer with broth and vegetables to make a delicious squash soup.

Toasted Squash Seeds

by Jody Main

Save all the squash seeds when cooking any type of winter squash, because they are both delicious and nutritious. The large seeds of the bigger squash, such as Kabocha, Blue Hubbard, and pumpkin, are wonderful when eaten raw. The edible seed inside is easier to remove with the teeth as a snack when it is not baked. Small seeds of the more diminutive varieties, such as Delicata and Acorn, are perfect for toasting. The hulls and all may be eaten.

To toast, remove stringy squash pulp from seeds by rubbing between paper towels. Spread seeds in a single layer on a baking sheet. Preheat oven to 300 degrees and bake seeds 10 to 20 minutes until crispy golden brown. Eat as a snack or sprinkle onto grain dishes, cornbread, salads, baked winter squash, or winter squash soup.

Pumpkin Seed Butternut Squash Soup

by Jody Main

Serves 8 to 10

This rich, creamy, and savory harvest soup is spectacular served in a pumpkin.

> 1 cup hulled raw pumpkin seeds
> 1 medium-small butternut squash
> 2 onions, chopped
> 2 chiles, seeded and chopped
> 9 cloves garlic, crushed
> 1 teaspoon sunflower oil
> 10 cups water
> Salt (optional)

Preheat oven to 350 degrees. Toast pumpkin seeds in a heavy skillet over medium heat for a few minutes, stirring constantly, until they are puffed, popped, and fragrant. Cool seeds, set aside half the seeds for garnish, and whirl the remaining half in a food processor until finely ground. Poke a few holes in the squash, set it on a baking sheet, and bake for 30 to 40 minutes or until tender. Peel skin and remove the seeds and fibers from cavity. Cut the squash into cubes.

In a skillet on medium-low heat, sauté the onions, chiles, and garlic in the oil for 10 minutes. Bring the water to a boil and add the squash and sautéed vegetables. Cover, lower heat, and simmer gently for 15 minutes or until vegetables are tender. Add the ground pumpkin seeds and simmer another 15 minutes. The soup will thicken. Add salt to taste if desired. Serve soup in a tureen (or a hollowed-out pumpkin) and sprinkle with the remaining seeds.

Winter Squash with Holiday Quinoa Stuffing

by Jody Main

Serves 4 to 6

Baked in a beautiful squash, this savory, toasty dish makes a flavorful and festive holiday main course. If you wish to make individual servings, use several smaller squash such as Delicata or sweet dumpling.

> 1 tablespoon sunflower oil
> 2 cups minced onion
> 2 cups minced fresh mushrooms
> 1 cup quinoa
> 2 cups water
> 1 cup chopped fresh sweet peppers
> 1 cup toasted pumpkin seeds (see page 51)
> 1 large winter squash (Blue Hubbard, Kabocha, or other)

Heat oil in a large, heavy skillet with a tightly fitting lid. Add onion and mushrooms, stirring over medium-low heat 3 to 4 minutes. Add quinoa, water, and peppers; bring to a boil. Turn heat down to low; cover, and simmer gently for 15 minutes. Remove from heat; add pumpkin seeds and toss tightly. Allow to stand 10 minutes, then fluff with fork.

Meanwhile, preheat oven to 400 degrees and cut the squash in half lengthwise. Scoop out seeds and place squash cut-side down in a large, lightly oiled baking pan. Bake about 45 minutes or until squash is firm but tender. Do not overcook. Remove from oven, turn cut-side up, and fill with quinoa mixture. Return to hot oven and bake another 15 to 20 minutes or until quinoa is hot. Serve immediately.

4 ≈

CENTRAL AMERICA, MEXICO, AND THE SOUTHWESTERN UNITED STATES

FOOD PATHS

The southern Mexican town of Oaxaca and the Bering Strait between North America and Asia have created some terrible dilemmas for the food historian, since food paths crossed these places millennia ago. These crop movements often make it difficult to locate the true origin of a food, and thus caused some difficulties in writing this book. For instance, some of the foods we describe as being part of ancient Central American and Mexican civilizations, such as amaranth, originated in South America, but because they were more important in Aztec than in Inca culture we chose to place them here.

Plants traveled the ancient path in the opposite direction as well: Purslane (*Portulaca*) most likely came to North America from the Old World in the eleventh century, after crossing the Bering Strait.

MAIZE (CORN)

Corn is what maize is called by most English-speaking peoples. A great gift to the world, acre for acre, corn plants can produce more food energy than many other grains. But let's keep in mind that yellow corn, the most popular in North American markets, supplies only half the protein of whole wheat, rye, quinoa, or amaranth. This

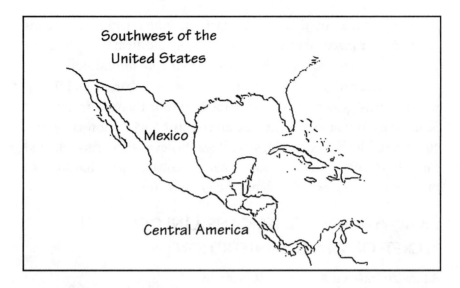

Southwest of the
United States

Mexico

Central America

caused tragic health consequences for both the Aztecs and the Incas when growing and eating amaranth and quinoa were forbidden by the Spaniards. Fortunately, corn mixed with beans, the combination you find today in every Mexican restaurant, gives protein of reasonable body-building quality. Blue corn, not the favorite of large growers today, is a different story, with about 6 grams of protein in a two-ounce serving (compared to 4 grams for yellow corn), which begins to approach that of other grains (about 8 grams of protein in two ounces). Blue corn is beginning to make a comeback and can be found in many specialty stores.

The years between 9000 and 5000 B.C. saw three key grains moving from the wild, where they grew as grasses, to cultivated fields, marking the beginning of farming and agriculture. Wheat and barley are probably the most ancient grains domesticated by humans, grown in Mesopotamia between 9000 and 7000 B.C. Soon after the sixth millennium B.C., corn began to be cultivated in the highlands of Tehuacan and in tropical Yucatan, and rice began to be cultivated in Asia. In South America, the oldest corn found dates back to about 3000 B.C., confirming that southern Mexico was the first region where corn was grown. Corn traveled not only to South America but also found its way to the American Southwest, where it was usually grown in fertile, friendly places. The ruins of Chaco Canyon in New Mexico, however, remind us that the Anasazi and other native Americans grew corn in places that were not as fertile and lush as the regions where corn originated, which attests to their agricultural skill.

Corn reached the Old World through Syria, Lebanon, and Egypt, where it was grown in the early 1500s. From there, it traveled to Spain, Italy, and other Mediterranean countries, where it was mistaken for a Middle Eastern grain, since it was believed that nearly all food came from that general region. This is probably why Italians call maize *grano turco*, which means "the grain of Turkey."

How Ancient Americans Unlocked the Secret of Maize's Nutrition

As maize traveled to Europe it brought along the great gift of a high-yielding crop. But it also contributed to a tragic disease, caused by Europeans' total disregard of the way ancient Americans prepared their corn before eating it. Perhaps the Old World inhabitants, who considered the ancient Americans inferior, did not believe that treating corn with lime had any beneficial effect. Whatever the reason, when corn became a major staple for the poor peasants of Italy (and for the people of the Southeast in America), a major epidemic developed, one unknown to native Americans. In 1771, an Italian named this disease *pellagra*, from the Italian "rough skin." It was not known until the 1930s that pellagra was caused mainly by a diet deficient in niacin, an essential B vitamin. This was not just a skin disease; pellagra became known as the "four Ds disease": dermatitis (skin inflammation), diarrhea (digestive system and loss of nutrients), dementia (poor brain function), and finally, if unchecked, death.

Still in doubt that these ancient Americans knew about "nutrition"? Here's another fact to convince you that they certainly did understand nutrition. Most of the corn they ate was treated with lime or another alkaline substance such as wood ash. Lime was the ultimate, as it also added calcium to the calcium-poor maize. When we treat corn this way, it becomes a reasonable source of niacin, and some of the essential amino acids, lysine and tryptophan, become more available. It also happens that tryptophan can be converted to niacin in the body.

In North America, the Anasazi and their descendants used blue corn. If the corn was treated with lime and then the lime was washed off, they lost the beautiful color and probably some nutrients with it. This color is a phenolic (anthocyanin) and could have protective properties. Did the Anasazi know that the "blue" was doing something for them? Perhaps they felt that when the corn was blue it was better for them than when the blue was washed out. Whatever the reason, the blue color was considered sacred and to preserve the blue, they mixed their ground cornmeal with either lime or wood ashes and did not wash it off before cooking.

When maize is *not* the basic staple and is balanced with a variety of other foods such as beans, fruits, and vegetables—in addition to milk, cheeses, and other animal products—an occasional use of "untreated" maize will not cause any problems. Remember also to use whole cornmeal, not the degerminated type. This will help to improve corn's nutrient balance and add the precious vitamins, minerals, oils, and proteins of the germ. Sophie Coe tells us in *America's First Cuisine* that "In the morning, the men went to their maize fields carrying tortillas, chiles, and salt, ready for whatever greens they could find." Here again the ancients felt that the protective factors of greens were a must.

Even popcorn is an ancient food, not a modern invention. Betty Fussell in *The Story of Corn* calls it "a truly indigenous fast finger-food that links all ages, places, races, classes and kinds." Fussell writes that the Aztecs scattered popcorn to honor the gods of the fishermen, and Aztec virgins adorned their heads with garlands of parched maize. Ancient pottery corn-poppers have been found in Peru.

AMARANTH: ANCIENT AMERICA TO ANCIENT GREECE

Where do we find the ancient, original amaranth? Like many other foods that originated in the Americas, amaranth, too, is probably native to South America. Millennia ago, it traveled to Central America and Mexico through Oaxaca. But it did not stop there; it was carried farther north across the Bering Strait and eventually reached ancient Greece. Amaranth's beautiful red leaves were appreciated then as they should be now. Aglaia Kremezi in her book, *The Foods of Greece,* reminds us that amaranth shoots were frequently mentioned by many classical Greek writers, together with cabbage and lettuce, and that the grain was used in sauces. Amaranth was considered medicinal, too. Kremezi tells us that Hippocrates recommended amaranth leaves with olive oil as a rub for headaches. We have no proof that this really works, but it shows that the plant was held in high esteem by the Greeks.

In the ancient language of the Incas, amaranth was called *kiwicha* (pronounced kee-wee-cha), and before the Spanish conquest of the Americas was as widely cultivated as corn. The amaranth plant is extremely resistant to adverse agricultural conditions—droughts, heat, and pests—and each plant produces about 100,000 seeds. Unlike many plants of tropical origin, which cannot adjust to varying day lengths, amaranth adapts to many different environments and latitudes.

The high nutritional value of amaranth seeds was well understood by the Aztecs. So revered was it as a life-giving cereal that annual religious ceremonies celebrated this grain. Amaranth was made into cakes with honey and human blood, and shaped into gods, mountains, deer, birds, and snakes. It was this celebration that caused amaranth's downfall soon after the Spanish invasion of Mexico. The Spanish considered the ritual unacceptable to their Christian principles. Rather than just forbidding the use of human blood or the amaranth "god cakes," they made it illegal to grow and sell amaranth. Cortez ordered total destruction of any field of amaranth found and had his troops cut off the hand of anyone found in possession of this grain. The Aztecs were thus deprived of their main staple, which is one of the most nourishing of all grains. The maize left to them was not as good as amaranth nutritionally, and perhaps this signaled the end of the Aztec civilization. The food that gave them strength, far beyond that provided by maize, had been taken away.

Perhaps amaranth is truly the "grain of the gods": While most plants' seeds will not sprout if kept for many years, some amaranth seeds, probably a thousand years old, have been planted, sprouted, and grown into amaranth plants!

THE GOODNESS OF AMARANTH

Amaranth is exciting to nutritionists because of its high protein content and its content of two precious amino acids, lysine and methionine. Compare 16 percent protein in this grain to an average 10 to 13 percent in typical wheats and ryes, and 7 to 10 percent in corn. Amaranth's percentage of lysine is about twice that of wheat. The good lysine content and the high protein make amaranth the ideal partner to wheat and corn. Use it to enrich wheat breads or pastas, cornmeal, and other grains without any loss of the good, natural flavors of these foods. Amaranth is making a faster comeback than some of the other lost foods of the Americas, perhaps because its protein is so good. And the amaranth leaves contain more calcium than many other common green vegetables, about twice as much as spinach, itself a reasonable source of calcium.

As was the case for quinoa, most of us today think only about the seeds of this great grain plant and do not eat the leaves. Let's bring back amaranth not only as a grain, but as a leaf as well. Grow it in your garden. Amaranth is a most beautiful plant and when in bloom all your friends will think it's an ornamental flower!

Today amaranth is becoming an important crop in the United States; in many European countries; in China, Nepal, and India; and in Mexico. Mixing amaranth with other grains or tubers can improve everyone's nutrition, and it could be particularly important for children and pregnant or lactating women.

CHIA

Chia, a small black seed, is another grain of the Aztecs and was used to make a gruel that was part of their regular diet. It is rich in a gum that limits the way we can use chia, but which may be very valuable. To the best of our knowledge, it has not been researched much but it is similar to other gums and mucilages that lower blood cholesterol and help proper elimination, like the popular bulk laxatives based on psyllium seeds.

AVOCADOS

Avocados originated in Central America and we believe they should be called "the olive of the Americas," because olives and avocados are extremely similar in the composition of their beneficial oils. They are both high in the friendly monounsaturated fats, moderate in polyunsaturated fats, and low in saturated fats. Avocados are a good diet food; they satisfy one's desire for a solid fat without using concentrated animal fats. If we magnify a cut olive and compare it to an avocado, they look just about the same, although they do not belong to the same botanical family. Its botanical name clearly links the avocado to America (*Persea americana*, a part of the laurel family). Ancient seeds of wild avocados, dating back to 8000 to 7000 B.C., have been found in a region that was the probable cradle of many Central American crops: the Oaxaca and the Tehuacan valleys in Mexico. Domestication took place about 6000 to 5000 B.C. in the same region. Other not-so-ancient seeds have been found in Peru (2000 B.C.).

It is unjust that avocados should be looked down on, as nuts are, for containing too much fat (about 30 percent). In a recent cholesterol-lowering study at our center, avocados, nuts, and olive oil were part of the diet. People were amazed that they not only could but *should* eat these foods. Some of them expected avocados to be "out." What's better than an avocado spread on bread for a sandwich? Use them in moderation, but use them with confidence. Remember that a food like avocado makes you feel more satisfied than a lowfat food. And avocados contain more protein than other fruits.

After the Spanish conquest, the avocado developed a reputation for producing sexual desire, and this made it very popular with the Europeans.

CACAO, COCOA, AND CHOCOLATE

What do we mean by cacao, cocoa, and chocolate? Cacao is the tree (*Theobroma cacao*) and the beans before processing. *Theobroma* gave the name to a sister of caffeine present in cacao seeds called *theobromine.* The terms "cocoa" and "chocolate" have meant various things over time. Today cocoa usually refers to the defatted powder from cacao beans, while chocolate refers to any of the manufactured products of the bean. Even though the cacao tree had its origin in the forests of the Amazon and the Orinoco in South America, it was in Central America and Mexico that cacao trees were widely cultivated and their products used as a beverage. For this reason, we have chosen to discuss the cacao bean here.

The Mayas introduced drinks made from the cacao bean to the Aztecs, who called this drink *chocolatl.* The Spanish found it pleasant and stimulating, enough so that Cortez brought it back to Spain in 1528 and introduced the drink there. In 1606, Antonio Carlotti introduced it to Italy and France. The use of chocolate spread to England, and by the early 1700s, there were about 2,000 chocolate houses in London. It was the first stimulant drink that became popular in Europe.

Caffeine and theobromine are the two closely related stimulants present in the cacao bean. Chocolate is quite low in caffeine, compared to coffee or even tea, but there is enough to give you a moderate lift. Theobromine, while not very stimulating to the brain, is mildly diuretic.

We have good news for the chocolate lover who's worried about the fat in chocolate. It's an unusual saturated fat—stearic acid. In a 1991 study, Drs. Margo Denke and Scott Grundy at the University of Texas discovered that stearic acid does not adversely affect blood cholesterol levels, as do some other saturated fats when consumed in large amounts.

CACTUS PADDLES

Prickly pear cactus grow on the Sonoran desert and are an ancient food of the Indians of that region—the Pima and Papago as well as peoples farther south. Both the fruits and the paddles are eaten. They are rich in vitamin C and beta-carotene (which becomes vitamin A in the body), and contain B vitamins and iron. Also called *nopales,* they're not hard to find in Western supermarkets and Mexican markets. They taste similar to green peppers but turn mucilaginous, like okra. Thorough cooking renders them free of that quality, however.

HERBS AND SPICES OF CENTRAL AMERICA, MEXICO, AND THE U.S. SOUTHWEST

by Cornelia Carlson

From earliest days, America's indigenous peoples must have noted the properties of local plants and gathered those that either tasted good or seemed to heal. In Mexico, this practice continues, with many herbs used alongside—and sometimes even in preference to—modern medicines. Walk along a side street off Mexico City's Calle Madero or an unpaved path in a Sonoran village, and you're sure to find an *hierberia* (herb store) or *cuandero's* (traditional herbalist) outdoor stall, filled with the rich, medicinal aromas of rue, creosote, and aloe, mixed with the spicy scents of mint, rosemary, and oregano. Some of the herbs are used just as therapeutic agents and others just for cooking. Many, like epazote (*Chenopodium ambrosoides*) and Mexican tarragon (*Tagetes lucida*), serve both functions.

EPAZOTE: THE HERB THAT LIKES BEANS

Epazote is one of the rankest herbs used in contemporary cooking. You'll find it mentioned in most books of authentic Mexican cuisine, usually to flavor its bean-based recipes. One suspects that this traditional combination relates more to epazote's reputed ability to relieve flatulence than to a harmonious taste. However, if you use just a pinch, its sharp flavor can add a pleasing edge to vegetable soups and quesadillas (cheese-filled tortillas) as well as to black or pinto beans.

For a sample of this medicinal-tasting herb, check your local Mexican grocery stores. If they don't carry it, you can grow it from seeds or plants available in your nursery, or from suppliers listed in the Sources section. The plants reseed themselves prolifically, so be prepared to weed most out.

Use epazote carefully. Small amounts, such as a teaspoon in a pot of beans, appear to be safe, and I've eaten this quantity often. But epazote has long been used in much of Latin America (and by the American Shaker communities) as a vermifuge. Its effectiveness is confirmed by its presence in many pharmacopoeias. In these books, you'll find that an overdose of the concentrated oil extracted from this plant can produce hallucinations, and even death.

MEXICAN TARRAGON

Hierbanis, or Mexican or winter tarragon as it's called in the United States, lies at the opposite end of the herbal spectrum. It is closely related to French tarragon in botany and chemistry, and thus shares the same sweet, delicious, anise-tinged flavor of its Old World kin.

Although Mexicans use it mostly in cooking, they've long used it also as a stimulating tea and a cure for colds, fright, and impacted intestines. According to *Badianus Herbal,* written shortly after Cortez invaded Mexico, the Aztecs also treated lightning-burned skin with hierbanis, added it to chocolate drinks, and, most gruesomely, ground it into a powder that was tossed at sacrificial victims as a pre-immolation anesthetic.

This herb grows well in any part of the United States, and far more vigorously than French tarragon in our hotter regions. In contrast to French tarragon, you can grow hierbanis from seeds as well as plants. Check the Sources section if your local nursery can't supply seeds or plants.

Use hierbanis in any recipe that calls for French tarragon—an equal amount is usually fine—and consider using it to flavor chocolate. Its taste hints of marshmallow, so if you hanker for a touch of Girl Scout s'mores in your cocoa, infuse the milk first with a sprig of this herb, or swirl it in your cup. It's a curiously pleasant combination.

Foods of Central America, Mexico, and the Southwest in Today's Cuisine

Many dishes referred to as "Mexican" are popular today in North America, such as the classic yellow corn tortillas. Yet dishes with amaranth, the greatest grain of this region, or blue corn are hardly known. Try to make all these a part of your meals. We think you'll find the following recipes intriguing as well as delicious. This is how excitement can become an intrinsic part of a good diet.

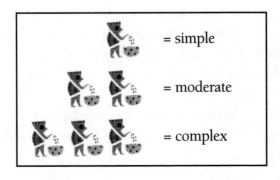

= simple

= moderate

= complex

Hot Amaranth

by Jody Main

Serves 4

Amaranth grains are creamy beige in color and only slightly larger than poppy seeds. Cooked as a hot cereal, amaranth has a nutty taste that is deliciously similar to wheat in flavor. Amaranth cereal is wonderful topped with a little honey and fresh or dried fruit for a hearty winter breakfast.

> **3 cups water**
> **1 cup amaranth**

Bring water to a boil in a large heavy pot; pour in amaranth. Return to a boil; stir, turn down heat, and simmer, covered, for 20 to 25 minutes or until thick and creamy. Serve immediately.

Amaranth Cakes

by Jody Main

Serves 6

Golden and deliciously rich, Amaranth Cakes are a wonderful weekend gourmet brunch. The amaranth may be cooked the day before, making it easy to just cut the cakes and sauté in the morning. Serve with fresh berries and honey.

> **3 cups water**
> **1 cup amaranth**
> **1 tablespoon sunflower oil**
> **Fresh berries, about 3 cups**
> **Honey**

Bring water to a boil in a large heavy pot. Add amaranth and return to a boil while stirring. Lower heat, cover, and simmer for 20 to 25 minutes until thick and porridge-like. Pour into a 9-inch x 13-inch glass casserole dish and cool. Cover and refrigerate overnight, if desired. Cut amaranth into 3-inch squares and sauté in the oil at medium heat for a few minutes on each side, until golden. Arrange cakes on a hot platter, topping each cake with fresh berries. Drizzle with honey to serve.

Amaranth Flat Bread

by Jody Main

Serves 4

Amaranth flat bread was a staple of the Incas, Aztecs, and other pre-Colombian peoples. Amaranth flour is best suited for unleavened breads because it lacks the gluten necessary for breads that require rising. It is also a perfect choice for those with gluten sensitivities. Freshly made Amaranth Flat Bread is delicious spread with jam for breakfast, folded over beans or other sandwich fillings for lunch, or served hot with any meal.

> 1 cup amaranth flour
> Sprinkle of salt (optional)
> ½ cup lukewarm water
> ½ teaspoon sunflower oil
> Additional amaranth flour for kneading and rolling

Blend flour and salt together, if adding salt. Add water and oil and blend a few seconds until dough clumps together. Sprinkle a cutting board with flour and roll the dough over this to ⅛-inch thickness. Press the dough flat, fold it over, and press flat again. Do this for a few minutes, adding flour as necessary until the dough loses its stickiness. Divide into four equal pieces and roll each into a ball. Pat or roll each ball of dough into a thin 6-inch circle. Heat a heavy, seasoned griddle to medium heat. Bake flat breads 3 to 4 minutes on each side until they are lightly browned and cooked through. Serve immediately.

Popped Amaranth

by Jody Main

Makes 1 cup

Popping the seeds is a traditional way to serve amaranth. The light little crisp puffs are delicious as a snack and taste very similar to toasty popcorn. The nutty taste makes popped amaranth a wonderful breakfast cereal or, mixed with a bit of honey, a delicious sweet and crunchy snack.

Three tablespoons of the tiny seed will make one cup of popped amaranth. The traditional way to pop this elegant grain is in a covered earthenware pot in an oven. Here is a quick and easy method, popping the tiny seeds directly on the stove top in a heavy skillet. The important thing is to have the heat high so that the amaranth seeds pop, while constantly moving the skillet so that the delicate seeds don't burn. Working with 1 tablespoon of seeds at a time produces the best results.

3 tablespoons amaranth seed

Heat a stainless steel skillet over medium-high heat. Pour in 1 tablespoon of amaranth seeds and cover quickly. The seeds will immediately begin to pop. For 30 seconds tip skillet back and forth while the seeds pop to prevent burning.

Immediately pour into a bowl. Do not worry about the unpopped seeds. They are toasted and delicious along with the popped amaranth. Return skillet to heat while still hot; add the next tablespoon of seed. Repeat as above until all three tablespoons are popped.

Blue Corn Mush (Chauquehue)

by Deborah Madison

Mrs. Zora Hesse of Albuquerque, who assembled the beautiful little Southwestern Indian Recipe Book for The Filter Press of Colorado in 1973, says baking powder is added to blue corn as a substitute for roasted shinbones, which originally supplied calcium carbonate. With the powder, the color also remains blue instead of turning grayish. Use it if you like.

Blue corn mush is basically the same thing as polenta and can be used in all the ways we've learned to use polenta. It can be eaten in its soft form or allowed to cool until set, then sliced and fried. Blue corn is eaten in the northern pueblos, especially in Hopi, where it can be ordered at the Cultural Center for breakfast, served fried with red chile as a side for eggs. It can also be eaten drizzled with honey.

Firm Style (About 4 cups)

3 cups water

¾ teaspoon baking powder (optional)

1 teaspoon salt, or to taste

1 cup blue cornmeal

Bring water to a boil in a pot; add baking powder and salt. Whisk in the cornmeal, then simmer, stirring constantly, until the corn tastes cooked, at least 20 minutes. If it becomes too hard to stir, add more hot water, but it should be very thick. Spoon it into a lightly oiled loaf pan, allow to harden, then slice and fry.

Soft Style (About 4 cups)

2½ cups plus 1½ cups water

1 cup blue cornmeal

1½ teaspoons salt

¾ teaspoon baking powder (optional)

1 tablespoon sunflower or safflower oil

Pepper

Bring 2½ cups water to boil in a pot. When boiling, mix the cornmeal with 1½ cups cold water to make a slurry. Whisk it into the boiling water; add the salt, baking powder, and oil. Cook, stirring constantly, until it tastes done, between 15 and 20 minutes. If it gets too stiff, thin with boiling water to the desired consistency. Taste for additional salt and season with pepper. Serve soft, like a cereal, poured onto the plate or bowl.

Corn Pudding with Pumpkin Seed Sauce

by Jody Main

Serves 4 to 6

Rich, hulled pumpkin seeds make a thick, creamy sauce when ground in a food processor. Toasting adds definitive depth of flavor, which the native people could easily have done over their fires. They probably mashed the seeds between two rocks, as we might today use a mortar and pestle. Serve the corn pudding warm, either creamy soft or in firm slices.

Corn Pudding

6 cups water

1 cup coarse ground cornmeal or polenta

Bring water to a boil in a large saucepan. Stir in cornmeal with a whisk to prevent lumping. Lower heat to medium-low; simmer gently, stirring occasionally, for about 1 hour. Serve immediately or keep warm in a double boiler until ready to use. If serving firm pudding, pour cooked mixture into a glass baking dish and cool. Cut into slices to serve.

Pumpkin Seed Sauce

1 cup hulled raw pumpkin seeds

2 cups water

4 cups chopped summer squash (3 to 4 medium squash)

2 fresh chiles, seeded and chopped

12 cloves garlic, crushed

Salt

Toast the hulled pumpkin seeds in a heavy skillet over medium heat, stirring constantly, until they are puffed, popped, and fragrant. Cool. Reserve half for garnish. Whirl the remaining seeds in a food processor until finely ground. Bring water to a boil in a large saucepan. Add the squash, chiles, and garlic. Cover, lower heat, and simmer gently about 15 minutes until the vegetables are tender. Combine the ground seeds, half the vegetables, and all of the cooking liquid in the food processor. Whirl until creamy. Add the mixture to the remaining vegetables in the saucepan; simmer together a few minutes. Add salt to taste. Pour creamy Corn Pudding into shallow bowls, or place slices into bowls. Ladle sauce over the top, sprinkle with the reserved pumpkin seeds, and serve immediately.

Zucchini Stew with Green Chile and Corn (Calabacitas)

by Deborah Madison

Serves 4

Calabacitas is the name of both a dish and the round zucchini-like squash that are grown in Northern New Mexico. It's a popular dish that combines two native foods—squash and corn—with green chile, which has been in the Southwest for several hundred years. You can omit the milk; just add a little vegetable broth or water so that there's a sauce at the end.

> 3 ears sweet corn
>
> 2 or more green chiles (Anaheim, Hatch, etc.)
>
> ½ pound zucchini (or yellow squash)
>
> 2 tablespoons sunflower or olive oil
>
> 1 white onion, diced
>
> 1 clove garlic, chopped
>
> ¼ cup milk or water
>
> 2 to 3 tablespoons dry crumbled goat cheese
>   or dry, grated Monterey Jack (optional)
>
> Salt

Shuck corn and slice off kernels. Roast the chiles (page 71); peel and remove skins and stems; chop. Quarter zucchini lengthwise; dice into chunks. Cut other summer squash into ½-inch chunks, if using.

Heat oil in a skillet; add onion and garlic and sauté for about 2 minutes. Add the squash and sauté, stirring occasionally, for 5 minutes or until it tastes cooked. (It shouldn't be tender-firm, but cooked enough in the end so that its squash flavor really comes out.) Add the corn and chile. Season with salt, then add the milk or water, and simmer, covered, until the corn is cooked, a matter of just a few minutes if the corn was tender to start with. When done, stir in the cheese, if using, then taste for salt.

How to Roast Chiles

by Deborah Madison

Place chiles over a gas burner, gas grill, or charcoal grill. Cook, turning them occasionally, until the skins are thoroughly blistered. (Do not char them as you would bell peppers. Since chiles are not as fleshy as bell peppers, it is easy to overcook them.) When the chiles are covered with blisters, place them in a bowl and cover the bowl with a plate. Let stand for at least 15 minutes to soften the skins. Slip off the skins with your fingers and discard them. Discard the stems and seeds as well, unless you want to retain the seeds for their added heat.

Anasazi Bean Soup with Juniper

by Deborah Madison

Serves 4

After they've boiled, cook the beans slowly to bring out all their flavors.

Sort through beans and rinse well. In a soup pot, heat the oil with the onion and garlic; fry 3 minutes, stirring occasionally. While this is cooking, bruise the juniper berries with a pestle and crumble the oregano, then add these to the onions with the coriander. Add the beans, whole chile, and 2 quarts water. Boil 5 minutes, then lower the heat and simmer very slowly, partially covered, until the beans are tender, but not quite done.

1½ cups Anasazi beans	1 teaspoon Mexican oregano
1 tablespoon sunflower oil	½ teaspoon ground coriander
1 onion, finely diced	1 whole dried New Mexican chile
2 cloves garlic, minced	Salt and pepper
8 juniper berries	

Add 1 teaspoon salt. Keep an eye on the liquid and replenish with boiling water if the beans become too dry. There should be some broth. When the beans are cooked through, taste for salt and season with pepper.

Anasazi Beans

by Deborah Madison

Serves 4 to 6

The Anasazi beans, which have recently been reintroduced, are said to have come from the time of the Anasazi peoples. They are quite similar in taste to the pinto, and don't require soaking. Traditionally they are cooked very simply, and red or green chile is usually served on the same plate. Epazote gives the beans a distinctive flavor and helps to make them more digestible. Dried oregano can be added if you like.

1 ½ cups Anasazi or pinto beans

6 cups water

Sprig of fresh epazote or 1 teaspoon dried

½ onion, diced

Salt

Sort through the beans, then rinse well. If using pinto beans, cover them with boiling water and soak 1 hour or overnight. Drain, rinse, then put in a pot with the water, epazote, and onion. Boil hard for 5 minutes; lower heat and simmer until they're tender. If the water cooks away, add more boiling water, as needed. Season with salt, to taste, after they're soft.

Thickened: If there's plenty of broth, thicken beans by making a roux. To make the roux: Warm 3 tablespoons sunflower oil with a few pinches dried oregano. Stir in 1 ½ tablespoons flour and brown. Whisk in a cup of bean broth, then add the roux to the beans. Cook another 15 minutes.

Anasazi Beans with Tomatoes and Serrano Chilies

by Deborah Madison

Serves 4

Serrano chiles have great flavor but they're fairly hot for the uninitiated. To tone down heat, remove veins and seeds, or use a milder chile, such as Anaheim. If you prefer pinto beans, soak them first.

> 2 cups Anasazi beans
> 1 small onion, peeled and diced
> 1 clove garlic, sliced
> ½ teaspoon salt
> 3 tablespoons sunflower or olive oil
> 4 tomatoes, peeled and diced, juice reserved
> 2 or 3 serrano chiles, finely diced, or 4 tablespoons chopped Anaheim chiles
> ¼ cup chopped cilantro
> 2 cloves garlic, minced

Cover the beans with 8 cups fresh water; boil 10 minutes. Skim off any foam. Add the onion and 1 clove garlic; simmer until the beans are almost tender, 45 minutes to an hour. Add salt and continue cooking until tender. Heat the oil in a medium skillet; add the tomatoes and their juice, chiles, cilantro, and remaining garlic. Fry over medium heat, pressing on the tomatoes until they break up and thicken into sauce, about 10 minutes. Add sauce to the beans and simmer 15 minutes more.

Serving Suggestion: Serve plain or with a little dry crumbled Mexican or feta cheese, cilantro sprigs, and corn tortillas. Or, strain off the broth and use the beans as a filling for warm tortillas or burritos.

Bean, Corn, and Summer Squash Stew

by Deborah Madison

Serves 4 to 6

This stew is based on a traditional pueblo stew, but also departs widely from it since most native American stews start with a few pounds of mutton, pork, or lamb. I've retained the plant elements and made up for the flavor of the meat by adding herbs and spices. This focuses on summer vegetables. Cactus paddles (page 85) could be added to this dish quite successfully.

3 cups cooked pinto or Anasazi beans, with broth

1 dried pasilla or New Mexican chile

2 tablespoons sunflower or safflower oil

2 onions, diced

½ teaspoon dried oregano

1 teaspoon cumin

½ teaspoon coriander

1½ tablespoons ground red chile

3 cloves garlic, finely chopped

1 pound ripe tomatoes, peeled, seeded, and chopped

1 teaspoon salt

1 pound zucchini, patty pan, or other summer squash, diced

4 ears corn, kernels removed, about 3 cups

½ pound green beans, cut in 1-inch pieces

¼ cup chopped cilantro, plus leaves for garnish

Have the cooked pinto beans ready and their broth reserved. Toast the chile in a cast-iron pan over low heat until it begins to smell good. Don't let it burn. Remove the stem, shake out the seeds, and cut, with a scissors, into thin strips. Put these in a bowl and add boiling water to cover. Set aside. Prepare the vegetables as suggested.

Heat the oil in a wide skillet or casserole and sauté the onions over high heat for 3 to 4 minutes. Lower the heat and add the oregano, cumin, coriander, ground chile, and garlic and cook 4 or 5 minutes, then add the chile strips and a cup of the bean broth or the chile soaking water to the pan. When the onions are completely soft, add the tomatoes, season with 1 teaspoon salt, and add the zucchini, corn kernels, green beans, chopped cilantro, and enough broth to moisten well. Cover the pan and simmer until the vegetables are completely cooked, about 20 minutes. Taste for additional salt. Serve with warm corn tortillas.

Posole and Winter Squash Stew with Red Chile

by Deborah Madison

Serves 6

Posole is flint corn that has been slaked with lime then dried. The lime gives it a unique flavor that's quite different from regular corn. Posole is sold in its dried form or, in the Southwest, fresh, usually in the meat department. Canned hominy is also corn treated with lime. It could be used here if you can't find posole, but remember it is precooked. Dried posole can take anywhere from 1½ to 3 hours to cook. If you have Red Chile Sauce (page 80) on hand, use it to flavor the posole instead of the chile that's called for.

1½ cups dried posole or 4 cups cooked hominy	Salt and pepper
1½ pounds butternut squash	2 tablespoons ground red chile
2½ tablespoons sunflower or light olive oil	1 whole dried red New Mexican chile pod
1 small onion, finely chopped	2 tablespoons tomato paste
½ teaspoon ground cumin	1 lime, cut in wedges
½ teaspoon dried oregano	Whole cilantro leaves

If starting with dried posole, cook it in 10 cups of water with a half onion and ½ teaspoon dried oregano until tender, between 1½ and 3 hours. Drain and reserve the broth.

Peel the squash, cut it in half, and scoop out the seeds. Dice into 1-inch chunks, more or less. In a soup pot, heat the oil, add the onion and squash, and sauté over medium heat until the squash begins to color. Lower the heat, add the cumin, oregano, salt, several twists of freshly ground black pepper, and the ground red chile. Stir everything together, then add the whole chile, 3 cups reserved broth (or water, if using hominy), tomato paste, and cooked posole. (If using hominy, add it 15 minutes later.) Simmer until the squash is tender, adding more broth if necessary to keep it stew-like. Taste for salt. Serve garnished with cilantro and a squeeze of lime juice. Warm, thick tortillas are the perfect accompaniment.

Pojaque Pinto Bean and Pine Nut Soup

by Deborah Madison

Serves 4 to 6

I came across a similar recipe years ago in the Pueblo Indian Cookbook *by Phyllis Hughes. It always seemed like the perfect soup to sip on a crisp Northern New Mexican fall day. Here is my version. Evaporated milk is often called for in recipes of this area. At one time it was undoubtedly more available than cow's milk. Actually, it's good with beans.*

> 4 cups cooked pinto beans and their broth
> 1 cup lowfat evaporated milk or vegetable broth
> 2 cloves garlic
> ¼ teaspoon coarse salt
> ¼ cup toasted pine nuts
> Salt and pepper
> 3 scallions, finely sliced
> 6 mint leaves, chopped
> 1 tablespoon Red Chile Sauce (page 80, optional)

Strain the beans, reserving the broth, and mash, purée, or pass them through a food mill. Make the soup perfectly smooth or leave it with some texture, as you like. Stir in enough broth and milk to thin it to the right amount. Pound the garlic in a mortar with coarse salt and 3 tablespoons of the toasted pine nuts. Stir this mixture into the soup and heat gently for 20 minutes. Season with salt and pepper or a tablespoon of Red Chile Sauce. Serve garnished with scallions, mint leaves, and remaining pine nuts.

Avocado, Corn, and Pepper Dip

by Jesse Cool

Serves 4 to 6

When avocados are at their best, this combination is not only strikingly beautiful but bursting with sweet sun-ripened flavors straight from the garden. Serve with homemade whole grain flat breads or corn chips.

> 2 perfectly ripe avocados
> Juice of 1 or 2 limes*
> 1 ear of corn, kernels removed
> ½ cup finely chopped sweet red pepper
> ½ cup chopped fresh cilantro leaves*
> 2 cloves garlic, minced fine
> Dash of cayenne pepper (optional)
> Salt (optional)

Cut avocados in half and remove the pit. Scoop out flesh and place in a medium-sized bowl. Pour the lime juice over the avocado. With a fork, mash avocado, leaving some chunks. Stir in corn, red pepper, cilantro leaves, and garlic. Season with cayenne and salt if you choose. Transfer to a small serving bowl and surround with flat breads or chips.

---

*Nontraditional seasonings used commonly today.

Masa Cakes Filled with Squash and Black Beans

by Jesse Cool

Makes about 16 cakes

On a trip to Guatemala, my sweetheart and I found a woman cooking these cakes over open coals at a small market near the bus station. They were one of the most intriguing and delicious foods we ate. The Guatemalan woman used blue corn masa, which is made from heirloom blue corn. You can find lime-cured fresh masa in most Mexican grocery stores.

> 2 cups cooked and mashed winter squash
> ½ cup cooked black beans
> 2 teaspoons grated onion
> 2 cloves garlic, finely chopped
> Salt
> 1 pound fresh lime masa

Put the squash into a small bowl. Stir in the beans, onion, and garlic. Season with salt to taste. Pinch off about 2 tablespoons of masa with your fingers. Flatten slightly with your hands. Place about a teaspoon of the squash and bean mixture in the middle, fold in half, and flatten, covering the squash completely and forming a flat, round, thick pancake. Continue until all the pancakes are formed. Heat a heavy, flat pan or cooking surface. Place stuffed masa cakes on hot surface. Brown for 2 minutes, turn, and brown on the other side. Eat immediately with or without a garnish of mixed chopped tomatoes, spicy peppers, and red onions.

Squash Blossoms Stuffed with Avocado, Corn, and Toasted Pumpkin Seeds

by Jesse Cool

Serves 3 to 4

A wonderful, light, refreshing way to enjoy squash blossoms.

> 8 to 10 medium-sized squash blossoms
> 1 large avocado, skin and pit removed
> 1 small ripe lime*
> ½ cup fresh corn kernels
> 1 tablespoon chopped garlic chives
> Pinch dried spicy chile
> Salt
> 2 tablespoons avocado or sunflower oil
> ¼ cup shelled, raw pumpkin seeds

Brush away any dirt from the squash blossoms. In a medium bowl, mash the avocado and squeeze lime juice over it. Stir in the corn, chives, and chile. Add a bit of salt if desired. Open the petals of the blossoms and fill each with a generous tablespoon of the corn mixture. Squeeze the petals around the filling. Set aside. In a medium-sized, heavy-bottomed skillet, heat the oil until it smokes. Toss the pumpkin seeds in the oil until they brown slightly Remove the seeds, reserving oil. Lightly salt seeds if desired. Return pan with oil to medium heat. Place stuffed squash blossoms in pan and brown lightly on both sides. Place on a plate and sprinkle with the toasted pumpkin seeds.

---

*Nontraditional seasoning used commonly today.

Red Chile Sauce

by Deborah Madison

About 2 cups

There has been a chile culture in New Mexico for more than 300 years. Red chile sauce can be made from the powder (molido) or whole chiles, which can easily be found in most groceries or Mexican markets. In Northern New Mexico, red chile, which is still hand-cultivated, is enjoyed for its own flavor and usually seasoned very simply—even cumin and oregano are not always used. Water rather than stock provides the liquid. As the sauce moves into Arizona and Texas, spices, tomatoes, vinegar, and other ingredients come into play. Red chile sauce is served daily in the Southwest. It's because of this sauce that other foods, such as beans and posole, are often cooked very simply. It's understood that this sauce, or a green chile sauce, will be offered.

> 10 dried New Mexican chiles
> 2 tablespoons safflower or sunflower oil
> 1 tablespoon flour
> 1 clove garlic, finely chopped
> Salt

Put on a kettle of water to boil. Break the stems off the chiles and shake out the seeds. If any places on the chiles are discolored (yellowish or gray) tear them out—it's usually a sign of earlier mold. Wipe them off if they're dusty. Put them in a cast-iron skillet warmed over low heat and toast until they just begin to smell good. Keep them moving so that they don't burn. (If they burn they'll turn bitter.) Put the roasted chiles in a bowl, cover with 2 cups boiling water, and let stand 30 minutes. Transfer to a blender and purée until smooth with the water they've been soaking in. Strain.

Heat the oil in a small skillet and stir in the flour. Cook the roux until it's browned, then stir in the strained chile and add the garlic and ½ teaspoon salt. Cook gently over a low heat, stirring frequently, for 4 to 5 minutes. Taste for additional salt. The finished sauce should be a rich brick-red and thick enough to coat a spoon. It will keep refrigerated for a week or more.

Note: If you like the addition of herbs and spices, add ½ teaspoon cumin and ¼ teaspoon oregano, crumbled into the oil when making the roux. A little minced onion can also be fried in the oil, if desired.

Green Chile Sauce

by Deborah Madison

About 3 cups

Green chile sauce is the counterpart to red and served just as frequently. I vary the traditional sauce by including tomatillos, another native Southwestern food, which give the sauce a little more body and complex flavor. A vegetable stock also helps. Natives use their local chile, which is much hotter and sweeter than the Anaheim or other chile hybrids. You can get more heat by including a few serrano or jalapeño chiles, seeded and diced. Allow time to roast, peel, and de-seed about a dozen large green chiles.

12 Anaheim or other long green chiles
½ pound tomatillos
2 tablespoons safflower oil
⅓ cup finely diced white onion
2 garlic cloves, chopped
¼ teaspoon dried oregano
¼ teaspoon cumin
2 tablespoons flour
1 to 2 cups water or vegetable stock
Pepper and salt

Roast the chiles (page 71), cover, and let them stand 10 minutes, then slip off the skins. Cut them open and scrape out the seeds, then chop. There should be about a cup. Remove the papery husks from the tomatillos and simmer in water to cover until they turn olive green. Drain, purée, and set aside.

In a small saucepan, warm the oil and add the onion, garlic, oregano, and cumin. Cook over low heat until the onions have softened, 6 to 7 minutes, Stir frequently and don't let them brown. Next add the flour and cook, while stirring, until the flour begins to color, then whisk in the water or stock. Add the chiles and tomatillos and season with pepper. Simmer, covered, for 25 minutes. Like the red sauce, green sauce should be thick enough to coat the back of a spoon. Taste for salt. Use immediately or cover and refrigerate for up to a week.

Cooked Chile Salsa

by Deborah Madison

About 1 cup

Here the chiles aren't roasted, as is usual, but sautéed. This is a delicious condiment to eat with beans, eggs, potatoes, squash, cactus, or wherever you like a little salsa.

> 4 large green chiles (Anaheim, New Mexican, poblanos, or a mix)
> 1 tablespoon safflower or sunflower oil
> 1 small white onion, finely diced
> 4 ripe red tomatoes, seeded and diced
> Salt

Remove the seeds, stems, and veins from the chiles—wear gloves if you're sensitive—and dice. Heat the oil in a large skillet, add the onion and chile and sauté over medium heat until both are soft and the onion is translucent. Add the tomatoes, raise the heat, and fry 3 minutes more. Season with salt.

Roasted Green Chile Salsa

by Deborah Madison

About 1 cup

Salsas of one kind or another are always on the table in the Southwest, to spoon onto beans, into tortillas, or wherever there's a hankering.

> 6 long green chiles
> 4 ripe tomatoes, seeded and diced
> 1 white onion, finely diced
> 1 teaspoon apple cider vinegar
> 1 tablespoon sunflower oil
> Few pinches dried Mexican oregano, crushed
> Few fresh mint leaves or pinches dried mint
> Salt

Roast the chiles (page 71), set in a bowl to steam 5 minutes or more, and then remove the skins, seeds (unless you want it hot), and stems. Dice finely and mix with the remaining ingredients. Taste for salt and make sure the balance of vinegar to oil seems right.

Black Bean, Pumpkin, and Chipotle Salsa

by Jesse Cool

About 3 cups

When winter rolls around and the last of the fresh tomatoes have been harvested, it is time to be innovative and use more seasonal ingredients in your salsa. Sweet, toothsome pumpkin or a similar winter squash is a perfect substitute for tomatoes. Use this salsa as a filling for tortillas or with any cooked bean dish.

  2 cups cooked and cubed pumpkin
    or firm winter squash
  1 cup cooked black beans
  3 to 4 dried and deveined or canned chipotle chiles
  ¼ cup chopped red onion
  ¼ cup chopped cilantro
  Juice of 1 lime
  Juice of 1 orange
  2 tablespoons sunflower or extra-virgin olive oil
  1 teaspoon cumin
  Additional dried chiles
  Honey
  Salt

In a medium bowl, combine all the ingredients and let stand, stirring occasionally, for at least 30 minutes before serving. Adjust seasoning with additional chiles, honey, and salt to taste.

Sautéed Cactus Paddles with Chile and Lime

by Deborah Madison

Serves 4 to 6

Traditionally cactus paddles would be simply boiled in water a good 25 minutes or so, but they can also be steamed, grilled, sautéed, and roasted in the oven—all methods that better preserve their nutrients and render them more interesting. Choose thinner rather than thicker paddles and, unless it's been done for you, remove the needles by scraping them off with a knife.

Serve cactus paddles as an accompaniment to eggs and beans, add them to vegetable stews, or serve them in a tortilla sprinkled with a small amount of feta cheese. Remember to limit the amount of cheese used because of its high saturated fat content.

> ¼ pound cactus paddles, needles scraped off
>
> 1 poblano or New Mexican green chile
>
> 2 tablespoons sunflower or light olive oil
>
> 4 tablespoons finely diced onion
>
> Salt
>
> 2 tablespoons chopped cilantro
>
> Juice of 1 lime

Rinse cactus paddles; dice into strips about ⅓-inch wide. Roast chile directly over a flame until the skin is loosened, then remove the skin and slice into strips. Heat oil, add the onion, and sauté for a minute or so, then add the cactus and chile. Season with salt and sauté a minute more. Lower the heat, cover the pan, and cook until the cactus is tender and its juices have cooked away, 15 to 20 minutes in all. Add the cilantro and season with the lime juice.

Baked Cactus Paddles

by Deborah Madison

Score the cactus flesh with a knife and season with salt and a little lime juice. Set on a sheet pan and bake at 375 degrees until tender, about 25 minutes. Remove and cut into strips or squares and serve as an accompaniment to other foods.

Lima Beans in Sorrel Garlic Sauce

by Jody Main

Serves 6

Rich, plump limas are enhanced with this piquant garlic sauce. The lima beans are delicious served over the crunchy Pumpkin Seed Quinoa (page 48).

> 5 cups fresh sprouted baby lima beans
> 2½ cups water
> 6 cloves garlic, minced
> 2 cups sorrel leaves or mustard greens
> 1 teaspoon avocado oil or vegetable oil
> ½ cup finely chopped parsley
> Salt

Bring the lima beans, water, and garlic to a boil. Reduce heat, cover, and simmer gently for 2 hours or until the limas are tender. Add water as necessary. Remove stems from the sorrel and slice leaves into thin strips, then cut in half. Add the oil to a large skillet; cook sorrel, tossing constantly, until sorrel turns brown. Add the cooked lima beans, parsley, and salt to taste, carefully stirring so as not to break up the limas. Heat together for a minute. Serve immediately with flat bread or over a grain dish.

Toasted Chia Seeds

by Rowena Hubbard

Chia seeds are tiny and black, even smaller than poppy seeds, and were one of the four ancient Aztec tribute grains that each province paid to the State. Toasting gives them a rich, nutty flavor that adds crunch and character to breads, cereal, vegetables, and salads. Just sprinkle them on top as you would sesame seeds.

1 tablespoon chia seeds

Place a small stainless steel frying pan over high heat. Add chia seeds and move pan back and forth over heat, about 2 minutes, until seeds smell toasty. Pour into a bowl to cool. Store in a small, tightly closed jar.

Chia Seed Tortillas

by Rowena Hubbard

Serves 6

Simple to make, these easy tortillas are perfect served with any squash or bean dish. If they are folded while hot, they make nice little pockets for any of the grain salads. Add a sprinkle of ground chiles to the tortillas along with the Toasted Chia Seeds if you like a spicier flavor.

> **6 corn tortillas**
> **2 tablespoons sunflower oil**
> **2 teaspoons Toasted Chia Seeds (recipe above)**
> **1 tablespoon toasted squash or pumpkin seeds**
> **Ground red chiles (optional)**

Grill the tortillas on one side (over electric unit, gas burner, or on top of a barbecue grill), moving often until lightly browned, about 2 to 3 minutes. Place on counter cooked side up. Brush cooked surfaces with sunflower oil. Sprinkle evenly with chia and squash seeds and with chiles to taste. Place uncooked side of tortillas down next to heat on grill, and cook until oil bubbles slightly, about 1 minute. Serve hot.

Hot Honeyed Chocolate

by Rowena Hubbard

Serves 4 to 5

This sweet, mellow drink comforts on a cold night. Originally the Aztecs crushed achiote seeds along with the cacao beans, giving the drink a deep red color. It tastes every bit as good without the fuss of adding achiote.

> 1 tablespoon cocoa powder
> 2 tablespoons honey
> Boiling water

Combine the cocoa and honey in a small bowl until blended. Add one heaping tablespoon to a large mug. Fill with boiling water and stir until well mixed.

Serving Suggestion: Cross the seas and add a dash of cinnamon or use a cinnamon stick as a stirrer for a little additional flavor.

5 ≈

MOVING NORTHWARD IN NORTH AMERICA

We now head to the northern plains of the U.S. Midwest and south central Canada, where ice and snow cover vast regions in the winter months. After we discover the uniqueness of wild rice, we take some side trips to find some other native North American foods.

WILD RICE

Botanically speaking wild rice is not a rice, but this name was probably given to it because it grows in water, as does Asian rice, and has a similar taste. Today, wild rice is grown in paddies, as well as in the wild. The root of the wild rice must anchor itself to mud deposits in the shallow parts of lakes and rivers. Since rivers and lakes in Europe have mostly sand and limestone bottoms, it's believed that these conditions, which are unfavorable to the root system of wild rice, prevented the plant from spreading into European waters. Wild rice was discovered, and found to be a good staple food, in regions with conditions friendly to this crop. It is certain that wild rice grew in the waterways and lakes of Manitoba, Minnesota, Ontario, Wisconsin, and surrounding regions in 500 B.C., and probably some millennia earlier, soon after glaciers receded from that region.

Thomas Vennum, Jr., in his book, *Wild Rice and the Ojibway People*, describes early explorers, missionaries, and traders traveling

in the regions around Lake Superior in the United States and Canada as being "struck with the beauty and ... the great abundance of a New World plant."

Wild rice is high in many nutrients. The protein content is close to 11 percent, compared to about 7 or 8 percent in yellow corn and rice. It contains reasonable amounts of vitamins, such as folic acid, and important minerals such as zinc.

CRANBERRIES

Some cranberries are native to North America and were used by American Indians, who called them *i-bimi* or bitter berries. They grow wild from Newfoundland to the Carolinas and westward to Minnesota and Arkansas. As with all berries, they're high in vitamin C and contain benzoic acid, a fruity acid that makes urine acidic. This property of benzoic acid is why cranberry juice is sometimes recommended to prevent urinary tract infections and kidney stones.

SUNCHOKES

Sunchokes (Jerusalem artichokes), a relative of the sunflower, are native to North America. When they arrived in Europe, it was soon discovered that their flavor when cooked was similar to that of the artichoke, hence the name "Jerusalem artichoke." They are low in calories and contain inulin, an unusual carbohydrate that is not totally absorbed by the digestive system (only about 50 percent). This makes sunchokes as satisfying to the palate as potatoes, but ounce for ounce, much lower in calories and thus valuable for weight control.

MAPLE SYRUP

Maple syrup, from the maple trees of the northeastern United States and eastern Canada, was one of the natural sweeteners of the natives. The maples were tapped in the early spring as the sap began to rise again, and the syrup was collected. Often they let it drip onto the snow and ate the snow as a sweet treat.

NORTH AMERICAN HERBS AND SPICES

by Cornelia Carlson

Americans have finally recognized the seasoning power of fresh herbs. Most supermarkets, which once carried nothing but frilly parsley, now at least carry cilantro and watercress year round, and in season stock sage, basil, dill, and others. Even better, many serious cooks enjoy a limitless array of flavors by growing their own.

No one deserves more credit for the resurgent interest in herb gardening than Adelma Simmons. More than half a century ago, she took over a decrepit farm in Coventry, Connecticut, and, working the land acre by acre, replanted it in herbs. The resulting Caprilands Herb Gardens is mecca for America's herb fans. To meander through its 50 acres and 30-plus varieties of herbs is to be transported back to the peaceful backdoor gardens of *simples* (herbal medicines) that graced this area two to three centuries ago.

Every August there you'll find one plant, which was a mainstay of those early gardens, flush with scarlet flowers, exuding a minty perfume. Botanists know it as *Monarda didyrria*, but most herb gardeners call it simply bee balm, noting the bee's fondness for it. Others refer to it as bergamot, since its lush, fruity taste is almost indistinguishable from that of the berg-amot orange, the defining flavoring of Earl Grey tea.

With time, the colonists would have discovered this New World herb on their own, but they probably learned about it by watching the local Indian tribes who reputedly used this fra-grant wild herb as a tea, spice, and therapeutic agent. The set-tlers must have grasped its potential as a tea substitute, for this *Oswego tea* became an instant favorite when the Boston Tea Party left them with none of the "real" beverage. About the same time, the Shaker community, newly arrived from England, must also have noted the Indians' medicinal use. This group, which became noted for its herbal cures, added bee balm to its pharmacopoeia for use as a diuretic and to soothe digestive upsets.

Bee balm is the best-known, and perhaps tastiest, of about a dozen native American herbs belonging to the *Monarda* genus, named for the Spaniard, Nicolas de Monardes, who brought them to Europe's attention. Several others deserve special con-sideration, especially the lemon-scented *Monarda citriodora,* which the Hopis used to flavor rabbit, and the harsher thyme and oregano-like horsemint (*M. punctata*) and wild bergamot (*M. fistulosa*), which other tribes added to cooked beans and meats.

While these herbs are little known outside the world of inveterate herb gardeners, they merit your attention. Bee balm is a spectacular seasoning for fruits—compotes of berries, fresh melon, poached nectarines, oranges with a sprinkling of liqueur, fruit tarts, orange marmalade—and an excellent way to add pizzazz to potato, millet, quinoa, or bean salads. Or try clip-ping this herb over warm new potatoes and olives or briefly steamed green beans. Above all, it's an excellent herb for bridg-ing sweet/fruity flavors with those of savory or piquant foods. For an idea of this potential, try the recipe for Wild Rice and Papaya Salad (page 331). Or for an herbal version of Earl Grey tea, use one tablespoon of the chopped fresh herb for each cup of soothing drink.

You won't find any of these native herbs in your local supermarket, either fresh or dried, but they're all easy to grow at home. If your nursery doesn't stock seeds or plants, you can order them from suppliers listed in the Sources section. Be sure to browse through their catalogs before you mail your order. In them, you'll find dozens of other neglected herbs. Order a few plants, and they'll snare you into a lifelong enchantment with herbs.

COOKING WITH WILD RICE

To complete our visit to the cold northern plains, let's learn the basics of wild rice cooking. Then, in Chapter 6, we'll find more wild rice recipes that combine wild rice and other northern foods with all the great foods we have encountered on our journey from South America to Canada.

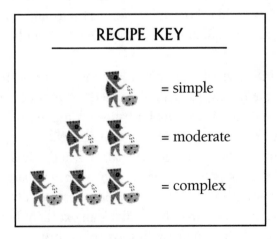

Basic Wild Rice

by Rowena Hubbard

Serves 4

The Ojibwa harvested their wild rice in lakes, but in California "wild rice" is a cultivated grain. It has a hard outer husk and thus requires a longer cooking time than Minnesota or northern wild rice. If you use California wild rice, cook it about 1¼ hours, until all the grains are opened and fluffy. Minnesota wild rice is available in specialty food stores.

> 1 cup wild rice
> 3 cups water
> 1 teaspoon salt
> 1 clove garlic, minced
> 1 tablespoon sunflower or light olive oil

Combine all ingredients in a 2-quart saucepan. Stir well. Bring to a boil, turn heat down to low, cover, and simmer about 40 minutes (1 to 1¼ hours if using California wild rice) until all liquid is absorbed. Fluff with fork before serving.

Wild Rice and Greens

by Rowena Hubbard

Serves 6

A richly flavored dish, pungent with aromatic mushrooms, this casserole is almost a meal in itself. Originally the Ojibwa would have used wild mushrooms and all manner of wild greens. Good substitutes today are the highly flavored dried shiitake mushrooms and a fresh baby lettuce and garden greens mixture, widely available in the produce sections of most supermarkets. This dish is delicious served with a squash and sweet pepper stir-fry.

> 3½ cups cooked wild rice (page 93)
> 1 cup broken, dried shiitake mushrooms
> ½ cup boiling water
> 2 tablespoons sunflower or olive oil
> 1 cup chopped onion
> 4 cups lightly packed baby lettuce and garden greens

Cool the wild rice to room temperature. Meanwhile, soak the mushroom pieces in the boiling water for 30 minutes until almost all liquid is absorbed and mushrooms are soft. Preheat oven to 350 degrees. Heat the oil in a small skillet and sauté the onion until it is translucent. Combine wild rice, mushrooms with all liquid, sautéed onion, and greens in a large bowl. Turn into a 3-quart casserole, cover with foil, and make slits in the foil using the point of a sharp knife. Bake for 30 to 35 minutes until hot.

Wild Rice Soup

by Rowena Hubbard

Serves 4 to 6

California-grown wild rice works well in this recipe.

> 2 tablespoons sunflower or extra-virgin olive oil
> 2 cups chopped onion
> 3 cloves garlic, finely minced
> 2 quarts water
> ½ cup California wild rice
> 1 cup broken, dried shiitake mushrooms
> Salt and pepper
> 1 bunch fresh spinach
> 1 bunch fresh dandelion greens

Heat the oil in a large soup pot. Sauté the onion and garlic until golden brown. Add the water, wild rice, mushrooms, and salt and pepper to taste. Bring to boil, turn heat down, and simmer, covered, for 1 hour or until wild rice is fluffy and cooked through. Meanwhile wash, stem, and drain spinach; wash and cut dandelion leaves into 2-inch lengths. Add to soup, stir a minute or two until wilted; simmer 5 minutes more for flavors to blend. Correct seasoning and serve.

6 ≋

PUTTING THE AMERICAS TOGETHER

COMBINING THE BEST FOODS OF THE TROPICAL, TEMPERATE, AND NORTHERN REGIONS

Now we are ready to combine all the foods of the Americas we have encountered in the first part of our journey. While difficult if not impossible in the days of the Inca Empire, today we can enjoy northern wild rice with Peruvian purple potatoes and other great combinations.

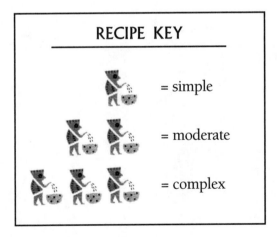

RECIPE KEY

= simple

= moderate

= complex

Amaranth with Mushrooms and Quinoa

by Jody Main

Serves 6 to 8

This dish combines amaranth and quinoa to make a delicious, nourishing grain dish. The fresh aromatic vegetables provide a bouquet of flavor and perfect moisture, so that only a small amount of Pineapple Sauce is needed for a gentle sweet touch.

>   4 cups water
>   1 cup amaranth
>   1 cup quinoa
>   1 pound mushrooms, finely chopped
>   1 cup chopped fresh sweet pepper
>   1 to 2 chopped fresh chiles
>   6 scallions, finely chopped
>   Pineapple Sauce (see below)

Bring the water to a boil in a medium-sized, heavy pot. Add the amaranth and quinoa. Stir grains, turn down the heat to very low, cover, and cook gently for 20 minutes or until all water is absorbed. Fluff with a fork and cool to about room temperature. Toss with the mushrooms, pepper, chiles, scallions, and Pineapple Sauce and serve immediately.

PINEAPPLE SAUCE

>   ½ cup unsweetened pineapple juice
>   2 tablespoons sunflower oil
>   2 cloves garlic, peeled

Whirl in blender or food processor until creamy smooth.

Quinoa with Corn and Potatoes

by Lorna Sass

Serves 4

It's no surprise that the flavors and textures of this Native American dish come together in such perfect harmony. The only foreign flavor is cumin, which adds a bit of excitement. To keep the dish authentic, you can use a sprinkle of dried chile flakes or mild ground chile in its place.

1 tablespoon sunflower oil

1 teaspoon whole cumin seed

2 large cloves garlic, minced

1½ cups water

2 tablespoons tomato paste

1 teaspoon salt, or to taste

1 teaspoon dried oregano leaves

1 cup quinoa, washed

2 cups fresh or frozen corn kernels

¾ pound potatoes, cut into ¾-inch cubes (peeling optional)

Heat the oil in a pressure cooker. Sizzle cumin seeds for 5 seconds. Immediately stir in the garlic and continue to cook for about 20 seconds more. Add the water (stand back to avoid sputtering oil) and then stir in the tomato paste, salt, and oregano. Bring to a boil. Add quinoa, corn, and potatoes. Lock the lid in place. Over high heat bring to high pressure. Reduce the heat just enough to maintain high pressure and cook for 1 minute. Allow the pressure to come down naturally for 10 minutes. Release any remaining pressure. Remove the lid, tilting it away from you to allow excess steam to escape. Stir well before serving.

Savory Sweet Potato and Wild Rice Crumble

by Jesse Cool

Serves 6

Inspired by the rich glory of deep wintry flavors, this dish is easily assembled and, like many baked dishes, can taste even better the next day.

> 2 pounds sweet potatoes, baked
> 1 cup sliced leeks
> 2 tablespoons fresh thyme
> Salt and pepper
> ½ cup sun-dried tomatoes
> 1½ cups cooked wild rice
> ¼ cup chopped pecans, toasted
> 2 tablespoons chopped chives

Cool the sweet potatoes, scoop out flesh, and transfer to a medium-sized bowl; mash. In a medium-sized sauté pan, cook the leeks in ¼ cup water until they are very soft. Mix the leeks and pan juices with mashed sweet potatoes. Add the thyme with salt and pepper to taste. Preheat oven to 350 degrees. While oven is heating, place the sun-dried tomatoes into a small bowl and cover with 3 tablespoons hot water. Cover bowl and let stand for 10 minutes. Remove tomatoes, reserving liquid. Chop tomatoes very fine and combine with the wild rice, pecans, and chives. Moisten with the sun-dried tomato liquid. Lightly oil a 2-quart baking dish. Fill with the sweet potato mixture. Spread wild-rice mixture evenly over the top. Bake about 30 minutes, until warmed through.

Wild Rice and Purple Potato Pancakes

by Jesse Cool

Serves 4

Rediscovering one of the oldest varieties of potatoes, Purple Peruvian, has been a visual treat for many cooks. Similar in quality to a white russet, purple potatoes take a common dish and make it spectacular.

1½ pounds purple potatoes
1 cup cooked wild rice
2 tablespoons sunflower oil
1 medium red onion, chopped fine
½ sweet bell pepper, chopped fine
Salt and freshly ground pepper (optional)
Additional sunflower oil for frying
1 large tomato, seeded and chopped (optional)

Peel and steam the potatoes. Drain; mash with a fork in a medium bowl. Combine with the wild rice. Place the 2 tablespoons sunflower oil in a medium sauté pan and sauté the onion and pepper until soft. Add the cooked onion and pepper to the rice-potato mixture. Season to taste with salt and pepper. In the same sauté pan, add just enough oil to cover the bottom. Heat over medium heat until oil just begins to smoke. Spoon large tablespoons of the potato mixture into the hot pan. Brown on each side. Serve warm or at room temperature. Garnish by sprinkling chopped tomato over the pancakes.

Amaranth Leaves Stuffed with Pinto Beans, Wild Rice, Corn, and Peppers

by Jesse Cool

Serves 4 to 6

An adaptation of the classic Greek stuffed grape leaves, this dish uses Native American ingredients. The beauty of the crimson amaranth leaves is further enhanced by vibrant bits of sweet red pepper, golden corn, and earthy wild rice.

> 12 to 15 medium-sized amaranth leaves
> ¼ cup cooked pinto beans
> ½ cup finely chopped sweet red bell pepper
> ½ cup cooked wild rice
> 1 ear of corn, kernels removed
> ¼ cup grated red onion
> Salt
> Juice of 1 to 2 oranges

In a medium-sized pot, bring 2 quarts of water to a boil. Lay the amaranth leaves flat in a steamer basket. Place the basket above the boiling water, cover, and steam leaves for about 3 minutes or until slightly wilted. Remove and cool leaves. Keep leaves covered with a moist cloth until ready to use. In a medium bowl, combine the pinto beans, bell pepper, wild rice, corn, and red onion. Season with salt if desired. Place amaranth leaves outer-surface-down on a flat work surface. Cut out any large veins or stems. Place a generous tablespoon or more of the filling near the bottom of the leaf. Roll the leaf around the stuffing, tucking the sides over the stuffing as you roll to completely encase the stuffing. Place finished rolls closely touching in a shallow casserole. When all the leaves are rolled, squeeze the orange juice over all. Cover with parchment paper or a cotton cloth. Place a heavy plate or similar flat weight on top of rolls. Refrigerate for at least an hour before serving.

Chayote Squash Stuffed with Red Beans and Wild Rice

by Jesse Cool

Serves 4

Succulent chayote squash is tender and sweet. With the addition of red beans and wild rice, this dish is perfectly balanced to serve as a light entrée next to a green salad or slices of perfectly ripe garden tomatoes.

> 2 large chayote squash
> ½ cup cooked red beans
> ½ cup cooked wild rice
> 1 green onion, finely chopped
> 1 medium tomato, seeded and finely chopped
> ¼ cup finely chopped basil*
> ¼ cup sunflower or extra-virgin olive oil
> Salt and freshly ground pepper

Cut squash into halves and steam over boiling water until tender, about 10 to 15 minutes depending upon the size of the squash. Cool. Using a spoon, scoop out center seeds. Set aside. Combine the beans, wild rice, green onion, tomato, and basil in a medium bowl. Moisten with the oil and season with salt and pepper to taste. Allow to stand 15 minutes, stirring occasionally. When ready to serve, place the squash halves on a plate. Using your hand, mound and press about ⅓ cup filling on top of each squash.

Borrowed from the Mediterranean for this modern dish.

Heirloom Bean Stew with Chile, Corn, and Tomatoes

by Deborah Madison

Makes 12 cups

Although this uses traditional foods, it is not a traditional Native American dish. If you can find them, use giant pinto or Madeira beans. The amaranth is used to thicken the stew.

> 1 cup dried giant pinto, black runner, or Madeira beans, soaked overnight
> 3 tablespoons sunflower or safflower oil
> 2 large onions, chopped
> 4 cloves garlic, finely chopped
> 2 teaspoons roasted ground cumin
> 1 teaspoon dried oregano
> 1 tablespoon ground red chile
> 1 whole, dried ancho (New Mexican) chile
> 2 teaspoons salt
> 2 cups peeled, seeded, and chopped tomatoes
> Kernels from 5 ears of corn (about 3½ cups)
> ½ pound summer squash, diced in large cubes
> ¼ cup amaranth
> ½ cup chopped fresh cilantro

Drain the beans, re-cover with water, and boil for 10 minutes. Drain again and set them aside. In a large, heavy pot, warm the oil with the onions and cook over medium heat, stirring frequently, until well browned. Add the garlic, cumin, oregano, and ground chile; cook together a few minutes more. Add the beans, 2 quarts water, and the whole chile to the pot. Bring to a boil, then simmer, partially covered, until the beans are soft, 1 to 1½ hours. Add the salt, tomatoes, corn, squash, amaranth, and half the cilantro. Cook until the vegetables are tender. Stir in the remaining cilantro just before serving.

Serving Suggestion: Serve as a soup, or, if thick enough, as a stew with Blue Corn Mush, firm style (page 68), and Red Chile Sauce (page 80).

Winter Squash with Warm Honey Cranberry Sauce

by Jody Main

Serves 6 to 8

There is nothing quite as festive as a dish of bright cranberries on the table. This tart-sweet cranberry sauce bursts with flavor and is especially delicious served in the cavity of a warm winter squash.

> 1 blue Hubbard, Kabocha, or other medium-large squash
> 3 cups fresh or frozen cranberries
> ½ cup light honey
> 1 cup water

Preheat oven to 350 degrees. Cut the squash in half, remove seeds and fibers, and rub cut ends with oil. Bake face down on a baking sheet for 30 minutes, or until tender when pierced with a knife. While the squash is baking, bring the cranberries, honey, and water to a boil. The berries pop as they cook, so be careful. Gently crush the mixture with a potato masher and turn heat down. Simmer gently, stirring frequently until thickened, about 10 minutes. Fill center of baked squash to serve.

Roasted Sunchokes and Purple Potatoes

by Jody Main

Serves 8

The sunchoke is a versatile but often neglected Native American vegetable. It is delicious simply scrubbed clean, sliced or chopped, and added raw to salads and sandwiches, or steamed with other vegetables. Here the sunchoke is teamed with an Incan vegetable, the purple potato. Similar in taste and texture when cooked, these combine to make a sweet, nutty, and hearty dish. Leftovers are perfect for breakfast.

1 pound sunchokes

1 pound purple potatoes (or red, yellow, or white)

4 scallions, sliced

6 cloves garlic, crushed

1 tablespoon sunflower or nut oil

1 teaspoon cider vinegar

Preheat oven to 350 degrees. Wash and slice the sunchokes and potatoes. In a baking dish, toss with the scallions, garlic, and oil. Roast, uncovered, for 1 hour or until vegetables are tender. While baking, turn a few times with a spatula for even flavor and browning. Remove from heat and toss with vinegar to serve.

Sunflower Pudding with Grape Sauce

by Jody Main

Serves 6

This warm pudding hits the spot for supper on cold, damp fall and winter evenings. Leftovers are wonderful reheated for breakfast, too. The Grape Sauce is a caramelized mixture, delicious warm or cold with the pudding or over cornbread.

> 2 cups nut milk, soy milk, or nonfat cow's milk
> ¼ cup sunflower seed butter
> 1 cup cornmeal, fine grind
> 1 cup sun-dried raisins
> ¼ cup pure maple syrup

Preheat oven to 325 degrees. Combine the milk and sunflower seed butter in a saucepan and heat to scalding. Add the cornmeal and raisins and cook, stirring constantly, until thickened, about 15 minutes. Stir in the maple syrup and pour into a lightly oiled 1½-quart casserole. Set casserole in a pan of hot water (1 to 2 inches deep) and bake for 2 hours. Serve warm or cold with Grape Sauce.

GRAPE SAUCE

> 4 cups seedless grapes, stemmed and washed*
> 1 cup water

Turn grapes into a large saucepan and crush them with a potato masher or fork. Add water and bring to a boil. Lower heat, cover, and simmer gently about 30 minutes. Preheat oven to 350 degrees. Pour grape mixture into a casserole and bake, uncovered, about 2 hours, stirring occasionally.

Concord grapes are native to the Americas, but any grape will do.

Purslane (Verdalagas)

by Deborah Madison

Serves 4 to 6

Purslane grows everywhere; it's probably growing in your garden right now, creeping flat to the ground in between rows of vegetables. A succulent, the leaves are flat and thick. Purslane, or verdalagas as it's called in Spanish, is eaten the world over—cooked, or raw in salads. We now know that, like other wild greens, it's very good for us. In New Mexico it's usually fried with onions and sometimes added to pinto beans. Like cactus paddles, it can become mucilaginous. Its taste is sharp and tart. In a salad it adds an acid bite.

> 2 to 3 cups purslane
> 2 tablespoons sunflower or safflower oil
> 1 small onion, finely diced
> ¼ teaspoon dried Mexican oregano
> 1 clove garlic, minced
> 2 tomatoes, peeled, seeded, and chopped
> Salt and pepper

Wash the purslane well since it tends to be sandy, and break it into small clumps. Heat the oil in a skillet, add the onion, oregano, garlic, and tomatoes, and cook until the onion is soft, 12 to 15 minutes. Add the purslane, season with salt and pepper to taste, and cook only until it's limp and heated through.

Lamb's-Quarters (Quelites)

by Deborah Madison

Serves 2 to 4

Lamb's-quarters, like spinach, is a member of the Chenopodiaceae *or goosefoot family. It grows wild in abundance and is still a popular green among native people.* Quelites *are gathered in the spring and early summer and are sold by Hispanic farmers in northern New Mexico's farmers' markets. Basically, cook it as you would spinach, or use spinach in its place. Sometimes cooked beans are added.*

> 2 tablespoons sunflower or olive oil
>
> 3 tablespoons finely diced onion
>
> Several pinches *caribe* or red pepper flakes
>
> 1 clove garlic, sliced
>
> 8 to 10 cups lamb's-quarters or spinach leaves
>
> Salt
>
> 1 cup cooked pinto beans (optional)

Heat the oil with the onion, pepper flakes, and garlic. When the garlic begins to color, add the lamb's-quarters, sprinkle with salt, and sauté, turning frequently, until wilted. If you like, add the beans as well. Taste for salt.

Native Sticky Corn

by Jody Main

Makes 25 cups

Around the time of the first American Thanksgiving, the native North Americans would mix popcorn and honey together and make sticky balls. This rendition adds toasted sunflower seeds, also grown at the time, for a sweet, crunchy snack. This recipe makes plenty to share.

> 1 cup raw sunflower seeds
> 1 cup popping corn
> ½ cup honey

Preheat oven to 350 degrees. Toast sunflower seeds in a dry skillet over medium heat, turning frequently with a spatula, for about 5 minutes, until they are golden and fragrant. Air pop the corn in an air-popping machine and then turn it into a lightly-oiled 11-inch x 15-inch baking pan with high sides. Drizzle with honey, then sprinkle with toasted seeds and bake 10 minutes. Turn with a spatula; bake 10 minutes longer. Turn again with spatula and bake 5 minutes more. Make sure corn does not burn. Turn oven off, open door, and cool corn inside oven. Turn while cooling to distribute sunflower seeds evenly. While mixture is still warm, but cool enough to handle, roll several tablespoons of mixture between your palms to form balls.

7 ≋

THE MEDITERRANEAN
AND THE MIDDLE EAST

As we journey to the Mediterranean Sea, we find a region steeped in ancient history, where advanced civilizations thrived millennia ago. The inhabitants of this region left a tremendous volume of historical writings, which we found to be sources of fascinating material about crops and foods. In this chapter, we'll visit southern Europe, North Africa, and the Middle East.

THE MEDITERRANEAN TRIAD

The healthful Mediterranean diet is founded on a triad of foods:

1. Grapes, their fermented or sun-dried products, and other fruits and vegetables
2. Grains (as breads and porridges) and beans
3. Olives and olive oil, sesame seeds, and nuts

Maguelonne Toussaint-Samat, in his *History of Food*, calls oil, bread, and wine the *fundamental trinity*. Beans, one of the super foods, were left out—again; but the concept of grapes, oil, and grain is so basic that, over the centuries, writers have found this trinity to be key in many civilizations.

The Mediterranean triad, with honey added, goes back to the Bible: "Until I come and take you to a land like your own, a land of grain and new wine, a land of bread and vineyards, a land of olive trees and honey." The Bible later says: "For the Lord your God is

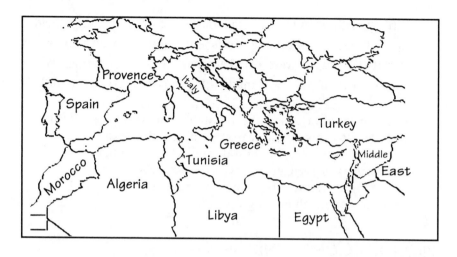

bringing you into a good land—a land with streams and pools of water, with springs flowing in the valleys and hills—a land with wheat and barley, vines and fig trees, pomegranates, olive oil, and honey."

Grapes—An Ancient Gift of Nature

Grapes are the first gem of the triad. Why put grapes and their products first? Because fruits and vegetables should always be at the top of our list of foods. Grapes are one of the great protective foods. In countries that surround the Mediterranean Sea, wild grapevines existed on the southern coast of France and in Sicily as far back as 10,000 B.C. Grapes were cultivated in the Bronze Age in Palestine, Syria, and Egypt. After 4500 B.C. the grape was used as a food in many Mediterranean regions. We know from the Bible—from Genesis—that Noah planted a vineyard.

The great Latin poet Virgil wrote in the last century B.C.: "As you look at the farmland, you'll see golden, gentle ears (of grains) and there will be rows of grapevines with ripe grapes." This loose translation from Virgil's *Bucolicon Liber* reminds us that, at the peak of the Roman civilization, grapes and grains were symbols of prosperity and of life itself. Other Latin writers frequently referred to grapes in their works. The breakfast of the Romans was often bread with sun-dried raisins and olives.

Although other fruits and vegetables were used, the grape held a very special place on the table of ancient Mediterranean people. To preserve them, grapes were dried to make raisins or fermented to make wine, or their juice was made into *vino cotto* (cooked wine).

Grapes have always had the reputation of being a healthful food. Perhaps this is one reason so much effort was made to have them available year round, and why for millennia they have been preserved either as sun-dried raisins or as wine. Sun-drying or fermenting into wine made it possible to have the flavor and goodness of grapes all year.

Precious Compounds in Grapes, Raisins, and Wine

Grapes and their dried product, raisins, in addition to being a great source of energy, contain a good balance of soluble and insoluble fiber and are a storehouse of phenolic compounds, a large group of powerful antioxidants. Grapes also provide the highest source of tartaric acid among common foods. Some of these beneficial compounds vary in fresh grapes, wine, and raisins. The highest concentration of phenolics is in the skin of the grapes. Because of the presence of the skin during fermentation, red wines have a much higher content of phenolics than do white wines. Raisins are also an excellent source of phenolics. Grape juices have not been studied as extensively as raisins and wines, but we expect that they can be used as part of our daily phenolic sources. Wines, with their alcohol content, need to be used with caution. Raisins, fresh grapes when available, and grape juices are more universal foods for people of all ages. In analyses performed in our center, we found 340 milligrams of phenolics in an old-fashioned, unfiltered French red wine, 25 milligrams in a French white Chablis, and 260 milligrams in a serving (about 1½ ounces) of sun-dried California raisins.

Some tartaric acid is lost in wines. Filtration removes some of it. and in unfiltered wines, some of it crystallizes at the bottom of the bottle. Studies at our center show that tartaric acid seems to work together with fiber in raisins to improve the function of the intestines, help proper elimination by preventing hard stools, and decrease intestinal transit time (time taken by food residues and other by-products of digestion to be "eliminated" from the body). And tartaric acid working with fiber in producing friendly compounds in the colon may aid in the prevention of colon cancer.

Raisins and fresh grapes when available combine carbohydrates, good fiber, phenolics, and tartaric acid more completely than beverages made from grapes. But these beverages, fermented or not, also have a great place in health maintenance. Make grapes and their products key foods in your meals and snacks. Always use caution when you choose the alcoholic beverages, however; avoid them during pregnancy, when nursing a baby, and early in life, and always drink them in moderation. Moderate consumption of red wine, about one glass a day with meals, may help prevent heart disease.

OTHER MEDITERRANEAN FRUITS AND VEGETABLES

To discuss the history and health-giving properties of all the Mediterranean fruits and vegetables would take volumes. Figs were highly respected, as were many berries, quinces, and an almost endless number of other fruits. Garlic and onions, purslane, spinach, and eggplant are all foods that were eaten by ancient Mediterranean people. The onion family (*Allium*) has recently been found to be a great source of unique compounds that benefit blood coagulation (prevention of abnormal blood clots, called *thrombi*) and blood cholesterol. Some garlic or onions should be eaten every week, if not every day. Purslane (*Portulaca oleracea*) is a weed that we have already encountered in the Americas, where it arrived from the Old World via the Bering Strait. Its leaves are very high in omega-three fats compared to other plants; these good fats help prevent abnormal formations of blood clots inside the blood vessels, clots that could lead to major heart trouble.

WHEAT, KAMUT, SPELT, AND BARLEY

These grains are the second gem of the Mediterranean triad. For millennia before Christ, Mediterranean peoples knew these grains would sustain life and help build healthy bodies. In Mediterranean countries, "food" meant *grain*. The Greek poet Homer called barley and wheat "the marrow of men." In Hebrew and Greek, words for "food" in general are *lehem* and *sitos*, meaning grain or bread.

Most archeologists believe that the cultivation of barley and wheat began at about the same time, about 8000 to 7000 B.C., although barley was probably more common as a food before wheat become the most important grain. At that time, barley was grown in Palestine, Syria, and Turkey. It was popular in primitive agriculture because it was resistant to weather changes, adaptable to various soils, and matured fairly rapidly. Barley porridge and toasted barley came before bread. At the same time, wheat was grown at higher elevations in Anatolia and Kurdistan and became a major crop in other European and African Mediterranean countries in the fifth and fourth millennia B.C. The Egyptians may have been the first to make "bread" by naturally leavening a dough made from wheat. Stone mills to grind grains in Egypt date back to the third millennium B.C., and from there moved into other Mediterranean countries. The resulting barley or wheat flour was far from our modern, highly refined "white flour." Some sifting was necessary, as poor grinding often resulted in sand-like particles in the flour, imparting an unpleasant taste. In Italian Pompeii, volcanic rocks were used for grinding, and the flour produced must have been quite good. As stone milling evolved, donkeys were often used to turn the grinding stone. Commercial bakeries, baking naturally leavened breads, began to appear in both Greece and Italy between 500 and 100 B.C. Before then, baking was done at home by women. That grains were held in high esteem is shown by the many ancient Roman coins that have grains engraved on them.

Kamut and spelt are ancient relatives (all part of the *Triticum* genus) of wheat. Spelt was cultivated in the Middle East as early as 2000 B.C. *Kamut* meant "wheat" in ancient Egyptian. It is said that kamut helped feed the workers that built the Egyptian pyramids. If wheat is to be a foundation of the diet, then kamut and spelt help to add variety to pasta and breads. They make great specialty homemade breads such as pita and other flat breads. Kamut and spelt are beginning to appear in North American markets, and some people find them particularly suitable for making pasta.

WHEAT AND BARLEY: THE STAPLES OF ANCIENT MEDITERRANEANS

What made wheat the basic breadmaking grain and propelled it to fame is that magic protein called *gluten*. It is so good for breadmaking that bakers today buy *gluten flour* to add to their mixtures to lighten some breads. This is the protein that makes light, leavened bread possible. While gluten is present in some other grains as well, the amount in wheat makes this grain ideal not only for breads, but for all the other baked goods we take for granted today. Wheat is also much higher in protein than barley, rice, or corn: with about 13 percent, compared to 8 percent for barley, and 7 or 8 percent for rice and corn. Wheat bread is even better if we add some flour from a New World grain high in superb proteins, such as amaranth (page 58). Wheat has a large germ rich in vitamins—including E, which is also a powerful antioxidant—minerals, plant sterols, and good oils. Never take the germ and bran away. Wheat bran is rich in minerals and one of the best sources of insoluble fiber. Constipation would be practically nonexistent if we always ate whole grains.

Barley makes great soups, but be sure to use barley that is only moderately pearled, where only the very outside layers of the bran have been removed. Barley contains *tocotrienols,* sisters to the tocopherols (vitamin E), which have been shown to lower blood cholesterol.

LENTILS, BROAD BEANS, PEAS, AND CHICKPEAS

Members of the *Leguminosae* family were the faithful nutritional partners of grains for ancient Mediterranean people, just as pinto beans and their relatives were for ancient Americans. They go with grains as the staples of a good diet, and as part of the triad of any continent and era.

Of the leguminous seeds that are common today near the Mediterranean Sea, we find the common green pea (think of split pea soup), chickpeas (garbanzos), lentils, and broad beans (fava beans). For the newcomer to beans as a part of the daily diet, the digestive system can become accustomed most easily to lentils.

The protein content of all common legumes is very similar, about 20 to 23 percent when dry. For a higher intake of high-quality protein, try combining these Old World legumes with the New World grains amaranth and quinoa.

THE SACRED OLIVE

The olive and its oil are the third gem of the Mediterranean triad. Just as the Aztecs made amaranth into cakes in the shapes of gods for rituals (page 58) and the Incas regarded quinoa as "the mother grain" (page 32), so the peoples of the Mediterranean region had the olive as their holy tree and fruit. The olive tree branches were symbols of peace, and its fruit provided holy oils, used not only as food but also for light, for religious ceremonies, for cleansing the body, and as a skin-friendly ointment. The olive tree seems to have originated in the Middle East. It was cultivated and its fruit pressed into oil at least five millennia ago in the Mediterranean region. From there it migrated into other Mediterranean countries, where it flourished. There is no close relative of the olive tree native to the Americas, even though the

fruit of the avocado, as we have seen (page 60), is very similar in many ways. The Jesuits brought olive trees to Mexico and California. Today, in California, excellent extra-virgin olive oils are pressed with great care, and more olive groves are being planted.

In ancient times, the olive tree was considered the king of fruit-bearing trees. Today, the traveler who drives the highways and byways of Mediterranean countries is overwhelmed by the seemingly endless fields of olive trees, some of which are a thousand years old. The Bible reflects how highly respected the olive tree and its fruit were in the last centuries B.C.: "One day the trees went out to anoint a king for themselves and said to the olive tree: Be our king. But the olive tree answered, Should I give up my oil, by which both gods and men are honored, to hold sway over the trees?" An olive branch was given to Noah. In Greek mythology, the goddess Athena and the sea god Poseidon wanted to rule Greece. Athena planted an olive tree and won, and Athens was named after her. Greek athletes were given a jar of olive oil for winning athletic competitions. Olive oil was preferred to butter by the ancient Greeks, who considered butter a part of the diet of northern barbarians, according to Dr. Thomas Braun of Oxford University. Another lesson in ancient wisdom, as we know today that olive oil is one of the safest oils to use.

FRIEND OF THE HEART

The inhabitants of the Mediterranean region knew that, together with their grains, pulses, fruits, vegetables, and cultured milks, they needed an oil to prepare their food, to make it taste better, and to make them feel good and stay healthy. Two or three millennia later scientists would discover the reason.

Monounsaturated fats have been found in recent years to be the safest fats, in more ways than one, and the principal fat in olive oil is *oleic acid* (the name "oleic" comes from "olive"), a monounsaturated fat. Olive oil is about 70 to 75 percent monounsaturated, 12 percent polyunsaturated (you want some polyunsaturated fats in oils but not an excess), and only about 15 percent saturated. This is as nearly perfect a fat as we can get, and, incidentally, is very similar in composition to almonds and hazelnuts (filberts). *The main fats in our diet should be monounsaturated.*

When olive oil replaces saturated fats, or the trans fats found in some margarines, the harmful blood cholesterol goes down while the good cholesterol remains unchanged. The occurrence of heart disease is very low in Mediterranean countries, where this oil is the main fat. The Greek island of Crete is famous for having an extremely low rate of heart disease; it also has a high consumption of olive oil.

A 1995 Italian study by Dr. Francesco Visioli and his colleagues at the University of Milan confirms that extra-virgin olive oils contain compounds that protect blood cholesterol from damage by oxygen.

Use oils that are predominantly monounsaturated, such as the oils of the olive and almond, and use unrefined oils, to be sure they are rich in antioxidants to preserve them on the shelf and to protect them from oxidation inside your body. Extra-virgin olive oil is the best one to use if you want not only a good-tasting oil, but an oil that is as rich as possible in natural antioxidants.

Whole olives, when properly prepared, can be used instead of olive oil to supply good fats to the diet, but care should be taken to select olives that have not been processed to the extent that some precious compounds are leached out. Olives preserved with sea salt, olive oil, or vinegar are the best choice, but be careful as they can be high in salt. Use them in place of salt as an addition to a salad or to make a dressing.

If people would consume most of their fats from olive oil, nuts, oil-rich seeds such as sesame, and avocados, some major forms of heart disease would become a rarity among nonsmokers.

Nuts and Oil-Rich Seeds of the Mediterranean

Each continent has its native nuts and oil-rich seeds. In the Americas, we find pecans, sunflowers, and a little-known variety of walnut. Around the Mediterranean Sea, we find the flavorful sesame seeds as well as almonds, hazelnuts, and pistachios, nuts that share many good things with the olive. Their main fat is monounsaturated; they contain fiber, vitamins, and minerals, and a reasonable amount of good protein. Nuts should be used more freely in the diet: they make people feel satisfied. In a recent study at our center, subjects consuming nuts were amazed that they did not feel as hungry between meals—a benefit of foods high in fat, as long as they are not used to excess.

For the history purist, we acknowledge that the almond tree is a gift of Asia, but we have chosen to talk about it here since it traveled to the Mediterranean region centuries before Christ and because it is important in Mediterranean cuisines. The almond tree was probably introduced to the Mediterranean by the Phoenicians. We find almonds used by ancient Hebrews, Greeks, and Romans.

Hazelnuts, sometimes called filberts, and pistachios—both native to the Mediterranean region—are very similar in composition to the almond and are excellent sources of monounsaturated fats.

Walnuts originated in Persia, Armenia, and around the Caspian Sea. Greeks and Romans cultivated them for centuries before the birth of Christ, and at the peak of their power, Romans introduced walnuts to many European countries. The walnut is a polyunsaturated nut and makes an ideal source of polyunsaturated fats. Walnuts are also a good source of omega-three fats. Be sure to keep them refrigerated or sealed in a can or airtight bag to prevent oxygen damage, or choose fresh walnuts in season. When you buy shelled walnuts in a package, check the expiration date carefully, or rely on a reputable supplier. Walnut oil can be used as an occasional flavoring for special recipes. Walnut oil should be stored in the refrigerator because it can become rancid if kept in a warm environment.

Sesame is the oil-rich seed of the Middle East. It's usually used as a "butter" (*tahini*), roasted, or raw. With chickpeas, it makes the famous Middle Eastern *hummus*. Mixed with honey, it makes *halvah*, a delicious candy. Sesame contains more polyunsaturated fats than olives, but the monounsaturated fats are still the major fats present.

Nuts and oil-rich seeds are among the greatest storehouses of nutrients and energy; it is sad that so many people have forgotten their great value.

CHESTNUTS

The chestnut tree is a native of the Mediterranean region, and we find it in southern Europe, Algeria, and the Middle East. Pliny, the Roman historian, places its origin in Asia Minor, a peninsula that comprises most of what is today Turkey. Chestnuts can be boiled in water or roasted and are a good source of easily digestible complex carbohydrates.

DATES: THE BLESSED FRUIT OF THE ARABS

"Honor your uncle, the palm: I call him your uncle because he was created from the earth left over after the creation of Adam... The palm resembles man by its separation in two sexes, and by its necessity for the pollination of the female." So Paul Popenoe, author of *Date Growing in the Old and New Worlds*, begins his book written in 1902, an excellent source of stories and facts about dates. He goes on: "The angel Gabriel appeared to Adam in Eden and designated the palm as his future food, saying: You were created of the same material as this tree, which shall nourish you." Ancient Arabic lore attributes healing properties to dates. In Roman times, Pliny wrote of their employment "to recruit the strength and allay the thirst of a patient"—a sensible use, since they are a concentrated source of easily digested energy.

In North African and Middle Eastern countries, dates are a staple food, and for many peasants in these regions, the only easily available and abundant food. The palm tree is still considered a holy tree by the Arabs and is worshipped not only for its fruits but for the shade it gives in the desert and for the usefulness of its leaves and other parts. Fibers from the leaves are used to make baskets, hats, and ropes; the stems and leaves are used to make huts. A juice from the upper part of the trunk is fermented to make palm wine, an alcoholic beverage (disapproved of by the Islamic religion). Today dates are also grown in the Coachella Valley in southern California, not far from Palm Springs, and in Arizona.

The Arabs have always considered yogurt and various other kinds of cultured milks to be good accompaniments for dates. This is a great nutritional combination: the sugar and quick energy of the dates and the proteins and calcium of yogurt. This concept can be expanded to include cultured milks with other dried fruits such as raisins.

Dates, raisins, figs, prunes, and other dried fruits are too often relegated to a secondary role in the meals of industrialized societies. These are the sweets (fiber- and nutrient-rich) that we should make an important part of our diet.

CULTURED MILKS

Ancient Middle Easterners discovered that milk from goats, cows, sheep, and camels would not keep very long in the hot desert temperatures. They also knew that the first and only food of newborn humans and other mammals was milk, an easy lesson in basic ancient nutrition. Milk had to be a body-building and energy-giving food. They knew also that milking did not kill the animal and thus was much more efficient—what we call today "ecological." From all of this, cultured milks were born, known by different names in different countries, with quite different flavors and consistencies as well. Cultured milks found in the Mediterranean region are often called yogurt or yoghurt. Needless to say, cultured milk contains some of the best proteins and is very high in calcium as well and makes an excellent addition to a plant-based diet.

In properly cultured milks, the milk sugar, difficult to digest and troublesome for some people, has been predigested by the culture and turned into the acidic flavor of these milks.

WHEN SWITCHING TO A PLANT-BASED DIET, WATCH YOUR PROTEIN INTAKE

In a recent study at our center, people with high blood cholesterol (remember Laurel's story, page 13) went on a diet based on whole grain breads and cereals, beans, nuts, fruits, and vegetables. No meat, fish, or fowl was allowed. Lowfat yogurts were used to supply the daily requirement of protein, because we feared that many of these study participants, used to a typical Western diet, would not eat enough cooked beans, tofu, nuts, and high-protein grains. One person went so far as to eat mostly grains and not enough beans or yogurts, and she began to feel weak before we discovered both the physiological and menu-planning switches were too drastic for her; she had not learned enough about the new way of cooking. You can eat a strictly vegetarian diet, but be sure you learn how to make the transition properly if you are used to the regular consumption of meats and fish.

MEDITERRANEAN HERBS AND SPICES

by Cornelia Carlson

The ancient Romans enjoyed one of the spiciest times in history, judging by the cookbook, *De Re Coquinaria by Apicius*. All but a few of its 500 recipes are flavored with at least one herb or spice and most are seasoned with several. The book, which may be the oldest known cookery manuscript, is filled with luxurious foods such as pheasant forcemeat spiced with black pepper and saffron-spiked wine. While the poorer classes couldn't have afforded the pepper or saffron, we can guess that they cooked with many of the other spices and herbs mentioned in this text. Virtually all were grown within the empire. Many were simply wild herbs that anyone could have gathered from the lush hillside stands.

The remnants of these fields remain today. In Spain, once the western reach of Rome's domain, borage still grows rampantly along the Costa Blanca south of Valencia; rosemary covers the thin soil of the desolate Maestrazgo hills; yellow fields of mustard blanket parts of Navarra; and low-growing lavender clings to the Extremaduran roadsides. To the east, in Greece, wild thyme, marjoram, and oregano still perfume the Peloponnesian air, attracting the bees that make its famed honey. Sage holds tenaciously to the land that once was Yugoslavia, despite horrific war. And throughout the British Isles, mint is as entrenched along damp waysides as it was 2,000 years ago.

In cooking and medicine, as in all matters, the Romans knew a good thing when they saw it, adopted it, and then took it one step further. From the Egyptians they learned how to make sesame and poppy seed oils, to season with coriander, cassia, and cinnamon, and to sprinkle their breads with poppy and sesame seeds. Perhaps they also learned that the Egyptians had strengthened their pyramid construction workers with onions and garlic. And from the Assyrians and Greeks, they may have acquired their taste for anise, cumin, dill, caraway, fennel, rosemary, marjoram, sage, mint, and capers. In fact, in their heyday, the Romans knew and used a majority of the spices and herbs that we employ today.

Just as in other ancient cultures, the Romans didn't segregate their spices into flavoring or therapeutic roles, but viewed most as helpful in both arenas. Dill was thought to induce sleep and cure indigestion and was also used to season bacon. Mint and parsley could soothe an ailing stomach or flavor a sauce for meat, fish, or fowl. Caraway was recommended as a tonic for pale girls and included in sauces for chicken. Savory, another favorite sauce flavoring, was used to treat bee stings. Mustard was given to hysterical patients, applied to scorpion bites, and added to vinaigrette for cooked beets. A few spices seemed to play yin/yang roles. To begin a meal, anise was used to perk up appetite; to end the meal, anise-seed cakes (called *mustacea*) were eaten to relieve the gluttonous aftermath. Saffron was used to flavor wine, then to cure hangovers.

If you read Apicius' cookbook, you'll find some delectable dishes among some seemingly bizarre. However, the cures, recorded in other Roman documents, are with a few exceptions the quaint relics of an ancient time. Yet, new scientific evidence suggests many of the herbs that played an important role 2,000 years ago may play a significant and beneficial part in our diet today. The mint family herbs are of particular interest. All the best-known members (basil, marjoram, oregano, lavender, rosemary, sage, savory, thyme) show strong antioxidant properties (see page 10), better even than the synthetic preservatives BHA and BHT that we see on too many of our food labels. As such, all may be helpful in preventing cancer, reducing inflammation, and retarding aging.

The flavor of each of these herbs is far more vibrant when they're fresh rather than dried. Your supermarket may sell bunches of cut herbs from time to time, but for a reliable supply you should grow your own. Even if your garden is no larger than your balcony, you can harvest a continual supply from plants grown in five-gallon cans. If you have more space, add some of the unusual varieties. There are at least 150 species of basil growing somewhere in the world, more than 1,000 varieties of mint, 30 species of savory, perhaps as many as 400 species of thyme, and numerous cultivated varieties of rosemary and sage. Some of these are wild plants you'll never find in nurseries. But you'll find enough exotic herbs offered by suppliers listed in the Sources section to fill an acre lot.

EXPLORING THE MEDITERRANEAN KITCHEN

As we visit the kitchens of Mediterranean countries, we'll find recipes that reflect the warmth of their people and climate. Remember that traditional Mediterranean food preparation is very simple, although we have included a few more elaborate recipes for special occasions.

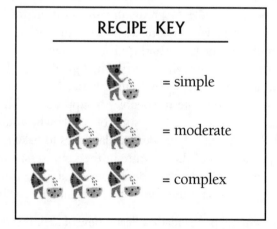

EGYPTIAN BREAD

by Monica Spiller

The ancient Egyptians are invariably given credit for being the first to make bread, but the actual shape of the bread and the actual wheat from which it was made are still unknown. Primarily though, the Egyptians must have been growing very good wheat for their style of breads. There is evidence that easily threshed bread wheat (*Triticum aestivum*) could have been grown in Egypt as early as 6000 to 5000 B.C., and this would have made a risen bread far superior in lightness to anything previously seen. The other wheats of that time were *einkorn* and *emmer*, both of which have very tough husks that are difficult to remove.

To be bread in the modern sense of the word, the first Egyptian bread must have been made from bread wheat and a ferment containing a yeast. A natural ferment containing yeast and accompanying lactic bacteria is readily made from whole grain wheat, as follows: bread wheat, as opposed to emmer wheat, is easily threshed free from its husk, so that the wheat berry would have kept its natural bloom of yeasts and lactic bacteria. If wheat grains are soaked and then sprouted, they are, as a result, enriched in vitamins and enzymes. These enzymes are capable of producing sugars from the wheat starch. Sprouted wheat is therefore an ideal source of nutrients for the growth of both the yeasts and lactic acid bacteria to be found occurring naturally on the wheat berry. The Egyptians probably sprouted their wheat, in a similar way to their barley for beer, and used it as a sweetener. It would be reasonable to suppose that they used some sprouted wheat with their mixture of whole wheat flour and water, which they quite likely made into flat cakes to bake on a hot stone. Daily preparation of this mixture in the same vessel, without cleaning it out, would allow the development of an optimal mixture of microorganisms, and these were the leavening for the bread.

The ancient Egyptians made at least some of their bread in ovens, and so this too could have contributed to their ability to be the first to make something more sophisticated than a flat unleavened hearth cake.

TIPS FOR BARM BREADMAKING

- A barm starter is a sourdough starter containing both a natural yeast and lactic bacteria in a batter of whole wheat flour, sprouted wheat flour, and water.

- A recipe for preparing a barm starter, as well as previously made barm starters, are available by mail order (see Sources).

- A sourdough starter can be used instead of a barm, provided it can be maintained by refreshment with whole wheat flour and a little sprouted wheat flour. Some kinds of sourdough starters need the addition of baker's yeast. Most sourdough starters give a strongly savory flavor to breads, and therefore may not give the fruity, buttery flavor notes that can be expected from a barm.

- Sprouted wheat, rye, or barley flour is also known as diastatic malt flour. This ingredient will help any sourdough starter to perform well by providing enzymes, which can release simple sugars from the grain starch. These sugars are the main source of energy for the sourdough microorganisms.

- The refreshment should always double the amount of starter. Thus one cup of starter is refreshed to give 2 cups, 2 cups of starter are refreshed to give 4 cups, and so on. Always remember to make enough refreshed starter both for the recipe and for some to keep for the next baking session.

- Approximately 86 degrees is a suitable room temperature for making barm breads.

- If you have a modern digital scale, measuring the ingredients by weight in grams will make it easier to exactly reproduce the bread recipes in this book. Commercial bakers also find it easier to scale up recipes by measuring ingredients by weight rather than volume (cups and spoons). The bread recipes in this and later chapters list gram equivalents for cooks using scales.

- When a barm has been stored in the refrigerator (at approximately 40 degrees) between baking days for more than 2 or 3 days, it should be refreshed at least three times at 12-hour intervals, at 55 to 60 degrees, before using in a final dough. Doing this prevents the accumulation of too much acid in the starter and allows the bread to have a lighter texture and milder flavor.

- A temperature of 55 to 60 degrees is wine cellar temperature; it can be achieved against warm room temperatures inside a cooler containing a bowl of ice. The ideal is a basement or room that is always at this temperature.

Egyptian Balady Bread
by Monica Spiller

Makes 8 pocket bread buns

One type of Egyptian bread which is popular today is balady bread, a puffy pocket bread. Modern balady bread is quite often still made with naturally fermented whole wheat flour made from a white wheat. Choose a hard white wheat, high in protein. Balady bread is baked in a very hot oven and is spectacular. It is made up as a thin, flat disk, but after it has been allowed to rise and is baked, it billows into a beautiful cushion with a hollow center in just a few seconds. The total baking time is usually less than three minutes.

WHITE-WHEAT BARM BREAD STARTER

(see Tips for Barm Breadmaking, page 127)

Refresh a barm starter with whole white-wheat flour, sprouted wheat flour, barley malt extract syrup, and water, using the proportions given below. Keep the refreshed barm starter at 55 to 60 degrees, and repeat the refreshment two or three times at 12-hour intervals. Six to twelve hours after the last refreshment, the refreshed barm starter can be used for balady bread dough.

If you are not baking daily, refrigerate (at approximately 40 degrees) a portion of the refreshed barm ready for the next barm breadmaking session. The barm starter can be kept refrigerated for up to 4 weeks and still be useful for making bread.

Ingredients for 2 cups (506 grams) white-wheat barm starter:

> 1 cup (250 grams) barm starter
> ⅔ cup (109 grams) whole white-wheat flour
> ½ teaspoon (1 gram) sprouted wheat flour
> 1 teaspoon (10 grams) barley malt extract syrup
> ⅔ cup (141 grams) water (at approximately 40 degrees)

BALADY BREAD DOUGH

1½ cups (250 grams) whole white-wheat flour
1 teaspoon (3 grams) sprouted wheat flour
1 cup (250 grams) white-wheat barm (6 to 12 hours since last
  refreshment, at 55 to 60 degrees)
1 tablespoon (25 grams) wheat or barley malt syrup
⅓ cup (88 grams) water (at approximately 86 degrees)
¼ teaspoon (1½ grams) salt

To a large mixing bowl, add whole white-wheat flour, sprouted wheat flour, white-wheat barm, and barley malt syrup. Dissolve salt in water and add it to the mixing bowl.

Mix all the ingredients together until just blended. Cover the mixing bowl and leave dough to rise at approximately 86 degrees for 45 minutes to 2 hours, to allow the dough to expand by about half as much again in volume.

Knead the dough to complete the mixing and to develop the dough, until it can be easily stretched into a paper-thin sheet (about 5 to 10 minutes). Divide the dough into eight equal pieces and round them into balls. Lightly coat each dough piece in flour and leave to rest between canvas cloths for 20 minutes.

On the canvas cloth, and using floured fingertips, gently press each dough piece into a flat disk, ¼ inch thick and 5 inches in diameter. Turn dough piece over at least two or three times during this process. Take care to work from the center of the dough piece so that the edge remains smooth and unbroken. Cover and leave to rise for 30 minutes.

Preheat oven and terra cotta baking tiles on middle shelf to 500 degrees. Arrange the buns, tops uppermost for the best puff, on the hot tiles. Bake for 1 to 2 minutes, until they puff. As soon as they have puffed, turn them over for another 1 minute or less of baking. These buns should be quite pale, even when fully cooked; browning should be kept to a minimum for the best flavor and texture.

ITALIAN BREADS

by Monica Spiller

Historically the Italians have preferred the white wheats for their bread, since these wheats have a bran color little different from the flour color. The red wheats have grown in popularity only since roller milling has been used, for roller mills can produce a white flour by efficiently removing the dark-colored bran and germ. Many white wheats produce a flour that can be made into a bread with relatively little kneading, and they are at their best when used to make flat rather than lofty breads. So it is reasonable to suppose that the grape bread of Tuscany, which is a flat bread, though nevertheless very well leavened, would once have been made with a stone-ground, whole white-wheat flour.

The grapes in Tuscany are not necessarily immediately made into wine, or even used to make grape bread, as soon as they are harvested. Instead, they leave some grapes to dry on the vine, or hang them from rafters so that they become intensely sweet raisins. These they use to make a very sugary must for their Vin Santo wine, or for transforming bread dough into a delectable sweet bread for breakfast or dessert, at any time of the year.

Not too far from Tuscany, in the Veneto—which is another wine making region of Italy—a similar flat bread is made with raisins, but with the addition of honey and black pepper. The black pepper probably dates from the Middle Ages, when Venice was at the center of the spice trade between Europe and the East.

The following raisin bread combines the elements of whole wheat flour from white wheat berries, richly flavored raisins, choice local honey, and just a trace of black pepper to add an intriguing warmth and spiciness. This bread is good for several days, especially if it is lightly toasted; the honey forms crunchy crystals of sugar and the raisins meld into the dough.

Whole White-Wheat Raisin Bread

by Monica Spiller

Makes one 10-inch diameter round flat bread

WHITE-WHEAT BARM BREAD STARTER

(see Tips for Barm Breadmaking, page 127)

Refresh a barm starter with whole white-wheat flour, sprouted wheat flour, barley malt extract syrup, and water, using the proportions given below. Keep the refreshed barm starter at 55 to 60 degrees, and repeat the refreshment two or three times at 12-hour intervals. Six to twelve hours after the last refreshment, the refreshed barm starter can be used for raisin bread dough.

If you are not baking daily, refrigerate (at approximately 40 degrees) a portion of the refreshed barm ready for the next barm breadmaking session. The barm starter can be kept refrigerated for up to 4 weeks and still be useful for making bread.

Ingredients for 2 cups (500 grams) white-wheat barm starter:

1 cup (250 grams) barm starter
⅓ cup (109 grams) whole white-wheat flour
½ teaspoon (1 gram) sprouted wheat flour
1 teaspoon (10 grams) barley malt extract syrup
⅓ cup (141 grams) water (at approximately 40 degrees)

RAISIN BREAD FILLING

1 cup (150 grams) sundried raisins or currants
Black pepper
1 to 2 tablespoons (60 grams) honey

Prepare the raisin filling by sprinkling a small amount of black pepper (1 to 4 twists from a pepper mill) onto the raisins. The amount of pepper should be small enough to provide the spicy warm notes rather than the pepperiness. Add the honey, and mix and toss until uniformly coated.

recipe continues next page

RAISIN BREAD DOUGH

1½ cups (250 grams) whole white-wheat flour

1 teaspoon (3 grams) sprouted wheat flour

1 cup (250 grams) white-wheat barm (6 to 12 hours since last refreshment, at 55 to 60 degrees)

1 to 2 tablespoons (60 grams) honey

⅓ cup (88 grams) water (at approximately 86 degrees)

⅛ teaspoon (1 gram) salt

To a large mixing bowl, add whole white-wheat flour, sprouted wheat flour, white-wheat barm, and honey. Dissolve salt in water and add it to the mixing bowl.

Mix all the ingredients together until just blended. Cover the mixing bowl and leave dough to rise at approximately 86 degrees for 45 minutes to 2 hours, to allow dough to expand by about half as much again in volume. While the dough rises, prepare the Raisin Bread Filling (previous page). Also prepare a 12-inch square of baking parchment paper by lightly coating it with olive oil followed by a light dusting of flour.

Knead the dough to complete the mixing and to develop the dough, until it can be easily stretched into a paper-thin sheet (about 5 to 10 minutes). Divide the dough into two equal-sized pieces and round them.

Lightly coat each piece in flour, and leave to rest between canvas cloths for 20 minutes. On the canvas cloth, and using floured fingertips, gently press each dough piece into a flat disk, ½-inch thick and 10 inches in diameter.

Lay one of the dough pieces on the prepared parchment paper. Spread two-thirds of the raisin filling over the dough. Press the raisins into the dough with your fingertips, and cover the entire surface. Take the second dough piece and gently place it on top of the raisins. Spread the remaining raisin filling on top, again gently pressing raisins into the dough. Seal the edges of the dough pieces together. Cover with a very large mixing bowl, and leave to rise for 30 minutes.

Preheat oven and terra cotta baking tiles, on middle shelf, at 400 degrees. Just before baking, gently coat entire top surface of bread with melted honey (1 tablespoon). To prevent the bread from forming pockets as it bakes, make a pattern of dimples all the way through the bread with a wooden pick or lemon reamer.

Transfer to oven on a baking peel. Bake for 20 minutes. Allow to cool on rack before removing the parchment paper.

OLIVE BREAD

by Monica Spiller

In the southern regions of the Mediterranean lands, the summers are very hot and dry, and the type of wheat favored is durum wheat. Durum wheat is used for making pasta, bread, couscous, bulgur wheat (which is a boiled and dried wheat), and frekeh, which is green wheat released from the husk by burning it.

In ancient times durum wheat for bread was used as a whole wheat flour, stone-ground locally, and leavened with a sourdough piece kept from one baking to the next. Durum wheat is wonderfully suited to making Italian pizza and focaccia. In Apulia and Sicily, it is used for much larger daily breads.

In the same regions where durum wheat is grown, olives are at their most prolific, so that it seems completely natural for breads to be flavored with olive oil and olives. The olives are prepared for the table in many ways, although almost all these ways include a step during which the bitter-flavored compounds are drawn from the olives by salt. Olives are at first green on the tree in the fall, but they turn black by the end of winter. At this point they can be prepared with salt to produce Greek-style olives, which in the final step are coated with olive oil and herbs such as thyme and oregano.

Focaccia with Black Olives

by Monica Spiller

Makes one 10-inch diameter flat bread

Durum Wheat Barm Bread Starter

(see Tips for Barm Breadmaking, page 127)

Refresh a barm starter with whole durum wheat flour, sprouted wheat flour, barley malt extract syrup, and water, using the proportions given below. Keep the refreshed barm starter at 55 to 60 degrees, and repeat the refreshment two or three times at 12-hour intervals. Six to twelve hours after the last refreshment, the refreshed barm starter can be used for the focaccia bread dough.

If you are not baking daily, refrigerate (at approximately 40 degrees) a portion of the refreshed barm ready for the next barm breadmaking session. The barm starter can be kept refrigerated for up to four weeks and still be useful for making bread.

Ingredients for 2 cups (500 grams) durum wheat barm starter:

> 1 cup (250 grams) barm starter
> 2/3 cup (109 grams) whole durum wheat flour
> 1/2 teaspoon (1 gram) sprouted wheat flour
> 1 teaspoon (10 grams) barley malt extract syrup
> 2/3 cup (141 grams) water (at approximately 40 degrees)

DOUGH FOR FOCACCIA WITH BLACK OLIVES

1½ cups (250 grams) whole durum wheat flour

1 teaspoon (3 grams) sprouted wheat flour

1 cup (250 grams) durum wheat barm (6 to 12 hours since last refreshment, at 55 to 60 degrees)

1 tablespoon (25 grams) barley malt syrup

1 tablespoon (5 grams) olive oil, for the dough

⅓ cup (88 grams) water (at approximately 86 degrees)

¼ teaspoon (1½ grams) salt

¼ cup (20 grams) pitted and halved black Greek-style olives

1 to 2 tablespoons (5 to 10 grams) olive oil, for coating the focaccia

To a large mixing bowl, add whole durum wheat flour, sprouted wheat flour, durum wheat barm, barley malt syrup, and olive oil. Dissolve salt in water and add it to the mixing bowl.

Mix all the ingredients together, until just blended. Cover the mixing bowl and leave dough to rise at approximately 86 degrees for 45 minutes. While the dough rises, halve and pit the olives. Prepare a 12-inch square of baking parchment paper by lightly coating it with olive oil.

Knead the dough very briefly to complete the mixing, for two or three minutes only. Then briefly knead the pitted olive halves into the dough. Form the dough into a ball, lightly coat in flour, and leave to rest between canvas cloths for 20 minutes.

Using olive oil–coated hands, coat the dough with olive oil and position it on the prepared parchment paper. Gently press the dough out from the center into a flat circle, until it is about 9 inches in diameter and ½-inch thick. Coat the entire top surface generously with olive oil.

Cover with a very large mixing bowl, and leave to rise for 30 minutes. Preheat oven and terra cotta baking tiles on middle shelf, at 400 degrees.

To prevent the bread from forming pockets as it bakes, make a pattern of dimples all the way through the bread with a wooden pick or lemon reamer.

Transfer to oven on a baking peel. Bake for 20 minutes. Allow to cool on rack before removing the parchment paper.

Spelt Pasta

by Gene Spiller

Serves 2 to 3

Choose freshly ground spelt flour or make this from freshly ground durum wheat flour. If the amounts are doubled, work with half the dough at a time to shape the pasta.

> 1 cup freshly milled spelt flour
> 3 egg whites
> 2 quarts water
> ½ teaspoon salt
> Herbs if desired (such as rosemary, thyme, and oregano)

Mound the flour into a pile on a large pastry board, making a well in the center. Lightly whip the egg whites and pour into the well. Working from the center, gradually combine flour and egg whites with your hands until a fairly stiff dough is formed. Form the dough into a ball and allow to rest in a covered bowl about 20 to 40 minutes. This allows the flour to absorb the moisture fully. Roll the dough out into a rectangle on a lightly floured board. Turn dough several times while rolling as thinly as possible without tearing. Use a wheel-style cutter to cut strips of pasta. Meanwhile, bring water and salt to a rolling boil in a large pot. Add fresh herbs to boiling water if desired. Add pasta; stir gently to separate pasta strands. Boil, uncovered, for 10 to 12 minutes. Strain and remove herb stems. Top with the Fresh Tomato-Basil Pasta Sauce that follows, or other sauces as desired.

Fresh Tomato-Basil Pasta Sauce

by Rowena Hubbard

Serves 2

This elegant, easy pasta sauce should be made when the garden is brimming with fresh ripe tomatoes and beautiful, fragrant basil. It perfectly captures the summer and the sunlight of the Mediterranean. Serve it tossed with Spelt Pasta (previous page).

> 2 cups chopped fresh tomatoes with juice
>
> 2 tablespoons Mellow Garlic Oil (page 177)
>   or extra-virgin olive oil
>
> 1 clove garlic from Mellow Garlic Oil
>   or 1 clove fresh garlic, chopped
>
> 2 ounces lowfat mozzarella cheese, chopped
>
> 2 cups coarsely chopped fresh basil leaves
>
> Freshly ground pepper
>
> Parmesan (optional)

Combine all ingredients, except Parmesan, in a large bowl. Toss with cooked Spelt Pasta and serve in warmed bowls, topped with a little freshly grated Parmesan if desired.

Speedy Fresh Pesto Sauce

by Rowena Hubbard

Makes 1 cup

This freezes well. In summer, when the garden is full of basil, make several big batches and freeze for use in the winter. This classic Italian pasta sauce is also excellent spooned into vegetable soup for vibrant, fresh flavor. I often toss it with cooked fresh vegetables, such as peas, green beans, or zucchini, and it is perfect as a topping for garden-fresh tomatoes. In Genoa, spelt pasta, tiny boiled new potatoes, and barely cooked green beans are tossed with pesto for a splendid dish.

> 2 cups fresh sweet basil leaves, packed
> 1 large clove garlic, coarsely chopped
> ¼ cup extra-virgin olive oil
> 2 tablespoons lightly toasted pine nuts
> Freshly ground pepper
> 2 tablespoons freshly grated Parmesan cheese (optional)

Combine the basil, garlic, oil, and pine nuts in bowl of food processor. Top with a few grinds of fresh pepper; process until a smooth paste is formed. Stir in the cheese by hand if using. Turn into a 1-cup glass container, cover well, and refrigerate or freeze.

Crunchy Almond Pasta Sauce

by Rowena Hubbard

Serves 2

Crunchy with almonds and sautéed whole wheat bread cubes, the flavors here blend well. Spicy arugula loses its bite when briefly cooked, but its color and flavor are intensified. Native to Italy, arugula is only now becoming widely available across America.

> 2 ripe medium-sized tomatoes, diced
> ¼ cup chopped fresh basil
> ¼ cup olive oil
> 1 large clove garlic, minced
> 1 cup small fresh whole wheat bread cubes
> 1 recipe of Spelt Pasta (page 136) or 16 ounces other whole grain pasta
> 2 cups shredded arugula
> ¼ cup toasted slivered almonds
> Freshly shredded Parmesan cheese

Toss the tomatoes and basil together and set aside. Heat the oil in skillet and sauté the garlic until pale golden. Stir in the bread cubes, tossing until they are golden brown. Remove from heat. Cook Spelt Pasta according to directions, adding the arugula during the last minute of cooking. Drain well. Toss pasta and arugula with the tomato mixture; then toss in the bread cubes and almonds. Serve at once, garnished with a little shredded fresh Parmesan cheese.

Pasta and Chickpeas with Tomato and Basil

by Deborah Madison

Serves 2 to 4

There are lots of ways to combine pasta and chickpeas. This is after the Napoletana style.

> 1 cup cooked chickpeas
> 1½ tablespoon extra-virgin olive oil, plus oil to finish
> 4 tablespoons finely minced onion
> 2 pinches red pepper flakes
> 4 ripe tomatoes, peeled, seeded, and chopped
> 2 cloves garlic, minced or pressed
> Salt
> 8 ounces spinach fettucine
> ¼ cup minced parsley
> 10 basil leaves, torn in small pieces
> Freshly ground pepper

Drain chickpeas. In a skillet, heat the oil, add the onion and pepper flakes, and cook over medium heat 12 minutes. Add the tomatoes, garlic, chickpeas, and ½ cup water; lower the heat to a simmer. Meanwhile, bring a large pot of water to boil, add salt to taste, then add the fettucine. Cook until al dente. Scoop it out and add it to the pan with the chickpeas. Don't worry about water dripping from the pasta—it will help make a little sauce. Add the parsley and basil; season with pepper and toss in the pan. Taste for salt and serve, drizzled with additional olive oil.

Homemade Pasta with Coarsely Ground Wheat Berries (Ksinohondros)

by Aglaia Kremezi

Makes about 2½ cups

This simple kind of homemade pasta was prepared with sour milk, because in the old days, without refrigeration, it was very difficult to keep fresh milk in the warm Mediterranean climate for more than one day.

The word ksino *means "sour" and* hondros *is the ancient Greek word for coarsely ground wheat. Traditionally the wheat berries are soaked in water overnight, then dried in the sun and coarsely ground in stone hand mills. I had the opportunity to follow the whole procedure of making ksinohondros in a completely primitive way, on the island of Kythera. The recipe that follows is my adaptation of Elini Kasimatis' way of making ksinohondros in the village of Drymonas, on Kythera.*

Ksinohondros is dried and then used in soups (as in the recipe that follows) or vegetable stews.

> 3 cups nonfat milk
> 1 cup medium-grain bulgur
> 1 cup nonfat plain yogurt
> Pinch of sea salt

In a nonstick pot pour the milk and add the bulgur. Bring to a boil over medium heat, stirring to avoid spilling. Lower the heat and simmer, stirring often at the beginning and constantly after the first 10 minutes. In about 20 minutes the mixture thickens. Remove from the heat, pour into a large shallow dish or pan, and let cool completely. Stir in yogurt and salt. Turn the somewhat hardened mixture over onto clean tea towels and let dry in the sun or at room temperature, separating the clumps into smaller pieces (like coarse bread crumbs). When completely dry, store in an airtight container until needed.

Note: You can speed up the process if you dry ksinohondros overnight in a just-warm oven. Heat oven to 200 degrees, then turn off. Place ksinohondros in oven and close door. Leave overnight.

Ksinohondros Soup

by Aglaia Kremezi

Serves 4

A simple Greek soup, combining ksinohondros and some typical Greek foods: olive oil, wine, and vegetable broth.

> 4 tablespoons chopped onion
> 3 tablespoons olive oil
> Freshly ground pepper
> ½ cup dry white wine
> 4 cups water or vegetable broth
> ½ cup ksinohondros (page 141)
> Sea salt
> A little dry feta cheese, crumbled
> 3 tablespoons chopped fresh parsley
> Olive oil croutons (see below)

Sauté onion in olive oil until soft, about 5 minutes. Add some freshly ground pepper and pour in the wine. Let it boil for a few seconds and add the water or broth and the ksinohondros. Stir and simmer for 6 to 10 minutes. Add a little salt, taste and adjust seasoning, taking into account the saltiness of the feta cheese. Divide into four individual soup bowls, and sprinkle with a little feta cheese and the parsley. Serve very hot, accompanied by whole wheat olive oil croutons.

OLIVE OIL CROUTONS

To make olive oil croutons, cut slices from a two-day-old whole wheat loaf. Brush the slices lightly with olive oil and cut into small cubes. Grill the bread cubes under the broiler, turning often, until golden. Let cool completely and store in an airtight box, until needed.

White Bean Soup with Spelt

by Deborah Madison

Serves 6 to 8

Spelt, an ancient form of wheat, is large and chewy, not unlike wheat berries and kamut, both of which can successfully be used in its place. The white beans can be navy beans or some of the larger varieties, such as cannellini or white Aztecs. A mound of steamed Savoy cabbage added to each bowl gives this winter meal a fresh and pretty look.

½ cup spelt, kamut, or wheat berries
1 cup large white beans, cleaned
2 quarts water or vegetable stock
2 bay leaves
4 cloves garlic: 1 sliced, 3 minced
3 tablespoons extra-virgin olive oil, plus oil to finish
½ teaspoon dried thyme
1 large onion, finely diced
2 carrots, finely diced
1 celery rib, finely diced, plus 2 tablespoons pale leaves, chopped
Salt and pepper
1 pound Savoy or green cabbage
Chopped celery or parsley leaves for garnish

In separate bowls, cover the spelt and beans with boiling water and set aside to soak for an hour. Drain. Put the spelt and the water or stock into a large soup pot; bring to a boil. Turn heat down and simmer, covered, for 30 minutes. Add the beans, bay leaves, sliced garlic, a tablespoon of the oil, and ¼ teaspoon thyme. Simmer, covered, 35 minutes.

While the beans are cooking, heat the remaining 2 tablespoons of oil in a wide skillet. Add the onion, carrots, celery, celery leaves, the 3 minced cloves garlic, and ¼ teaspoon thyme. Sauté over medium heat until the onions are completely soft, 12 to 15 minutes. Add the vegetables and 2 teaspoons salt to the spelt and beans. Cook until the beans are completely tender. Taste for salt and season with pepper. Just before serving, steam the cabbage until tender. Ladle the soup into soup plates, add the parsley or celery leaves, and mound cabbage in the middle of each bowl. Thread extra-virgin olive oil over each serving, add a dusting of pepper, and serve.

A Thick Pottage of Mixed Legumes

by Deborah Madison

Serves 6 to 8

Since all the beans are cooked in the same pot, this isn't really any more work than making a soup with a single legume. I rather like mixing beans—some fall apart while others stay whole and there's a pleasing play of textures, colors, and shapes. Since chickpeas usually take a lot longer to cook than other beans, I give them a 30-minute head start. This recipe is somewhat modified from the traditional, cutting back significantly on the fat. Beans do need some oil to come into their own, however.

Legumes

½ cup chickpeas

½ cup borlotti or pink or red kidney beans

½ cup cannellini or navy beans

½ cup green lentils

Salt

Aromatics

1 onion, peeled and halved

2 bay leaves

3 tablespoons chopped parsley

3 cloves garlic, peeled

Pasta

1 cup farfalle or other pasta shapes, cooked later

Grated pecorino cheese

Vegetables

    3 tablespoons extra-virgin olive oil

    1 large onion, finely chopped

    1 carrot, peeled and diced

    4 sun-dried tomatoes, cut in thin strips

    1 ounce dried porcini mushrooms, soaked in warm water
      20 minutes

    1 cup sliced fresh mushrooms

    Salt and pepper

    ½ pound Savoy cabbage, shredded

Soak the chickpeas in one bowl and the borlotti and cannellini beans in another bowl overnight. Clean and rinse the lentils. In a large pot, combine the soaked chickpeas with 10 cups water and the aromatics, reserving 2 cloves garlic. Bring to a boil, then simmer, partially covered, 30 minutes. Drain the remaining soaked beans; add them to the pot and cook until all are nearly tender (about an hour). Add the lentils and salt to taste; continue cooking until the beans are completely tender, another 25 to 35 minutes.

In a separate pan heat the oil; add chopped onion, carrot, sundried tomatoes, and reserved garlic. Fry for 5 minutes, stirring frequently. Drain the soaked porcini mushrooms, reserving the liquid, and add them to the pan with the fresh mushrooms. Fry another 4 to 5 minutes and season with salt and pepper. Add the cabbage, cooked beans, and enough broth plus the mushroom soaking water, strained, to give the soup the consistency you want. Simmer 25 minutes. Check for salt and season with pepper.

If possible, let the soup stand a few hours before serving, or overnight, so that the flavors can merge and deepen. Serve with pasta and a little grated cheese in each bowl.

Spelt Soup (Zuppa di Farro)

by Lorna Sass

Serves 6

In traditional Italian cookbooks, you will often find a recipe for Zuppa di Farro, *a hearty spelt and vegetable soup such as this one. Most whole grains remain a bit chewy—even when properly cooked—giving this soup a hearty texture. This is one of those simple preparations that nourishes both body and soul. It makes a satisfying dinner, accompanied by a green salad and a hearty peasant loaf. This soup thickens on standing. Thin it, as needed, with water or vegetable stock.*

> 1 tablespoon olive oil
> 1 tablespoon coarsely chopped garlic
> 2 cups coarsely chopped onion
> 1 cup spelt (wheat berries), soaked overnight in 3½ cups water
> 3 large ribs celery, sliced
> 3 large carrots, halved lengthwise and sliced
> 3 cups chopped plum tomatoes
> ½ cup tomato juice or water
> ½ pound potatoes, cut into ½-inch slices
> 1 teaspoon dried basil
> 1 teaspoon dried oregano
> ½ teaspoon dried rosemary
> ½ cup loosely packed, finely chopped parsley
> Salt and freshly ground pepper
> 1 to 2 tablespoons balsamic vinegar (optional)

Heat the oil in a pressure cooker. Sauté the garlic, stirring constantly, until lightly browned. Add the onion and cook, stirring, for 1 minute. Add the spelt and soaking liquid (stand back to avoid sputtering oil), celery, carrots, tomatoes and juice, potatoes, and dried herbs. Lock the pressure cooker lid in place. Over high heat bring to high pressure. Reduce heat just enough to maintain high pressure and cook for 10 minutes. Allow the pressure to come down naturally, about 10 minutes. Remove the lid, tilting it away from you to allow any excess steam to escape. Stir in parsley and salt and pepper to taste. Add balsamic vinegar to punch up the flavors, if needed.

Spinach and Chickpea Soup

by Rowena Hubbard

Serves 4

If you have cooked chickpeas on hand, this tasty soup comes together in half an hour. It has a mellow quality that is counterbalanced and complemented by the lemon juice.

> 3 tablespoons olive oil
> 2 large yellow onions, peeled and coarsely chopped
> 3 cloves garlic, minced
> 1 pound spinach
> ½ cup chopped fresh cilantro, lightly packed
> 2 tablespoons minced parsley
> 1 tablespoon minced fresh oregano
> 3 cups cooked chickpeas
> 2 cups chopped fresh tomatoes
> 3 cups vegetable broth
> Salt and freshly ground pepper
> 1 tablespoon lemon juice

Heat the oil in a large heavy soup pot. Sauté the onion and garlic until soft and transparent. Wash the spinach well; remove stems and coarsely chop leaves. Add spinach leaves to onion and sauté until they start to wilt. Stir in the cilantro, parsley, and oregano until just wilted. Add the chickpeas, tomatoes, vegetable broth, and salt and pepper to taste. Cover and simmer 20 minutes for flavors to blend. Stir the lemon juice into the soup just before serving.

Chickpea Soup with Condiments (Leblebi)

by Deborah Madison

Serves 6 or more

Leblebi is one of Tunisia's national dishes. In the markets I've seen tiny leblebi stands crowded with young men waiting for this hearty breakfast. Chickpeas, their broth, and bread are served in a bowl. An egg, if one wants, is whipped into it, then an assortment of condiments are added to each person's liking. It's an enormously sustaining dish. I used to serve a similar dish of boiled white beans with condiments at Greens in San Francisco. It was more in a Southern American style (I'd never heard of leblebi) and people always liked it. Condiments seem to make legumes much more appealing and fun to eat. This makes lots of chickpeas, but the leftovers are wonderful to use in salads, stews, and soups.

Soup Ingredients

2 cups dried chickpeas, soaked overnight
1 tablespoon olive oil
2 bay leaves
1 onion, finely diced
4 sprigs parsley
6 cloves garlic, roughly chopped
Salt
2 tablespoons *Harissa* (page 179)
1½ teaspoons cumin

Rinse the chickpeas and set them aside. Heat the oil in a soup pot with the bay leaves, add the onion, and sauté 3 to 4 minutes. Add the chickpeas, 10 cups of water, and parsley and bring to a boil. Lower the heat and simmer, partially covered, until the beans are soft but not completely cooked, anywhere from 30 minutes to 1½ hours.

Meanwhile, using a mortar, pound the garlic with 1 teaspoon salt, *harissa*, and cumin until it makes a smooth purée. Add it to the chickpeas along with another teaspoon salt and continue cooking until they're tender.

Condiments

> 4 thick pieces day-old country bread, chunked
> 6 lemon wedges
> 1 small finely diced onion or 1 bunch scallions, sliced
> ⅓ cup capers, drained
> ⅓ cup *Harissa* (page 179)
> Pickled turnips*
> Salt and freshly-milled pepper
> Extra-virgin olive oil

Prepare the bread and other condiments. Put a few pieces of bread into each serving bowl, ladle the chickpeas with some broth over them, and spoon in a little olive oil and freshly ground pepper. Let each person add his or her own condiments.

---

*Available in Middle Eastern food stores.

Chunky Gazpacho
by Rowena Hubbard

Serves 6

Traditional to Andalusia, this light soup of cool liquid and crisp vegetables is a perfect counterpoint to the searing heat. In oppressively hot weather, food seems unappealing and cool refreshing liquids are a must. I added the bread in the form of croutons rather than adding it to the base soup. It is a delightful entrée on a hot day or perfect as a light snack after strenuous exercise.

3 ½ cups chopped ripe tomatoes, with their juice
2 ½ cups cubed cucumber (¼-inch cubes)
1 cup finely minced onion
1 cup finely minced green pepper
1 large clove garlic, pressed
3 cups cold water
¼ cup fresh lemon juice
¼ cup extra-virgin olive oil
Salt and freshly ground pepper
Whole wheat croutons (see below)

Combine all ingredients, except croutons, in a large bowl, mixing well. Cover and chill at least 2 hours or overnight. Serve garnished with whole wheat croutons.

WHOLE WHEAT CROUTONS

¼ cup extra-virgin olive oil
1 cup whole wheat bread cubes

Heat the oil in a large skillet. Add the bread cubes and fry until golden on all sides. Drain on paper towels and cool.

Mashed Yellow Split Peas (Fava)

by Aglaia Kremezi

Serves 4

What Greeks call "fava" is not made with fava beans, but with yellow split peas, which are cooked to a thick paste and then mixed with chopped scallions or onion, oregano, virgin olive oil, and fresh lemon juice or vinegar. This is very similar to the ancient gruels. We know from ancient texts that Greeks ate a lot of legumes. Because the legumes were tough and needed endless hours of boiling to become edible, they were often roasted in the oven and then ground and just mixed with water or briefly cooked to be made into a kind of gruel. Boiling the split peas requires a lot of attention, and a low fire, because if they are left unattended and the water evaporates, they stick to the bottom and burn very easily, giving a disgusting smell to the dish. There is no alternative but to throw everything away and start again. The Greeks have a saying that characterizes disgusting things: "It tastes so bad, like burned fava."

½ pound yellow (or green) split peas

6 cups water

Sea salt

2⅔ teaspoons dried oregano

⅓ cup olive oil

Juice of ½ to 1 lemon

1 teaspoon Dijon mustard

3 scallions, chopped, white part plus 2 inches of green part

Freshly ground black pepper

½ cup chopped fresh dill

½ cup chopped arugula or cilantro

3 tablespoons capers for garnish

Rinse the peas and put them in a pot with the water. Turn the heat on and as they start to boil, add 1 teaspoon salt and 1 teaspoon oregano. Reduce the heat and let the split peas simmer, watching closely and stirring frequently, for about ½ to ¼ of an hour. By that time they should have absorbed most of their water and turned into a smooth paste. Do not let the fava cook unattended. It has a tendency to burn and stick at the bottom of the pan. So stir very often and add more water, if needed, during cooking. When done, remove from the heat and let cool for about 15 to 30 minutes. It thickens and can even be cut with a knife when completely cold. Just before serving, stir in the oil, lemon juice, mustard, scallions, and the rest of the oregano, adding a few tablespoons of water if it is too thick. Fava is eaten with a fork, so it should not be runny. Add salt and pepper to taste. Sprinkle with fresh dill and arugula or cilantro and top with the capers.

Cold Cucumber and Yogurt Soup

by Rowena Hubbard

Serves 4

Light, refreshing, and easy to make, this is a wonderful soup for a hot day. Versions of this as soup or sauce are still served all over the Middle East. To use it as a sauce, simply leave out the water. Serve sauce with baked falafel balls tucked into pita pockets and other Middle Eastern dishes.

    1 cup peeled, seeded, and grated cucumber
    2 cups plain nonfat yogurt
    1½ cups cold water
    1 tablespoon fresh lemon juice
    2 teaspoons chopped fresh mint
    1 teaspoon olive oil
    1 teaspoon chopped fresh dill
    Salt and freshly ground pepper
    Mint sprigs for garnish

Combine all ingredients except mint sprigs, adding salt and freshly ground pepper to taste. Chill about 1 hour. Serve garnished with mint sprigs.

Note: This soup can be made up to a day ahead and kept refrigerated. Stir well before serving.

Oven-Baked Chickpeas (Revithia Sto Fourno)

by Aglaia Kremezi

Serves 6 to 8

Ancient Greeks loved to eat chickpeas, not only cooked, but also roasted and munched as a snack or dessert. Roasted chickpeas, together with sultana raisins, dried figs, and nuts, were called tragemata *and made the perfect companion foods during the* symposion *(drinking party), which was the conclusion of every ancient dinner. In Greece, Turkey, and all over the Middle East, you will still find roasted chickpeas eaten as a snack, much like Americans eat popcorn today. On the island of Sifnos, they still make special clay casseroles for this dish, which was originally left to cook slowly overnight in the wood-burning village oven.*

> 1 pound dried chickpeas
> 2 tablespoons dried oregano
> 1 cup olive oil
> 3 onions, sliced
> ½ cup dry white wine
> ½ to 1 teaspoon freshly ground black pepper, or to taste
> 4 cloves garlic, minced
> Sea salt

Soak the chickpeas in water overnight. Drain and place them in a pot. Cover with cold water and bring to a boil. Skim any scum off the surface. Reduce the heat; sprinkle with one tablespoon of the oregano, and simmer for about one hour or more. The chickpeas should be almost done. Drain and reserve the liquid. Preheat oven to 300 degrees. Heat the olive oil in a skillet and sauté the onions for about 5 minutes, until soft. Add the wine and pepper; allow to boil for a few seconds. Remove the skillet from the heat and add the garlic, the rest of the oregano, and the chickpeas. Mix well and transfer to a clay or glass ovenproof casserole. Add about two cups of the reserved liquid. Toss, cover the casserole, and bake for 1½ to 2 hours, until the chickpeas are tender. A little more liquid may be needed during cooking. Taste, add salt, and adjust seasoning. Cook a little more if needed. Serve warm or at room temperature.

Country Zucchini Pies
(Kolokythopites)

by Aglaia Kremezi

Serves 8 (16 little pies)

The paper-thin phyllo pastry we buy today was originally a thin, flat bread, to which ancient Greeks added cheese, onion or garlic, and other toppings. The various Greek vegetable pies have their roots in those ancient breads, which were called plakous *and were similar to modern pita bread. Pita, in Greek, also means "pie." The village cook takes a piece of her bread dough to make the pie crust and fills it with whatever is in season: wild greens gathered from the fields, leeks, zucchini, pumpkin, eggplant, or a combination of several vegetables and greens.*

If you can find hard (durum) wheat flour—not to be confused with semolina flour—the crust has a better texture. If you're serving less than eight people, you can freeze the surplus. As you take the pies out of the freezer, let them warm in a 400-degree oven for 15 to 20 minutes before serving.

For the Pastry

> 4 cups all-purpose whole wheat flour*
> 1 teaspoon dry yeast
> 1 teaspoon coarse sea salt
> ⅓ cup olive oil
> 1⅔ to 2 cups warm water
> Cornmeal to sprinkle the baking sheets

In the bowl of a food processor equipped with dough hooks, add the flour, yeast, and salt. Work for a few seconds to combine. Add the olive oil and half the water and process for 3 minutes. Add more water as needed and work for another 3 minutes. The dough should be soft. Turn it onto a lightly floured board and knead until soft and silky. Form into a ball. Oil the bottom of a large 4-quart bowl and roll the dough in it. Cover with a plastic film and let rise for 1½ to 2 hours, until doubled. You can also leave the dough overnight in the refrigerator. (The next day, let it stand at room temperature for about 2 hours before proceeding further.)

Or use 2 cups hard wheat (durum) flour and 2 cups all-purpose whole wheat flour.

For the filling

> Sea salt
> 4 to 5 medium zucchini, grated (about 1 pound)
> ½ cup olive oil
> 2 cups chopped onions
> Freshly ground black pepper
> 1 cup nonfat milk
> ⅓ cup bulgur or *Ksinohondros* (page 141)
> 4 egg whites
> A little grated pecorino cheese or Greek *kefalotyri*

Salt the grated zucchini and let it drain for at least 45 minutes in a colander. In a large, deep skillet warm the olive oil and sauté the onions until translucent, about 5 minutes. Squeeze the zucchini with your hands; add to the skillet. Sauté over high heat until most of the liquid has evaporated, about 10 minutes. Add the pepper, the milk, and the bulgur and lower the heat. Simmer for about 5 minutes and remove from the heat. You can prepare the filling up to this stage a few hours or even a day in advance. Let the mixture cool a little. Add 3 of the egg whites and a little cheese to the vegetable mixture and stir well. Taste and adjust the seasoning.

To Assemble and Bake:

Bring the risen dough to a lightly floured working surface and divide it into 16 pieces. Cover all but one with plastic film. On a lightly floured surface, sprinkle the piece of dough with flour and flatten it with your palms. Using a floured rolling pin, roll the dough to make a disk about 6 inches in diameter. It doesn't matter if it is not a perfect circle. Spread about 3 tablespoons of the filling on half the disk, leaving about an inch of clear border. Fold the pastry to cover the filling and press with a fork to seal.

Preheat the oven to 400 degrees. Oil a large baking sheet and sprinkle it with cornmeal. Continue to assemble the pies and transfer them to the baking dish. Mix the remaining egg white with a little water, and brush over the pies. Bake for about 30 to 35 minutes, until golden. Let cool on a rack before serving.

Egyptian Brown Beans (Ful Medames)

by Claudia Roden

Serves 6 to 8

An Egyptian dish which has become "the" national dish. Ful medames is pre-Ottoman and pre-Islamic, claimed by the Copts and probably as old as the Pharaohs. According to an Arab saying: "Beans have satisfied even the Pharaohs."

Although basically a peasant dish, the rich and the middle classes also delight in these small dark beans. Ful medames is eaten in the fields and in village mud houses, in luxury restaurants and on town terraces by masters and servants alike. It is sold in the streets, sometimes buried in Arab bread, garnished with tahini salad, and accompanied by a tomato and onion salad. It is the usual substantial breakfast, traditionally cooked overnight in an earthen vessel buried up to the neck in ashes or on the lowest flame of a primus stove.

The small brown beans can be bought in all Greek stores and some delicatessens. Ready-cooked, tinned beans can also be found.

> 2 pounds *ful medames,* soaked overnight
> 2 to 4 cloves garlic, crushed (optional)
> Finely chopped parsley
> Olive oil
> Quartered lemons
> Salt and freshly ground pepper
> 1 teaspoon cumin (optional)

Boil the soaked beans in a fresh portion of unsalted water in a large saucepan until tender. In the past this took at least 7 hours, but the qualities available now are soft after 2 to 2½ hours of gentle simmering. A pressure cooker will reduce the time considerably—to 30 or 45 minutes—but care must be taken not to overcook the beans. When the beans are soft and the liquid reduced, drain them and add crushed garlic to taste, or instead pass some around with the other garnishes for people to take as much as they want. Serve in soup bowls and sprinkle with chopped parsley. Pass around olive oil, quartered lemons, salt, black pepper, and cumin for each person to season as he wishes.

Variations:

• A pleasant way of thickening the sauce is to throw a handful of red lentils into the water at the start of the cooking.

• In Iraq large brown beans are used instead of the small Egyptian ones in a dish called *badkila*, which also serves for breakfast in the street.

• It is common to serve *hamine* eggs (cooked in water under a simmer for at least 6 hours, a Middle Eastern way of preparation). Put one of these, or a hardboiled egg, on top of the beans.

• Another way of serving *ful medames* is to smother it in a tomato sauce flavored with garlic.

• Yet another way is to top it with a chopped mixed salad and thinly sliced onions or spring onions.

Pepper and Tomato Stew (Chakchuka)

by Deborah Madison

Serves 4

This vegetable stew is definitely one of my favorites, especially when the big fleshy peppers and ripe tomatoes come in. It's not dissimilar to the Basque pipérade of peppers, onions, tomatoes, and eggs. Adding the eggs adds protein to the dish, making it more of a meal, but it's perfectly good without them and is often served that way.

> 1 big red and 1 big green bell pepper, or 2 red peppers
> 1¼ pounds ripe tomatoes
> 2 tablespoons olive oil
> 1 medium onion, chopped
> 1½ teaspoons *Harissa* (page 179)
> Few pinches red pepper flakes
> 2 cloves garlic, minced
> Salt
> 4 eggs (optional)

Cut the peppers into thin strips or small pieces, removing the seeds and membranes first. Peel the tomatoes and dice them into small chunks. Heat the oil in a skillet and add the onion and peppers and sauté over high heat until the peppers begin to soften. Add the *harissa*, pepper flakes, and garlic; stir so that everything is well mixed, then add the tomatoes. Season with ½ teaspoon salt, add a few tablespoons water, and simmer until the tomatoes break down to make a little sauce, 4 to 5 minutes. Taste again for salt.

Optional: Make four slight impressions and crack an egg into each one. Lower the heat and cook gently until the eggs are set.

Baked Falafel

by Rowena Hubbard

Serves 4

Baked falafel make delicious appetizers with a simple dipping sauce of ground cumin and fresh, chopped cilantro stirred into plain nonfat yogurt. Tucked into whole wheat pita bread with chopped tomatoes and cucumbers and this same sauce, they become a hearty lunch. Traditionally falafel are deep-fried, but they are much easier to bake. Although they lose a little in texture, they make up for it in preparation time saved.

½ cup bulgur wheat, medium grind

1½ cups whole wheat pita bread crumbs

2 cups cooked and drained chickpeas

¼ cup fresh lemon juice

1 large clove garlic, chunked

¼ cup fresh cilantro leaves, packed

1 teaspoon salt

1 teaspoon ground cumin

1 teaspoon crushed red peppers

Freshly ground pepper

2 tablespoons olive oil

Pour the bulgur into a small bowl; cover with cold water and soak for 15 minutes. Do the same with the bread crumbs. Meanwhile, combine remaining ingredients, except oil, in the bowl of a food processor. Whirl to a smooth paste. Drain the bulgur very well; drain bread crumbs and squeeze all the water out with your hands. Add both to the food processor and whirl to combine. Turn mixture out into a large bowl. Line a cookie sheet with waxed paper. Wet your hands and form the mixture into balls about 1 to 1½ inches in diameter; drop onto the cookie sheet. Allow to stand 1 hour to dry.

Preheat oven to 400 degrees. Spread the oil in a 9-inch x 12-inch glass baking dish. Roll the balls in the oil and arrange in rows so that they are not touching. Bake 30 to 40 minutes until golden. Serve warm.

Spring Vegetable Ragout with Artichokes, Chickpeas, and Greens (Tbikhit Khoothra)

by Deborah Madison

Serves 4 to 6

According to Mohammed Kouki's recipe, which was the inspiration for this stew, cardoons and dried fava beans would also be included. In place of the hard-to-find cardoons and dried fava beans, I've suggested using artichokes and canned favas (or fresh, if they're available). Although it's not called for, I have sometimes added grilled peppers, finely diced, which nicely sweeten the stew. Although turnips and artichokes are spring vegetables, they also make a second appearance in the fall.

> 2 medium artichokes
> 3 tablespoons extra-virgin olive oil
> 1 onion, diced
> 4 teaspoons tomato paste
> 1 tablespoon *Harissa* (page 179), or more to taste
> ¼ teaspoon red pepper flakes
> 2 to 3 small turnips (about ½ pound), peeled
>   and cut into quarters
> 3 medium carrots, peeled and sliced in rounds
> 1 large bunch chard or beet greens, washed and sliced into ribbons
> 1 cup cooked chickpeas
> 1 can cooked fava beans or 1 cup fresh, peeled or not
> Salt
> 1 green pepper, or yellow, if available, chopped in ½-inch pieces
> Lemon juice
> 3 tablespoons chopped parsley

Trim the artichokes, quarter them, and remove the choke. Dice the hearts and set aside in a bowl of water to cover, mixed with a tablespoon lemon juice or vinegar.

In a casserole, heat the olive oil, then add the onion and fry until it begins to color, stirring frequently. Add the tomato paste, stir it around in the oil and fry for a minute, then add the *harissa* and red pepper. Lower the heat and cook several minutes more.

Next add the turnips, carrots, artichokes, greens, chickpeas, and fava beans. Stir well and season with $1\frac{1}{2}$ teaspoons salt. Cook, stirring occasionally, for 10 minutes, then add 2 cups water (or chickpea broth) and stew, covered, 15 to 20 minutes. Add the bell pepper and cook 15 to 20 minutes more. Check the liquid to make sure there is some—you'll want to end up with a little juice. The vegetables will be softer than we're used to. Stir in the lemon juice and parsley and taste for salt.

Eggplant, Tomatoes, and Chickpeas

by Rowena Hubbard

Serves 4 to 6

A wonderful, slightly sweet, mellow vegetable dish, which is excellent served hot, at room temperature, or cold. It can be stuffed into pita bread for a grand lunch, served on lettuce as a cold salad, or served hot as an entrée with steamed rice.

1 pound eggplant
1 teaspoon salt
4 tablespoons extra-virgin olive oil
1 large onion, sliced
2 large cloves garlic, minced
1½ cups cooked chickpeas
¼ cup currants
3 cups chopped fresh tomatoes, with their juice
⅛ teaspoon ground nutmeg
⅛ teaspoon cinnamon
Dash cayenne pepper
Freshly ground black pepper
¼ cup chopped parsley

Preheat oven to 400 degrees. Cut the eggplant into cubes 1-inch by ½-inch thick. Turn into colander, toss with the salt, and allow to sit 30 minutes. Meanwhile, place 2 tablespoons of the oil into a large ovenproof skillet. Sauté the onion and garlic until the onion is translucent and the garlic slightly browned. Remove and reserve. Rinse and drain eggplant; pat dry on paper towels. Add the remainder of the oil to the skillet and heat. Add the eggplant and sauté until browned on all sides. Return the onion and garlic to the skillet. Stir in the chickpeas. Top with the currants. Add the tomatoes, nutmeg, cinnamon, cayenne pepper, and black pepper. Sprinkle parsley over top. Bring this mixture to a boil, cover tightly, and bake in lower third of oven for 40 minutes. Allow to cool slightly before serving.

Couscous

by Deborah Madison

Traditionally, couscous is cooked through a series of steamings, which render it light, golden, and incomparably delicate. It's a more involved process, but the results are far superior to the dump-and-soak method on the back of the box. Whole wheat couscous is used in North Africa; it's not just some health food idea. Once steamed, it is every bit as light as the "white" couscous. Both are cooked the same way and take about the same amount of time. Usually, couscous is steamed over the broth, meat, and vegetables in a specially designed pot called a *couscousière*. You can fashion your own apparatus by setting a colander over a pot of boiling water and tying a dampened cheesecloth around the seam.

Steamed Couscous

by Deborah Madison

Makes about 5 cups

*Allow 50 minutes in all from start to finish. You can leave the second
steaming until just before serving. This method works perfectly with couscous
that I buy in bulk from my natural-foods store (which appears to be the same
as the boxed variety) and tends not to lump very much. If your couscous
turns excessively lumpy, see page 166, in Moroccan-Style Couscous.*

1. Put 2 cups couscous in a large, shallow bowl, cover it with water, and
   swish it about with your fingers. Pour off the water, let it stand 15 minutes, then rake it with your fingers or a fork to break up any lumps.
   Some people add a few tablespoons of oil at this point, which helps with
   the lumps.

2. Meanwhile, prepare a steamer; improvise with a colander and a pot if
   you haven't a proper steamer or *couscousière*. Bring 3 inches of water or
   broth to a boil in the bottom part and set the steaming unit on top. Aim
   for as close a fit as possible. Wet a piece of cheesecloth, dip it in flour,
   and wrap it tightly around the two units to make a good seal if you don't
   have a tight-fitting rig.

3. Slowly add the couscous to the steamer, letting it fall through your
   hands into a pile. Steam, uncovered, 20 minutes over medium heat.
   Gently move it around with a fork a few times so that the grains cook
   evenly. Then empty it into a shallow bowl and spread it out with a fork.
   Over a period of a few minutes, sprinkle 1 teaspoon salt dissolved in 1
   cup cold water over the couscous. Then lightly oil your hands and rake
   the grains with your fingers, gently breaking apart any lumps. Let it
   stand up to an hour or until you're ready to finish cooking your meal.

4. Check the water level in the steamer, then steam a second time, for 20
   minutes, and turn it out into a wide, shallow serving bowl. If lumps have
   formed, lightly oil your hands again and break them up, gently rubbing
   them through your fingertips. (Moroccan couscous typically has you
   work butter through it.) If there's more couscous than you think you'll
   eat, set some aside to use the next day in a salad. If you're serving it with
   a stew, fluff the couscous with a fork, mound it on a round, shallow
   platter, and sprinkle a half cup or so of the warm broth from your dish
   over it.

Vegetable Couscous

by Deborah Madison

North African couscous dishes are rich with vegetables and legumes. They also invariably begin with a pound of lamb or beef (or a smaller portion of dried meat or fish), which provides a few bites for each person and lends flavor to the broth. Since these are meatless versions, I have made adjustments from traditional recipes to compensate for the flavor the meat provides.

The basic components of couscous are a flavorful stock or broth, the vegetables and legumes, and the couscous. I get my stock two ways: if I'm cooking my own chickpeas, I add spices and vegetables to the water, strain once the chickpeas are cooked, and use that as the stock. (See the Moroccan-Style Couscous on page 166 for an example.) If I'm using canned chickpeas, I make a basic vegetable stock, browning the vegetables first in olive oil. I begin the stew by cooking the onions and harder vegetables until lightly browned in ample olive oil, which as generous as it sounds, is extremely reduced from the original recipes that often call for a cup or more.

Making couscous looks terribly complicated at first. You are doing several things at once, but there's a sensibility to the steps that becomes obvious after you make it a few times, hopefully in quick succession.

Couscous vegetables need a large pot. If you don't have a *couscousière* or a very large steaming unit, you'll be better off steaming the couscous independently of the vegetables, even though they won't get the benefit of being bathed in aromatic steam.

Moroccan-Style Couscous with Seven Vegetables, Raisins, and Almonds

by Deborah Madison

Serves 6 to 8

Moroccan couscous doesn't have the fiery element that harissa brings to the Tunisian version, although it's often served on the side or mixed into the broth. It does, however, include warm spices like saffron, turmeric, cinnamon, black pepper, and ginger.

For the Chickpeas

> 1 cup chickpeas, soaked

Aromatics

> 2 quartered onions
> 2 carrots
> 4 garlic cloves
> 1/2 bunch each parsley and cilantro, tied together
> 1 teaspoon paprika
> 1 teaspoon dried ginger
> 1 teaspoon cinnamon
> 1 dried chile

Cook the chickpeas with the aromatics in 10 cups of water. After 1 hour, add 2 to 3 teaspoons salt, to taste. When the chickpeas are tender, drain them, reserving the broth. Discard the vegetables and set the chickpeas aside.

For the Couscous

(For the complete description of the steps, see page 164.)

Rinse and soak the couscous, then rake it with a fork or your fingers to get rid of any lumps. Do the first steaming over water, then turn it out, add the salted water, and let it stand 30 minutes to 1 hour. Do the second steaming over the vegetables, if you have a couscousière, or over water in a separate pot.

For the Vegetables

6 tablespoons olive oil

2 onions, chopped

1 pound carrots, cut in 2-inch lengths

Good pinch saffron threads

½ teaspoon turmeric

½ teaspoon cinnamon

2 teaspoons salt

1½ teaspoons freshly ground black pepper

12 ounces winter squash, peeled and cut into chunks about twice as large as the carrots

4 red potatoes, peeled and quartered

3 medium turnips (about 12 ounces), peeled and quartered; or whole baby turnips, scrubbed

5 ripe tomatoes, peeled, seeded, and quartered

1 pound zucchini, cut diagonally into ¾-inch slices

½ cup sun-dried raisins

½ cup chopped parsley and cilantro, mixed

½ cup whole blanched almonds, toasted in the oven until golden

1 tablespoon *Harissa* (page 179)

Cooking the Vegetables:

1. In a wide soup pot or the bottom of the couscousière, heat the oil, add the onion, carrot, saffron, turmeric, and cinnamon, and cook over medium heat for 5 minutes, stirring frequently. Season with the salt and pepper, then add the squash, potatoes, and turnips and stir to coat. Pour in vegetable broth to cover, then bring to a boil and simmer, covered, 10 minutes.

2. Add the tomatoes, zucchini, raisins, reserved cooked chickpeas, and more broth, if needed, to cover. Bring to a boil. If steaming the couscous over the vegetables, add it now to the top unit and seal with a piece of cheesecloth. Otherwise, begin cooking it in another steamer. Simmer the vegetables, uncovered, for 20 minutes, making sure the heat is high enough for the steam to rise. Fluff it a few times so that it will cook evenly.

3. Turn the couscous into the serving dish, breaking up any lumps as you do so. Form the couscous into a mound and make a well in the top. Add the parsley, cilantro, and almonds to the vegetables. Check to make sure they and the broth are sufficiently seasoned, then remove the vegetables with a slotted spoon and set them in the well of the couscous. Spoon some of the broth over the grains, then bring the rest of it back to a boil and stir in a tablespoon of *harissa* or to taste. Pass this sauce separately.

Tunisian Vegetable Couscous

by Deborah Madison

Serves 6

Tunisian couscous uses harissa, caraway, and coriander for seasonings rather than the saffron, cinnamon, and ginger of Morocco. Season a vegetable stock with ½ teaspoon caraway seeds, ¼ teaspoon each coriander and cumin seed, and a few pinches of red pepper flakes in place of the saffron, ginger, turmeric, and cinnamon. Dried meat and fish are frequently used in Tunisian couscous. I often use dried tomatoes, which have a deep, concentrated flavor. This follows the same procedure as the Moroccan-Style Couscous (page 166). Do the first steaming over water or broth and the second over the vegetables.

> 2 cups couscous
> 4 red or white potatoes, about a pound
> 2 medium turnips or 8 small (about 1 inch across)
> 4 carrots
> 2 large red or green bell peppers
> 4 fresh tomatoes
> 1 jalapeño pepper
> 1 small green cabbage
> 1 pound zucchini
> 1 large onion
> 1 bunch scallions, with half the greens
> ¼ cup olive oil
> 6 cloves garlic, peeled and crushed with a knife
> ½ bunch each parsley and cilantro, chopped,
>   plus a few sprigs for the top
> 5 sun-dried tomatoes, cut in strips or broken in pieces
> 1 teaspoon paprika
> 1½ teaspoons black pepper
> 2 teaspoons salt
> 1 tablespoon *Harissa* (page 179)
> 2 tablespoons tomato paste diluted in ½ cup water
> 1 cup cooked chickpeas

1. Rinse and soak the couscous, then do the first steaming (see page 164 for instructions). While it's steaming, peel the vegetables and cut them all into neat-looking, fairly large pieces: quarter the potatoes and turnips (leave baby ones whole), cut the carrots into 2-inch lengths. Cut the peppers lengthwise into eighths and trim away membranes and seeds. Peel, seed, and chop the tomatoes. Halve the jalapeño and leave the seeds in for heat, or take them out. Cut the cabbage into quarters, if very small, or sixths, leaving the core intact so that the leaves don't fall apart. Slice the zucchini in thirds, if small, or diagonally into slices about ¼-inch wide. Finally, dice the onion and slice the scallions.

2. Heat the oil in the bottom of a *couscousière* or wide soup pot and add the onion, scallions, garlic, parsley and cilantro, and dried tomatoes. Cook over medium heat, stirring frequently, for 5 or 6 minutes, then add the paprika, pepper, salt, and *harissa*. Stir to break up the *harissa*, then add the diluted tomato paste. Add the carrots, potatoes, and turnips to the pot with stock or water to cover, bring to a boil, then simmer 10 minutes.

3. Add the remaining vegetables and the chickpeas. If you're using a *couscousière* or other suitable pot, add the couscous and steam over the simmering vegetables for 20 minutes, uncovered. Break it up with a fork occasionally so that it will cook evenly.

4. Turn the couscous out onto a platter and moisten it with a half cup of the broth. Break up any lumps, then mound it and arrange the vegetables attractively over the top and around the sides. Garnish with the parsley and cilantro sprigs. Taste the broth, make sure it's well-seasoned and has plenty of *harissa*, and pass it separately. Each person can spoon it over his or her couscous to taste.

Fast Tunisian Vegetable Couscous

by Deborah Madison

Serves 4

This recipe is the simplest couscous of all and doesn't follow the usual rules. It's based on one of many recipes given to a group of us who were touring the largest couscous factory in the world, Diari, in Sfax, Tunisia. It seems too simple to be as good as it is, but the vegetables yield a surprisingly delicious broth, part of which is used to cook the couscous pilaf-style, staining the couscous red. You can vary this dish by including 1 cup of chickpeas or fava beans.

¼ cup plus 2 tablespoons fruity olive oil

1 large onion, chopped

1½ teaspoons dried spearmint

½ teaspoon crushed red pepper flakes

1 pound potatoes, peeled and cut in sixths

6 cloves garlic, peeled and crushed with a knife

1¼ teaspoons salt

3 red bell peppers, cut into eighths, then into large pieces

1 green and 1 yellow bell pepper, cut as above

4 tomatoes, peeled, seeded, and chopped

3 cups water

1½ cups couscous

Harissa (page 179)

Chopped parsley

In a wide, deep skillet or soup pot, heat ¼ cup oil; add the onion, mint, pepper flakes, potatoes, and garlic. Fry over medium heat, stirring occasionally, for about 6 minutes or until the onions begin to color. Add the salt, bell peppers, and tomatoes. Stir well, then add the water. Cook, partially covered, until the potatoes are tender. When done, remove 2 cups of the liquid and set the vegetables aside while you make the couscous.

Heat the remaining olive oil in a 10-inch skillet, add the couscous, and cook, stirring constantly, over medium heat 4 to 5 minutes, without letting it brown. Add a dash of salt, remove the pan from the heat, and pour in the reserved warm broth. It will instantly spurt up if there's a lot of residual heat in the pan, but give it a stir, put a lid on, and set it aside to steam for 5 minutes. Fluff the grains with a fork to break up any lumps, then spoon another ½ cup of the juices over them and cover again for a few minutes. (It will not swell nearly as much as properly steamed couscous, but the grains will come out nice and separate, not mushed together.) If there's any juice left, use some to thin the *harissa* a little so that it has the texture of soft butter. Mound the couscous in a dish, add the parsley to the vegetables, and spoon them around the couscous. Include a spoonful of *harissa* on each plate.

Couscous with Seven Vegetables for Spring

by Deborah Madison

Serves 6 to 8

Make the Moroccan-Style Couscous (page 166) and omit the squash and either the turnips or the potatoes but include the following among the vegetables:

> **1 to 2 pounds fava beans, in their pods**
>
> **4 medium artichokes**

Shuck the beans from their velvety pods. If they're small and tender, and less than $\frac{1}{2}$-inch long, you can leave them in their skins. If they're larger, or if you have the time, boil them for 1 minute, then pop off the skins with your thumb.

Trim the artichokes of their rough outer leaves, slice off $1\frac{1}{2}$ inches of the tops, then quarter and remove the chokes. Rub them with lemon juice to keep them from browning. Sauté the artichokes when you add the onions to the Moroccan couscous and add the fava beans during the second 20-minute cooking.

Simple Tuscan Salad

by Rowena Hubbard

Serves 4

Greens found in the fields and along the pathways were plucked young and tender in ancient times and dressed in the most simple way. A little olive oil, maybe an herb or two, and a little lemon juice was all it took to make a wonderful fresh salad. This simple salad is just as easily assembled and just as refreshing to eat.

> 6 handfuls fresh mixed baby greens
>
> 1 clove garlic, peeled
>
> 3 to 4 tablespoons extra-virgin olive oil
>
> Salt and freshly ground pepper
>
> 1 to 2 tablespoons fresh herbs (optional)
>
> 1 to 2 tablespoons fresh lemon juice or balsamic vinegar

Wash and dry the greens well. Rub the garlic clove on the inside of a large wooden salad bowl. Add the olive oil and salt and pepper to taste to the bowl. Blend until salt is dissolved. Toss greens lightly with oil until coated. Sprinkle with herbs if desired and toss with lemon juice. Serve at once.

Salade Tunisien

by Deborah Madison

Serves 4

Salade Tunisien is a very popular dish composed principally of diced peppers, tomatoes, and onions. It's garnished, always very decoratively, with a small amount of protein-rich food—tuna, eggs, or strips of cheese—and olives. Often two of the three—tuna and eggs or tuna and cheese—are used.

>   4 ripe tomatoes
>   2 red bell peppers
>   1 bunch green onions
>   1 tablespoon extra-virgin olive oil
>   1 teaspoon red wine vinegar
>   3 tablespoons fresh mint leaves or 1 to 2 tablespoons dried
>   Salt
>   8 green olives
>   8 black olives
>   2 hard-cooked eggs (quartered), or a little dry goat cheese,
>   crumbled

Seed the tomatoes and peppers, trim the onions of their roots and ragged greens, and slice these vegetables into small pieces or strips. Toss with the olive oil, vinegar, and mint, to taste. Season with salt. Divide among four plates and arrange the olives and the tuna, eggs, or cheese decoratively over the top.

Grilled Vegetable Salad (Slata Michwiya)

by Deborah Madison

Serves 4

Initially, this salad may look a little wet and soupy to our taste, but many Tunisian salads are that way and they're very good.

> 1 onion
> 2 large bell peppers (1 red, 1 yellow)
> 1 Anaheim or other long green chile
> 3 ripe tomatoes, seeded and finely diced
> 1 preserved lemon (page 180) or 1 fresh lemon
> 2 tablespoons capers
> Juice of 1 fresh lemon
> 1 tablespoon finely chopped parsley
> Salt
> Extra-virgin olive oil
> 4 ounces gouda or ricotta salata cheese (optional)
> Black and green olives
> Small romaine or butter lettuce leaves

Peel the onion and slice about ⅓-inch thick. Secure each slice by inserting a toothpick into the middle; brush with oil; grill on both sides until browned and soft. Dice finely. (Or, grill a whole onion until tender; then peel and dice.) Grill the peppers and chile until the skins are loose and flesh is soft; remove skins and seeds, and dice. Combine the onions and peppers in a bowl with the tomatoes. Scrape flesh from the preserved lemon; dice the skin; add to the vegetables. (If you don't have preserved lemon, use the grated zest of a whole lemon.) Add the capers, lemon juice, and parsley. Season with salt and toss gently with olive oil. Arrange on plates and decorate with cheese, if using, and the olives. Garnish with small romaine or butter lettuce leaves.

Green Beans with Garlic and Coriander

by Rowena Hubbard

Serves 6

Marinated beans are a perfect make-ahead salad. Sometimes in Portugal fresh fava beans are used, but their season is so short that green beans are often substituted. However, there is no adequate substitute for the fresh cilantro. Don't add the lemon juice until just before serving as it will turn the beans dark.

1 pound tender young green beans
2 quarts boiling salted water
1 cup coarsely chopped fresh cilantro (coriander)
2 cloves garlic, mashed
3 tablespoons extra-virgin olive oil
2 tablespoons fresh lemon juice
Freshly ground pepper

Snap ends off the beans; cook in boiling salted water 3 to 5 minutes until just crisp-tender. While beans are cooking, place the cilantro in the bottom of a heatproof glass casserole; sprinkle the garlic over the top of the cilantro. When beans are crisp-tender, drain well, and put back in the pot over low heat, stirring for a minute to dry the beans. Turn out on top of garlic and coriander. Cover with plastic wrap and allow to stand 10 minutes to cool. When cool, toss with olive oil; cover again with plastic wrap and refrigerate overnight. When ready to serve, sprinkle with lemon juice and pepper to taste and toss lightly.

Mellow Garlic Oil

by Rowena Hubbard

Makes 2 cups

Easy to make and filled with soft garlic flavor, this mellow oil is perfect for salads and to drizzle over freshly steamed vegetables.

> 6 large cloves garlic, peeled
> 1 tablespoon light olive oil
> 2 cups fruity (extra-virgin) olive oil

Combine the garlic and light olive oil in a small microwave-safe dish. Microwave on high heat 2 minutes, just until garlic cloves are soft. Spoon the garlic and cooking oil into the bottom of a sterile pint jar. Add the fruity olive oil. Cover with plastic wrap and screw on lid. Allow to stand at least two days for flavor to develop before using.

Fresh Herb Vinegar

by Rowena Hubbard

Makes 2 cups

Use almost any herbs from the garden, either singly or in combination. Herb vinegars are wonderful on salads, sprinkled on steamed vegetables, or stirred into soups to perk up the flavor.

> 3 or 4 sprigs fresh herbs (such as basil, thyme, or rosemary)
> 2 cups red wine or rice wine vinegar

Wash herbs well; pack into a sterile pint jar. Bring vinegar to a boil and pour over herbs. Cover tightly and store at least 2 to 3 days for flavors to develop.

Herb and Olive Spread

by Aglaia Kremezi

About 1 cup

The Roman Cato (234 to 147 B.C.) describes a preparation made with black, green, and mottled olives, pitted and chopped, and mixed with coriander, fennel, cumin, rue, and mint, together with olive oil and vinegar. My olive spread was inspired by this ancient recipe. Serve it with toasted bread as an appetizer.

1½ cups juicy black olives
1½ cups cracked green olives, preferably Greek
3 tablespoons chopped fresh coriander
½ cup chopped fresh fennel tops or wild fennel
2 cloves garlic
3 tablespoons chopped fresh mint leaves
1½ tablespoons red wine vinegar
1½ to 2 tablespoons balsamic vinegar, or to taste
4 to 5 tablespoons extra-virgin olive oil
Freshly ground white pepper
Additional virgin olive oil to top the jar

Rinse the olives in running water. Taste them and if they are still very salty, soak them for 1 to 2 hours in warm water and rinse them again. Dry on paper towels. Pit and chop them coarsely. In a food processor or blender, add the olives, coriander, fennel, garlic, mint, red wine vinegar, and 1 tablespoon of the balsamic vinegar. Process to obtain a homogeneous paste, then slowly add the olive oil. Taste and adjust the seasoning, adding pepper and more vinegar if necessary. Transfer the olive paste to a jar, top with a little olive oil, cover, and refrigerate for one day before serving. It keeps for up to two weeks in the refrigerator.

Harissa
by Deborah Madison

Makes I cup

Harissa, a brick-red paste of chile, garlic, and spices, is an essential part of Tunisian cooking, where it's used as both a seasoning and a condiment. I've always made harissa with New Mexican chiles, both the big commercial varieties and the smaller native chiles. In Tunis I once watched a woman grinding red, fresh chile, which was spread out on a screen to dry. It looked exactly like our native New Mexican chile. You can buy harissa in cans and tubes, but it's not as good as what you can make; it lacks that fiery color and it's often quite hot. Since it keeps several months in the refrigerator, you might as well make a quantity of your own—especially if you like using harissa. A heavy stone mortar and pestle works best for breaking up the leathery skin of the chile.

> 3 ounces dried New Mexican red chiles (10 to 14 chiles)
> 3 guajillo chiles
> 4 plump cloves garlic, roughly chopped
> ½ teaspoon sea salt
> I tablespoon caraway seed
> 1½ teaspoons coriander seed
> 1½ teaspoons ground cumin
> Olive oil

If you're sensitive to the oils in the chiles, wear a pair of rubber gloves when handling them. Wipe off the chile if it's dusty, break off the stems, and shake out as many seeds as you can. Pull out any large veins. Areas on the skin that have turned grayish should be broken out and discarded since they may have a moldy taste. Tear the chile into pieces and put them in a bowl; then cover with boiling water and let stand at least 30 minutes to soften. Drain, then cut them into smaller pieces with a pair of scissors.

In a mortar, pound the garlic with the salt, caraway, coriander, and cumin. Add the chile and keep pounding until you have a smooth paste. (This can be done in a small food processor.) Taste for salt and stir in a tablespoon of olive oil. If you prefer it to be hotter, add cayenne or chile pequin to taste. Pack into a clean jar, cover the surface with oil, and refrigerate.

Preserved Lemons

by Deborah Madison

Preserved lemons are another frequently used condiment in Tunisian and other North African cuisines. The skin, which is the part that's used, becomes soft and mild. Though preserved in salt and lemon juice, they're neither too salty nor too sour, but pleasantly lemony. Chopped in small pieces, preserved lemon adds a note that's uplifting, lively, and a little unexpected. They keep for months. Make a batch in the winter when lemons are in season, and keep them in the refrigerator to use over time.

> **2 pounds ripe but firm lemons,**
> **plus 5 or more extras for the juice**
> **½ cup fine sea salt**

Make two circular incisions into the lemons—one around the poles and the other around the equator—without cutting all the way through. Rub salt into the flesh, then squeeze the lemons closed. Sterilize a wide-mouthed quart jar with boiling water, pour water out, then pack the lemons tightly into the jar. Cover them with freshly squeezed lemon juice, put on a lid, and refrigerate. As they sit, they will soften and mellow. They're ready to use after three weeks. To use, rinse them briefly, cut them in quarters and discard the flesh. Chop the peel into small pieces and add to salads and stews.

Classic Chickpea Hummus

by Rowena Hubbard

Makes 2 generous cups

This is the classic hummus made with homemade tahini. If you particularly like the flavor of cumin, you can blend ½ teaspoon into the chickpea mixture as well as using the ½ teaspoon on top. It is equally delicious served with crisp, fresh vegetables—cucumber, zucchini, carrots, and celery sticks, small whole radishes, bell pepper strips, small broccoli florets—or with the traditional pita bread triangles, either toasted or plain.

> 2 cups cooked chickpeas, drained and cooled
> 2 large cloves garlic
> Salt
> ½ cup lightly toasted tahini (page 182)
> ½ to ¾ cup fresh lemon juice
> 1 tablespoon extra-virgin olive oil
> ½ teaspoon paprika
> ½ teaspoon ground cumin
> 1 tablespoon finely chopped parsley

Combine the chickpeas, garlic, dash of salt, tahini, and lemon juice in a food processor. Whirl until well blended and smooth. Taste and adjust salt seasoning. Turn into a 1-quart bowl. Drizzle with the olive oil. Sprinkle with the paprika and then the cumin. Finally sprinkle with the chopped parsley to serve.

Tahini (Sesame Paste)
by Rowena Hubbard

Makes a generous ½ cup

Tahini is used throughout the Middle East in various sauces and dips, and can be made from either raw or toasted sesame seeds. The toasted version has a much richer depth of flavor. Since it is so easy to make using a food processor, you can experiment by making it from untoasted seeds to all levels of toasted seeds, until you find a flavor level you like. I prefer lightly toasted tahini in hummus and a more heavily toasted tahini when mixing it with yogurt and garlic for sauces and dips.

> **1 cup sesame seeds**
> **About 3 tablespoons cold water**

Heat a large stainless-steel skillet over medium heat. When hot, add the sesame seeds and toast to desired degree of doneness by stirring constantly with a wooden spoon. Remove from heat and pour into the bowl of a food processor. With metal blade in place, process seeds, adding cold water, one tablespoon at a time, through the feed tube until a smooth paste is formed.

Yogurt Tahini Dip
by Rowena Hubbard

Makes about 1½ cups

Delicious as a dip with fresh vegetables or pita bread triangles, this mixture also can be thinned with a little water to make a sauce or salad dressing for fresh vegetables.

> **2 small cloves garlic**
> **Salt**
> **½ cup tahini (recipe above)**
> **½ cup plain nonfat yogurt**
> **⅔ cup lemon juice**
> **1 tablespoon olive oil**
> **Parsley, chopped, for garnish**

Crush the garlic with about ¼ teaspoon salt, using a mortar and pestle. When ground to a paste, place in a food processor with tahini, yogurt, lemon juice, and olive oil. Whirl until thick and smooth. Garnish with parsley to serve.

Split Pea Hummus

by Lorna Sass

Makes 2 generous cups

Here is a quick-to-prepare and lowfat variation of the popular Middle Eastern chickpea spread. Serve a dollop on its own or stuff into pita pockets with shredded lettuce and tomato.

> 1 tablespoon olive oil
> 1 teaspoon whole cumin seeds
> 2 teaspoons minced garlic
> 1 cup finely chopped onion
> 2 large ribs celery, finely chopped
> 2¼ cups water
> 1 cup yellow split peas, picked over and rinsed
> ½ teaspoon salt, or to taste
> 3 tablespoons finely minced parsley
> 1 to 2 tablespoons fresh lemon juice

Heat the oil in a pressure cooker. Sizzle the cumin seeds for 5 seconds. Add the garlic, onion, and celery and continue to cook, stirring frequently, for 1 minute. Add the water (stand back to avoid sputtering oil) and the split peas. Lock the lid in place. Over high heat bring to high pressure. Reduce heat just enough to maintain high pressure and cook for 9 minutes. Allow the pressure to come down naturally or quick-release the pressure by placing cooker under cold running water. Remove the lid, tilting it away from you to allow any excess steam to escape. Stir well to create a coarse purée as you add salt to taste. Set the mixture aside to cool and thicken. (For a finer texture, process the mixture in a blender while still warm.) Just before serving, stir in the parsley and lemon juice to taste.

Note: This mixture becomes quite solid when refrigerated. To soften, bring to room temperature and mash with a few tablespoons of boiling water.

Herb-Marinated Olives

by Rowena Hubbard

Makes 1 quart

These appear all over the Mediterranean made with the olives of the country or a blend of olives from the region. They have served as breakfast with a handful of raisins and a hearty whole wheat bread as far back as ancient Roman times, and perhaps before that.

> 4 cups mixed olives (Amphissa, Arbiquena, Manzanilla, Elitses, Ionian, Kalamata, and a few pimento-stuffed olives for color)
> 4 large cloves garlic, slivered
> Zest cut from 1 lemon (use a zester)
> 2 tablespoons fresh lemon juice
> 10 small sprigs fresh thyme
> 6 (2-inch) sprigs fresh rosemary
> ½ cup extra-virgin olive oil

Combine all ingredients in a large bowl, tossing well. Pack into a sterile quart jar. Cover top with plastic wrap and screw lid on tightly. Place jar on its side and turn jar one-quarter turn every couple of hours (just as you pass it in the kitchen) or at least every twelve hours for two days before using. Store in the refrigerator up to a month (if they last that long!).

Almond and Honey Cookies (Rosedes)

by Aglaia Kremezi

About 40 cookies

These simple cookies have a deep, delicious flavor, especially if you make them using Greek thyme honey. I believe that these cookies must be one of the oldest Mediterranean sweets made. This recipe comes from the island of Kythera, situated halfway between the southwestern tip of the Peloponnese and the island of Crete.

4 1/2 cups ground blanched almonds

1/2 cup brown sugar

6 tablespoons honey, preferably Greek thyme honey

2/3 teaspoon ground cinnamon

1/3 teaspoon ground cloves

1/2 cup whole wheat semolina flour

About 1/4 cup water

Olive oil to oil the baking sheet

Preheat the oven to 350 degrees. In the bowl of a food processor add the almonds, sugar, honey, cinnamon, cloves, and semolina. Add some water and process, with an on-and-off motion, until you obtain a rather hard dough. Add a little more water if needed. Wet your hands and, taking 2 tablespoons of the mixture at a time, shape them into oval cookies. Place the cookies on an oiled baking sheet. Bake the cookies for about 20 minutes. They don't need to turn golden and should not be overbaked. They will be soft when taken out of the oven, but they will harden as they cool.

Khoshaf (Dried Fruit Salad)

by Claudia Roden

Serves 8 to 10

A great Middle Eastern favorite in which the fruit is not stewed but macerated. A superb dessert. Various fruits may be used, but purists feel that only apricots and raisins should go into this classic dish, together with the nuts and almonds.

> 1 pound dried apricots
>
> 8 ounces prunes
>
> 4 ounces raisins
>
> 4 ounces blanched almonds, halved
>
> 2 ounces pistachio nuts or pine nuts
>
> Sugar*
>
> 1 tablespoon rose water
>
> 1 tablespoon orange blossom water

Wash the fruits if necessary and put them all in a large bowl. Mix with the nuts and cover with water. Add sugar to taste ($\frac{1}{4}$ to $\frac{1}{2}$ pound is usual but you need not add any at all), and sprinkle with rose water and orange blossom water. Let the fruits soak for at least 48 hours. The syrup becomes rich with the juices of the fruit and acquires a beautiful golden color.

Variations

- A less common variation is to add 4 ounces each of dried figs and peaches, and a few fresh pomegranate seeds when these are available. Their luminosity brings out the rich orange, mauve, and brown of the fruit, and the white and green of the nuts.

- Some people dissolve *amardine* (sheets of dried compressed apricot) in the water to thicken and enrich it. Three soaked apricots put through the food processor with a little water will achieve the same effect.

---

*Author's Note: To stay within the realm of truly ancient foods, replace the sugar with honey.

Honeyed Almond Paste

by Rowena Hubbard

Makes about 1 cup

Probably one of the oldest forms of sweetmeats, almonds pounded using a mortar and pestle and sweetened with honey were not too time-consuming or difficult to make in ancient times and a treat for all. Today, with a food processor, this honeyed almond mixture can be made in a flash. Use the paste to stuff dates or prunes as a special holiday sweet. Or, if you want to include American ingredients and make multicultural sweets, form into small balls by rolling between your palms and then roll these in unsweetened cocoa.

> 1½ cups slivered, blanched almonds
> 3 to 4 tablespoons honey
> Pinch of salt

Turn the almonds into the bowl of a food processor with the metal blade in place. Grind almonds until fine. Add 3 tablespoons of honey and blend until a ball of paste forms on the blades. Add the additional tablespoon of honey if mixture is too stiff. (The quantity depends on the moisture in the air.) Almond paste can be used at once or wrapped in plastic wrap and kept in the refrigerator for a couple of days, or in the freezer for up to 6 months.

Date Paste

by Rowena Hubbard

Makes 1½ cups

Date paste can be used as a spread for whole wheat toast or crackers, thinned with a little yogurt and spooned onto fresh fruit; mixed with chopped walnuts, almonds, or pistachios and eaten as sweetmeat; or used as stuffing for baked apples. Other seasonings also blend well with dates. Add grated orange peel, cinnamon, pumpkin pie spice, or cloves to taste. Start with a small amount, just a sprinkle, and taste before adding more. This paste will keep about two weeks in the refrigerator.

> ½ pound Medjool or other dates, pitted
> ½ teaspoon grated lemon peel
> Water

Combine the dates and lemon peel with water to cover in a heavy, stainless-steel saucepan. Cover the pan and soak overnight. Bring the mixture to a boil, turn heat down to medium-low, and simmer slowly about 15 minutes, stirring constantly with a wooden spoon. Mash the dates as they soften during cooking by pressing into the bottom and sides of the pan. Cook until the mixture has the consistency of thick jam and holds its shape in the pot when a spoon is run through the mixture. Cool, cover, and refrigerate.

Pistachio, Date, and Banana Dessert

by Rowena Hubbard

Serves 4 to 6

A quick, easy dessert that is best made the day before it is served. If you like rose water, a drop or two added to the yogurt will provide an exotic flavor. No honey is needed, since the dates and bananas both have abundant natural sweetness.

> 2 ripe bananas
> 8 large Medjool dates or 12 to 14 medium-size dates
> 1 cup plain nonfat yogurt
> ½ teaspoon grated orange peel
> ¼ cup coarsely chopped pistachio nuts

Peel and slice the bananas into a small bowl. Pit and sliver the dates; add to the bananas. Fold the yogurt and orange peel into the bananas and dates until well coated. Cover and refrigerate 3 to 4 hours or overnight. Sprinkle with pistachios just before serving.

8 ≈

NORTHERN EUROPE

Now we'll visit some countries with cold, harsh climates, long winter nights, and often months with fields covered by snow. We cannot find many native food plants here; rather we often find plants native to milder climates that moved northward over the centuries. Despite the difficult climate, the ancient peoples of this region harvested healthful greens, grains, and fruits and became particularly skilled at producing delicious cultured milk products.

THE DARK GREEN *CRUCIFERAE*

In these unfriendly climates, greens are an especially good source of protective factors, including the antioxidants of the carotene family and some vitamin C, precious in the absence of other fresh vegetables and fruits. Dark green leaves also are some of the highest sources of calcium in the vegetable kingdom. These Nordic greens are a good source of both soluble and insoluble fibers, fibers that round out our fiber intake from grains and beans. Greens, along with local berries, were crucial in health maintenance for ancient northern European populations.

> Always remember that dark green leaves are a good source of beta-carotene, other carotenes, and calcium. White leaves in vegetables are usually low in carotenes and other vitamins and minerals.

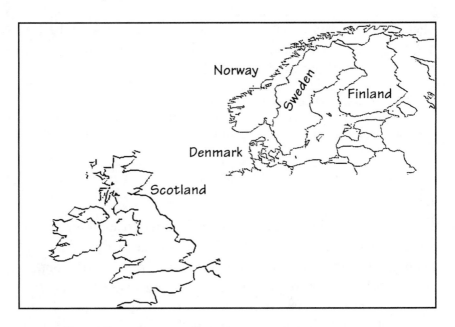

THE KALES OF NORTHERN EUROPE

The predecessors of modern head cabbages were the kales. In northern Europe kales grow wild, even in the bleakest places. They are actually at their sweetest when grown in frosty weather. Kales were also cultivated; in Scotland they were once grown so frequently that their vegetable gardens were called "kale yards." To appreciate kale at its best, choose one that has been grown in cold, wintry conditions.

Kale, which comes in many varieties, is one of the dark green vegetables that deserves a better place in the modern North American diet. Kale is a member of the *Cruciferae*, or mustard vegetables, making kale a sister to cabbage, broccoli, and cauliflower. You may also see the Latin name *Brassica* when scientists refer to the cabbages. (*Brassica* vegetables belong to the *Cruciferae* family.) This group of vegetables has made the news often in recent years as being protective against cancer. As far back as 1982, the National Academy of Science has touted the cancer-protective role of the cabbage and its relatives.

> The diverse *Cruciferae* family includes kales and cabbages, broccoli, cauliflower (white and purple), turnips, brussels sprouts, kohlrabi, the leaves of the horseradish, watercress, and many others.

NETTLES

Nettles, in Latin *Urtica*, are known for delivering a painful sting when touched. They have been used for centuries and not just for food, although they make a hearty and beautifully green contribution to soups. Their fiber was used from the Bronze Age to as late as the seventeenth century in some northern countries to make ropes, fishing lines, and cloth. Even paper has been made from nettles. The leaves, when cooked, are delicious and contain more iron than spinach, as well as beta-carotene and vitamin C.

Use the real stinging nettles that appear early in the spring, and then select only the top four or five leaves from the youngest plants. Nettles collected in the fall are said to be harmful. Wear protective gloves when picking stinging nettles. Curiously, when the leaves are soaking wet, they do not sting. Nettle soup appears in both Scottish and Norwegian recipe books as a very healthful and cleansing dish, which is highly recommended at the end of the winter. If you do not know your plants, do not assume that something is a nettle. Do not pick or use it until you have consulted a knowledgeable person. There are many poisonous plants around, so don't take a chance.

> One of the "new" carotenes recently discovered in green leaves is lutein, which plays a protective role in the retina of the eye. Spinach and collard greens have been found to be particularly good sources of this carotene.

PARSNIPS

Parsnips are probably native to northern Europe and are in the same botanical family as carrots (*Umbelliferae*), which contains compounds that appear to have cancer-protective properties. Certainly parsnips are at their best when grown in cold climates, becoming incredibly sweet and delicious in frosty conditions. They are absolutely wonderful when baked, which allows their spicy-sweet flavor to emerge. When potatoes were first introduced into the British Isles, they were coaxed into acceptance by being described as "a sweet roote which farre exceedeth our English parsnep."

APPLES, FRESH OR SUN-DRIED

Apples are a wild native fruit in northern Europe and their cultivation dates back to the beginning of the Stone Age. It appears that, even then, apples were preserved by drying, probably sun-drying. Ancient peoples knew the value of fruits, and the drying of apples to have fruit year-round reminds us how much these people knew about good nutrition! Apples became popular in antiquity, as they are today, because they could be used in so many different ways. Today there are hundreds of varieties of apples, probably more than any other domesticated fruit tree. And just as grapes were fermented into wine, apples in northern Europe were fermented to make hard apple cider.

Apples have always had the reputation of being a healthful fruit, perhaps because they are a great source of pectin, the substance that "jells" jams and jellies. Pectin is one of the best food fibers for lowering blood cholesterol. In a study in our center, pectin was one of the key components of a fiber concentrate fed to people with high blood cholesterol. In four weeks, with no other change in their diet, their blood cholesterol was lowered an average of 10 percent. Apples also have a reputation for helping digestion; again, pectin and other fibers from apples are probably the reason. Apples are also a good source of phenolic antioxidants.

THE CEREAL GRAINS OF NORTHERN EUROPE

Oats, barley, rye, and some wheats are among the hardiest of the cereal grains and can be grown in northern Europe. Barley was probably the first cultivated grain grown in northern Europe, followed by some hardy wheats, and then oats and rye. Rye is native to central Asia, where it still grows wild. Today Russia, Poland, and Germany are some of the largest growers of rye. Oats were first known best as an animal feed, and developed a reputation as a good food for horses. This use of oats might have originated in the Bronze Age, when farmers noticed that some of their oxen would choose to eat oats instead of other grasses available in the area. Later oats, like beans, were considered the food of the poor. This might have slowed the acceptance of this great grain as human food in many countries. The Crusaders found that this overlooked grain was indeed a source of strength for their soldiers, and was easy to cook as well. When they returned home, the Crusaders encouraged the cultivation of oats in many northern European countries, including Scotland, Wales, England, Ireland, and Germany. In the early 1600s, British settlers brought oats to Massachusetts, where they became one of the foundations of the Pilgrim diet.

Removal of the tough husk of these grains was difficult. Some types of barley, rye, and wheat could be threshed free of husks, but oats and other wheat and barley types needed to be roasted before the husks could be loosened or knocked off in a stone mill. The grains with loosened husks were then soaked in water and the husks floated away from the grains. A small-scale alternative was to set fire to the top of a stalk of grain, burn off the husk, and so release the grain. Yet another method was to soak the husked grains, sprout them, and then lightly roast the sprouted grain so that it became sweet, as well as easier to separate from the husk. The product became known as malted grain, and the sweet solubles were extracted with water and used to make ale.

Grinding the grain into meal was at first achieved with grinding stones, and later with a hand-operated stone mill called a *quern*. Roasted and dry grains could be coarsely or finely ground. Unroasted, moist, soft-textured grains produced flakes of grain in the meal when ground in a quern. However, for a porridge or pottage, it was not essential to grind the grains—they could simply be soaked, then boiled in water until the grains swelled and burst.

A natural fermentation of these prepared grains could occur whenever the grains were moistened and left untouched for more than a day, or when grain preparation processes were carried out repeatedly in the same vessel without a thorough cleaning between batches. Fermentations favorable for bread and beermaking could occur while the grains were soaking, or sprouting, or in porridges saved from the previous day.

Prepared oats, barley, and rye are the basis for a variety of porridges, soups or pottages, hearth breads, steamed breads, and oven breads, which have been made for millennia in northern Europe.

THE FIBER AND PROTEINS OF OATS AND RYE

Oats became nutritionally famous in the 1980s, when it was found that the "soluble" fiber of their bran lowered blood cholesterol. Many soluble fibers lower cholesterol, but some of them are not present in common, widely accepted foods. Oat bran and oatmeal should be considered an important part of breakfast, not just for people with high cholesterol, but for anyone who wants to keep their blood cholesterol low. The protein content of oats is about 14 percent, making an oatmeal breakfast with milk or yogurt a great way to start the day.

Rye, like wheat, contains "insoluble" fiber, the kind that keeps the digestive system functioning well, regularly eliminating its by-products. Its protein content is 12 to 13 percent. It adds texture and variety to breadmaking, important factors when breads are the staff of life. And, as with all whole grains, both whole rye and oats are rich sources of B vitamins and vitamin E in their germ and bran layers.

THE CULTURED MILKS OF NORTHERN EUROPE

Since Neolithic times in Scotland and Scandinavia, cows, and to a lesser extent goats and sheep, have been skillfully cared for so that they would produce a good supply of milk for people. Milk has been available even at times when crops failed and is a highly regarded food in all of northern Europe. Because all of the cultured milk products—curds, whey, and cream—were eaten and appreciated, the eating of a disproportionately high amount of cream and butter did not occur as readily in ancient times as it does now. Culturing milk under cold conditions has been common practice until recently; it is now jeopardized by modern dairy practices. Fortunately Finland and Sweden still have a large population of cultured-milk connoisseurs and cold-cultured milks are still produced there. From each of these two countries' examples of cold cultures, *viili* from Finland and *filmjölk* from Sweden, are continued here in the United States, through suppliers of these natural cultures (see the Sources section).

SCOTTISH HATTED KIT

That "hatted kit" is actually the phonetic rendition of "heated curd" by a Scotsman is a wild presumption. Nevertheless, hatted kit is indeed heated curd! Dr. Samuel Johnson, who documented his travels to the Western Isles of Scotland in 1775, found little difference between English and Scottish dinners except in their desserts. Whereas in England they ate a variety of tarts, in Scotland they served milk dishes, which must have included hatted kit.

The Scots had wonderful ways with their cows. They chose the richest pastures for them and milkmaids with the best singing voices to sing to the cows, to keep them contented at milking times. It is not surprising, then, to learn that milk dishes were so popular.

Although *filmjölk* is a Swedish cultured milk, it is probably similar to the cultured milks that were once so much a part of Scottish food. It is cultured at such a cool temperature that the curds do not separate easily from the whey. In old recipes for hatted kit, the heating was the result of adding milk hot from the cow (101.5 degrees) to some of the cool cultured milk, and then at the next milking adding more of this hot milk. After this mixture had been left to culture, the curds and whey separated easily. The whey could be drained off and the curds compressed into a mold. These molded curds were served as hatted kit, together with honey originally, and later with sugar and spices such as nutmeg. A less spectacular but still delicious way to serve the curds was as a soft cheese to spread on oatcakes. The chilled, separated whey is a wonderfully refreshing beverage, especially after exercise.

Peas

Small beans, similar to peas, were grown by the Celtic people long before the Romans introduced peas to the British Isles. Hardy varieties of peas suited to the climate of northern Europe were selected, and have been grown there ever since Roman times. However, the pea soups of northern Europe have nothing to do with modern fresh peas. For centuries, almost all the peas harvested were dried and used to supplement the grain supply throughout the year. Variation in the drying process produces either yellow or green split peas. They are split because the skins are removed during processing, thus allowing the two parts of the seed to separate. Alt of northern Europe is proud of its pea soups, which they can make all year from dried peas.

Vegetation From the Sea

The instinct that draws people to the smell of the sea and fresh seaweed is a sound. Many seaweeds are delicious and have been appreciated for thousands of years by coast- and island-dwelling people. Sea vegetation is usually associated in North America with the Japanese diet, but sea plants have been used by people living along the coasts of other continents since ancient times. Our first recipes using sea plants appear as we arrive in northern Europe, so this is a

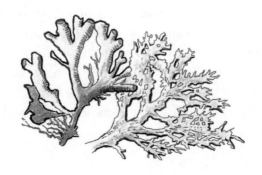

good time to explore these healthful vegetables. And by placing sea plants in this chapter, we hope to show that the use of sea plants for food is not just limited to the Pacific coast of Asia, but has been as universal as fishing, for people living near the sea.

Dulse (*Palmaria palmata*) is dark purple and has a characteristically delicate seafood flavor. Dulse is a delicious snack when eaten dried, but it also can add a wonderful seafood flavor to soups. Traditionally, in Aberdeen, Scotland, it was collected in May and then sold from baskets by girls in the markets. In North America, dulse is gathered extensively on the Maine coast.

Laver (*Porphyra laciniata*) is a delicately textured, purplish-brown seaweed that is rather tough to eat raw. Prolonged boiling of the laver transforms it into a wonderful green jelly-like paste with a mild seafood flavor. Laver jelly was taken out to sea by fishermen to spread on their oatcakes, and the combination is indeed a good one. The Japanese also have harvested a *Porphyra* seaweed since ancient times and eaten it with rice. They call their variety nori (*Porphyra tenera*) and use it to make the immensely popular sushi.

Carrageenan (*Chondrus crispus*) is another seaweed that has been used as a food since ancient times by the people of the northwestern coasts of Europe, especially as a thickener for milk and fruit juices. Although the common name, "Irish Moss," suggests that the Irish alone appreciated carrageenan, dishes originally prepared with carrageenan are still popular all over the British Isles and western Scandinavia. "Jelly and blancmange" are essential at children's parties all over the British Isles, and red fruit jelly is a frequent dessert in Denmark and Norway. None of these desserts is made at home nowadays with seaweed fresh from the beach; instead, the blancmange is made with a corn flour thickener, the British jelly with gelatin, and the Danish jelly with potato flour. Yet carrageenan has become the basis of a major industry producing thickeners for a variety of applications as well as food. The gelling carbohydrate is extracted from the seaweed as a nearly white powder, in which form it is still used for making desserts. An American company sells it in a packet, premixed with sugar, whey solids, cornstarch, sodium citrate, polysorbate, flavorings, and artificial coloring, ready to cook with milk for a dessert.

We find a lot of potassium and very little sodium in sea vegetables. An ounce of washed and dried dulse contains about 2,200 milligrams of potassium for 500 of sodium, and yet still adds that "salty" taste so many crave and miss when on low-salt diets. In an ounce of dulse we also find 1,500 milligrams of iodine, 9 milligrams of iron, and many other essential minerals and vitamins. Sea plants are high in fiber. For dulse, more than 50 percent of the fiber is soluble, the kind that should be a part of good cholesterol-lowering diets. The beneficial effects of these fibers on cholesterol deserve more clinical studies.

Many other varieties of sea plants with different flavors and textures are now available in specialty stores. Let's use them for their good fiber and mineral content and as a natural high-potassium, sea salt replacement.

HERBS AND SPICES USED IN NORTHERN EUROPE

by Cornelia Carlson

In the midst of the chaotic centuries that followed Rome's decline, much of what remained of Western "civilization" centered around the monasteries. Herb gardens were one of their central features, as crucial for the monks' bodies as the library and chapel were for their minds and souls. Here parsley and garlic were planted in the vegetable beds alongside the cabbages and carrots they might flavor, while other herbs were allotted to the *physic garden*, where the doctor/monk would have ready access to his sage, rue, fennel, mint, poppy, and tansy—the medicines of his day.

In the northern reaches of Christianity the monks must have raced against time each year, hoping to produce enough herbs in the brief summer warmth. Two herbs, however, must have thrived in this cold clime, and these—dill and caraway—

have become staples of the northern European kitchen. Both seem exceptionally well suited to the bone-warming, filling dishes of this region's cuisines—hearty soups, rye breads, pickled beets, potatoes, sauerkraut, wild mushrooms, cooked apples, cheese, and not the least, warming aquavit.

Taste the two seeds in sequence and you'll be amazed, not by their different flavor but by their striking similarity. Not surprisingly, the same two molecules dominate the taste of both: warm and medicinal d-carvone and lemony-flavored d-limonene. These two are probably responsible not just for the similar taste, but for the two herbs' effectiveness as folk remedies, usually to soothe upset stomachs or as a carminative agent to relieve flatulence. Both show some antioxidant and antimicrobial effects, and, more excitingly, may inhibit cancer. The evidence for the latter comes from studies of mice, showing that either the herbs or the isolated limonene or carvone rev up an enzyme that detoxifies various carcinogens. Whether reasonable amounts of dill and caraway can do the same job in humans isn't known, but the data is tantalizing all the same.

You don't need cold weather to enjoy these spices. Rye or whole wheat breads flavored with either dill or caraway are as tempting for summer sandwiches as they are for sopping up hot soup. Caraway is also an excellent choice to spice cakes and cookies, or baked apples, pears, or plums. The compatibility of sweetness with this sharp, medicinal spice will please as much as surprise you.

Dill weed is more delicately flavored than its seed, and an excellent choice to flavor grains or other starchy vegetable-based salads like bulgur, potato, couscous, beet, rice, quinoa, or millet, or to perk up beans and other vinaigrette-soaked vegetables. It's as luscious with fresh, vine-ripened tomatoes as it is classic with pickles, and superlative with any soured milk product such as yogurt, sour cream, or soft cheese.

Dill and caraway seeds' antioxidant properties may help them retain flavor longer than most spices, so you can easily keep them for up to a year. Dill weed is a different story. On drying, the herbal leaf loses its delicate zest, leaving its hay-like undertone to prevail. Always buy it fresh or grow your own. It grows best from seed (those in your spice cabinet are fine), rather than from established plants. Sow in loose soil as soon as the weather warms in spring.

Exploring Northern European Kitchens

The flavors of the foods we have just encountered in northern Europe are reflected in the aromas of the local cuisines. For the seeker of variety in a healthful diet, we find here a drastic change from the Mediterranean flavors—and variety is important if we want to avoid boredom. Let's begin with some grain-based dishes.

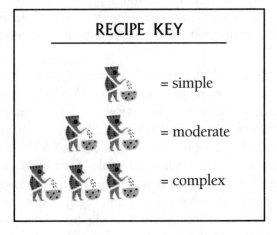

RECIPE KEY

= simple

= moderate

= complex

Oatcakes

by Monica Spiller

Serves 4

Oatcakes are most characteristic of Scotland. In their simplest form, oatcakes are made from portions of a thick oatmeal porridge flattened out into thin cakes, which are then baked on a hot griddle. Including a portion of roasted oatmeal (Burstin, page 206) in the porridge adds an extra nutty note to the final flavor. The Scots use a thick stick-shaped utensil, called a spurtle, to stir their porridge, and it is much more effective than using a spoon for the stirring. The Scots might also have added some butter when preparing their oatcakes, but it is not at all necessary and can be omitted.

Rather than increasing the recipe amounts for more of these oatcakes, it is usual that each batch is mixed while the previous one is baking for ease in handling the dough. The manner of baking, first on the griddle and then under the broiler, is intended to simulate the traditional methods of first baking on a hearthstone and then toasting in front of the fire. These oatcakes do not stick to the griddle because they are coated with oatmeal.

Ingredients for 4 pieces or farls:

1 cup stone-ground oatmeal	1 teaspoon butter (optional)
Salt	½ cup freshly boiled water

In a mixing bowl, rub together oatmeal, a pinch of salt, and butter, until well mixed. Using a wooden spoon or *spurtle*, mix in the freshly boiled water to produce a fairly stiff dough. Stir the mixture until it is cool enough to handle.

Form the dough into a ball, pressing it together as though it were a snowball. Coat the ball of dough lightly with oatmeal by dropping it into a bowl of oatmeal. Lightly dust a wooden pastry board with oatmeal. Press the dough into a thin, flat circle, 8 to 10 inches in diameter, ⅛-inch thick, using your fingertips and turning the dough over often with the aid of a dough cutter. Keep the rim of the circle thick until you have almost finished, in order to make a true circle with an uncracked edge. Finish one side of the oatcake with a grooved rolling pin rolled in two directions at an angle, to produce a square or diamond pattern. Use a knife or a dough cutter to cut the circle into four quadrants or *farls*.

Preheat a griddle at two-thirds full heat. Bake the *farls*, patterned side down, on the griddle for 5 to 10 minutes. Complete the baking by toasting under the broiler, on baking tiles, still with patterned side down, for 1 to 2 minutes.

Oat and Flax Seed Cakes

by Monica Spiller

Serves 4

*Flax seed is an oil-bearing seed and was an important part of the diet of the
ancient Britons and Danes. A freshly ground mixture of oatmeal and flax seed
meal makes a delicious oatcake that is immensely satisfying, especially after
a winter day outdoors. Flax seed can be obtained in many specialty food
stores. It can be ground with a pestle and mortar or in a hand mill (see
Sources).*

Ingredients for 4 pieces or farls:

⅞ cup stone-ground oatmeal

⅛ cup freshly ground flax seed

Salt

½ cup freshly boiled water

In a mixing bowl, rub together oatmeal, flax seed, and a pinch of salt, until
well mixed. Using a wooden spoon or *spurtle*, mix in the freshly boiled
water to produce a fairly stiff dough. Stir the mixture until it is cool enough
to handle.

Form the dough into a ball, pressing it together as though it were a snowball. Coat the ball of dough lightly with oatmeal by dropping it into a bowl
of oatmeal. Lightly dust a wooden pastry board with oatmeal. Press the
dough into a thin, flat circle, 8 to 10 inches in diameter, ⅛-inch thick, using
your fingertips and turning the dough over often with the aid of a dough
cutter. Keep the rim of the circle thick until you have almost finished it in
order to make a true circle with an uncracked edge. Finish one side of the
oatcake with a grooved rolling pin rolled in two directions at an angle, to
produce a square or diamond pattern. Use a knife or a dough cutter to cut
the circle into four quadrants or *farls*.

Preheat a griddle at two-thirds full heat. Bake the *farls*, patterned side down,
on the griddle for 5 to 10 minutes. Complete the baking by toasting under
the broiler, on baking tiles, still with patterned side down, for 1 to 2 minutes.

Oatcakes with Whey

by Monica Spiller

Serves 4

Milk from cows has been important in northern Europe since Neolithic times, and cheesemaking was carried on at least as early as the Bronze Age. The first cheeses would have been made from the naturally separated curds produced in a fermented milk, and the whey consumed as a deliciously refreshing beverage. When cheese production was at its peak, there was an abundance of whey available for cooking. Whey separated from a fermented milk (Hatted Kit, page 214) is ideal for making these oatcakes.

> 1 cup stone-ground oatmeal
> Salt
> ¾ cup freshly boiled whey

In a mixing bowl, mix together oatmeal and salt. Using a wooden spoon or *spurtle*, mix in the freshly boiled whey to produce a fairly stiff dough. Stir the mixture until it is cool enough to handle.

Form the dough into a ball, pressing it together as though it were a snowball. Coat the ball of dough lightly with oatmeal by dropping it into a bowl of oatmeal. Lightly dust a wooden pastry board with oatmeal. Press the dough into a thin, flat circle, 8 to 10 inches in diameter, ⅛-inch thick, using your fingertips and turning the dough over often with the aid of a dough cutter. Keep the rim of the circle thick until you have almost finished it in order to make a true circle with an uncracked edge. Finish one side of the oatcake with a grooved rolling pin rolled in two directions at an angle, to produce a square or diamond pattern. Use a knife or a dough cutter to cut the circle into four quadrants or *farls*.

Preheat a griddle at two-thirds full heat. Bake the *farls*, patterned side down, on the griddle for 5 to 10 minutes. Complete the baking by toasting under the broiler, on baking tiles, still with patterned side down, for 1 to 2 minutes.

Laver Bread

by Monica Spiller

Serves 4

Rather than spreading laver jelly (page 219) on their oatcakes, the Welsh used to sometimes make up their oatcakes with laver jelly. The laver bread would be fried for breakfast as a much appreciated delicacy. In the following recipe, the laver bread is baked on a floured griddle without the use of any fat, and is soft and surprisingly light.

> 1 cup stone-ground oatmeal
> Salt
> 1 cup freshly boiled water
> 2 tablespoons laver jelly (page 219)

In a mixing bowl, mix together the oatmeal and a pinch of salt. Separately dissolve the laver jelly in the freshly boiled water, and bring to a boil again. Pour the freshly boiled water and laver jelly mixture onto the oatmeal, and stir well using a wooden spoon or *spurtle* to produce a very soft dough. Wait a minute or two until the dough is cool enough to handle.

Form the dough into a ball, pressing it together as though it were a snowball. Coat the ball of dough lightly with oatmeal by dropping it into a bowl of oatmeal. Lightly dust a wooden pastry board with oatmeal. Press the dough into a thin, flat circle, 8 to 10 inches in diameter, 1/8-inch thick, using your fingertips and turning the dough over often with the aid of a dough cutter. Keep the rim of the circle thick until you have almost finished it in order to make a true circle with an uncracked edge. Finish one side of the oatcake with a grooved rolling pin rolled in two directions at an angle, to produce a square or diamond pattern. Use a knife or a dough cutter to cut the circle into four quadrants or *farls*.

Preheat a griddle at two-thirds full heat. Bake the *farls*, patterned side down, on the griddle for 5 to 10 minutes. Complete the baking by toasting under the broiler, on baking tiles, still with patterned side down, for 1 to 2 minutes.

Burstin

by Monica Spiller

Serves 4

When the husks of oat or barley grains are removed by soaking, the grains must be dried if they are to be kept for later use. Drying these moist grains in a pan over the fire expands and pops the grain and simultaneously roasts it. The result is burstin, which has a rich, roasted flavor and a similar, though less expanded, texture to modern popped or puffed grains. But perhaps the ancients had a technique that produced burstin as well-expanded as our modern puffed grains; the following is by no means a perfected recipe! Previously soaking the grains before making the burstin may improve the expandability of the grains.

2 cups oat groats or hull-less barley

Add the oats or barley to a stainless steel saucepan, one that is large enough for the cereal to form a single layer on the bottom.

Heat the saucepan over medium to high heat, gently shaking the pan constantly, until the cereal begins to pop. Heat only until the cereal turns a deep golden brown, taking care not to blacken it. This is now burstin.

When cooled the burstin can be eaten as is, with milk, or ground to a coarse flour and served with hot milk.

RYE AND BARLEY BREADS

by Monica Spiller

Rye is widely grown and enjoyed in northern Europe. Rye is easily milled into a whole grain flour that retains the nutritionally valuable germ and bran, and it is the whole grain rye that has sustained northern Europeans since the Bronze Age. The characteristics of rye protein and carbohydrates differ from wheat. Rye has a very weak gluten that does not require strong kneading and gummy carbohydrates that have the reputation of only giving a good bread texture if they are fermented with a lactic starter, such as the leavening barm described on page 127. The flour from whole rye is usually dark grayish brown and can be made into bread with a dark-colored crumb. However, a really dark rye bread, one that is almost black and deliciously interesting in flavor, can be made by cooking the bread at a relatively low temperature, close to the boiling point of water, for a long time. In a cottage with only a simple hearth, the bread would be covered and then steamed inside a large pot of constantly boiling water. The adding of flavorsome seeds such as caraway to rye breads must be an ancient custom that originally was an addition of seeds to supplement the grain supply.

Although barley can be milled to a flour and is used to make certain flat breads such as the Scottish bannock, it is much more frequently used in breads in the form of barley malt extract. Barley malt extract is flavorful and sweet and also naturally adds a considerable supply of extra nutrients, such as B-vitamins, to the bread. These extra nutrients encourage a good growth of the microorganisms in the leavening barm, as well as being good for us when we eat the bread.

The Old English words for a bread starter or leavening were *yeast* and *barm*. The word "yeast" is now used for the microorganism recognized as responsible for the leavening action. The word "barm" can still be used for the mixture of whole grain dough that ferments naturally and is perpetually used as a starter for the next batch of bread. A barm naturally contains lactic acid bacteria (*Lactobacilli*) as well as a yeast. Because of these lactic bacteria, whole grain breads leavened with barms are more flavorful, keep longer, and are more nutritious than breads leavened with yeast alone.

Dark Barley-Rye Bread

by Monica Spiller

Makes one 1¼-pound loaf

Rye Barm Bread Starter

(see Tips for Barm Breadmaking, page 127)

Refresh a barm starter with whole rye flour, sprouted rye flour, barley malt extract syrup, and water, using the proportions given below. Keep the refreshed barm starter at 55 to 60 degrees, and repeat the refreshment two or three times at 12-hour intervals. Six to twelve hours after the last refreshment, the refreshed barm starter can be used for the Dark Barley-Rye Bread that follows.

If you are not baking daily, refrigerate (at approximately 40 degrees) a portion of the refreshed barm ready for the next barm breadmaking session. The barm starter can be kept refrigerated for up to four weeks and still be useful for making bread.

Ingredients for 2 cups (500 grams) rye barm starter:

      1 cup (250 grams) barm starter

      ⅔ cup (109 grams) whole rye flour

      ½ teaspoon (1 gram) sprouted rye flour

      1 teaspoon (10 grams) barley malt extract syrup

      ⅔ cup (141 grams) water (at approximately 40 degrees)

Dark Barley-Rye Bread Dough

½ cup (100 grams) water (at approximately 86 degrees)

½ teaspoon (2 grams) salt

¼ cup (50 grams) barley flour

1 teaspoon (2½ grams) sprouted rye flour

1 tablespoon (25 grams) barley malt extract syrup

1 cup (250 grams) rye barm (6 to 12 hours since last refreshment, at 55 to 60 degrees)

1¼ cups (200 grams) coarsely ground whole rye flour

In a mixing bowl (stainless steel or glass), dissolve the salt in the water. Add the barley flour, sprouted rye flour, barley malt extract, and rye barm. Mix just until completely blended. Gradually mix in the rye flour. If necessary, add more water to accommodate all the rye flour in the dough, or add extra rye flour if the dough is too soft. The dough texture should be just firm enough for the dough to hold its shape as a loaf. Moisten your hands with a little water and form the dough into a ball, as though you were making a snowball. Allow the dough ball to rest in the bowl for 10 to 20 minutes.

Select an unglazed terra cotta pan with matching domed lid. Butter the pan and remove the excess with a cloth.

Gently complete the formation of the dough into a cylinder, and fit it into the buttered terra cotta pan. Make two or three diagonal cuts across the surface of the loaf. Cover the pan, and set to rise in a warm place (approximately 86 degrees) until nearly doubled in volume (45 to 60 minutes).

Preheat oven to 250 degrees. Bake, covered, until springy to the touch and a wooden pick comes out almost dry, 1 to 2 hours.

Allow to cool completely on a wooden rack before slicing. This bread is delicious served fresh or after several days.

Danish Rye-Bread and Beer Porridge (Øllebrød)

by Monica Spiller

Serves 2 to 4

Books written in the 1960s suggest that Danes could easily become enraptured by their nostalgia for øllebrød, which then was fast disappearing from Danish breakfast tables. Indeed this porridge is wonderful. It is a porridge for everybody from weaned babies to the strongest seaman.

Øllebrød seems to be a perfect example of the way in which cereal grains were used from the earliest days of cereal use; it is a porridge made from both bread and beer!

When grains were first fermented to make beers, they were probably much less alcoholic than modern beers. Ancient beers, generally called ales, were a food made from malted grains, so they could not have been as intoxicating as modern beers. Food ales would have been possible if they were made with a naturally mixed fermentation (yeasts and lactic bacteria), and if they were boiled after the fermentation, so that any alcohol that had formed would be evaporated off. The food ales were made without the addition of hops. The effect of hops is to reduce the fermentation due to the lactic bacteria, with the result that the fermentation is due mostly to yeast, causing more alcohol to be produced from a given amount of sugar in the malt extract. When hops came into general use after the fourteenth century, the word "beer" began to mean an ale made with hops, but even today the distinction is not a clear one. The hops also add a characteristically bitter flavor to beers, and nowadays it is almost impossible to buy a beer without hops.

The bread used in øllebrød would have been made from whole grain rye, and it would most certainly have been fermented with a natural mixture of yeasts and lactic bacteria. It would also most likely have been steamed rather than baked, so that it was dark and flavorful.

The following recipe was made with Dark Barley-Rye Bread (page 208) and a purchased nonalcoholic barley beer made with hops, although ideally a food ale made without hops would have been chosen. The recipe needs planning, but the actual steps are not time-consuming, and a batch can be refrigerated for three days if necessary. Perhaps the Danes no longer want to make øllebrød because both the breads and beers are so much changed by modern processing.

½ loaf dry dark rye bread
3 cups nonalcoholic barley malt beer
1¼ cups water

Remove the crust from the bread and slice it. Break the bread into small pieces, and soak it in the beer and water overnight, in a cool place.

Strain the bread pieces from the liquid and pour it into a saucepan (stainless steel or glass). Sieve the bread pieces, or break them up into fine doughy pieces in a food processor, and then add them to the saucepan. Bring to a simmer over medium heat, stirring frequently with a wooden spoon, until the porridge thickens. Serve hot, with a cool-cultured milk such as *Filmjölk* (page 213), and honey to taste.

Finnish Cultured Milk (Viili)

by Monica Spiller

Makes 2 quarts

Viili, from Finland, has a wonderful glutinous texture and a mild creamy flavor. The culture can be maintained by preparing the viili with fresh milk every day, or at least every week, and then keeping a portion of the prepared viili to mix with the next batch of milk to be cultured. Even milk fresh from the cow can be chilled rapidly in cold winter weather, and indeed this cultured milk can be prepared with pasteurized milk straight from a modern refrigerator, at about 40 degrees. It is then kept at about 60 degrees for approximately 24 hours, by which time it has set, with the cream nicely layered on the top. Modern homogenized milk does not give this nice separation of cream, and therefore removes the choice of whether or not to use the cream. Viili is also very sensitive to additives in the milk. For some time in the early 1990s it was possible to prepare the viili from any bought milk, but in 1993, our culture failed with several northern California commercial milks. The viili could only be continued with milk directly from a local cow, and with organically produced milk. Our assumption was that antibiotics were present in the milks that failed to support the viili culture. (Viili is available in the form of previously cultured milk from the supplier listed in Sources.)

Ingredients for 2 quarts, from which one cup is saved for culturing the next batch:

> 8 cups (2 quarts) whole milk, at 40 degrees (pasteurized, nonhomogenized, organic)
>
> ½ cup (¼ pint) viili (previous batch, at 40 degrees)

Select a large (2½-quart) container and a small (1-cup) container made of food-grade plastic or glass, with lids. Prepare the containers by washing them well with soap or detergent and hot water, rinsing them well, and drying them well.

Add all the milk to the large container, followed by the viili from the previous batch as culture. Stir very well until completely mixed. Pour a portion of the newly cultured milk into the small container. Add lids to both containers. Label both containers with time and date of preparation.

Leave containers of new viili in a cool place, 55 to 65 degrees, until set (approximately 24 hours). Store in refrigerator, at about 40 degrees.

Swedish Cultured Milk
(Filmjölk)
by Monica Spiller

Makes 2 quarts

Filmjölk from Sweden should be prepared with the freshest possible pasteurized milk, taken directly from the refrigerator at about 40 degrees. The cold milk is mixed with a small amount of previously prepared filmjölk, and then left to set at a cool temperature, approximately 60 degrees, for about 24 hours. It is preferable to prepare filmjölk with nonhomogenized milk, so that the cream forms a protective layer above the set milk. Filmjölk has a custard-like texture and a delicate, creamy flavor similar to some modern buttermilks. It is possible that some of the cultured milks of Scotland were once like this filmjölk. The Swedes often serve their filmjölk sprinkled with a mixture of cinnamon and sugar, but long ago they would have used honey alone. Later, in the Middle Ages they would have added cinnamon, and perhaps only during the last 200 years would they have used cane sugar. (Filmjölk is available in the form of previously cultured milk from the supplier listed in Sources.)

Ingredients for 2 quarts, from which one cup is saved for culturing the next batch:

> 8 cups (2 quarts) whole milk (pasteurized, nonhomogenized, organic, at 40 degrees)
> ½ cup (¼ pint) filmjölk (previous batch, 40 degrees)

Select a large (2½ quart) container and a small (1-cup) container, with lids and made of food-grade plastic or glass. Prepare the containers by washing them well with soap or detergent and hot water, rinsing them well, and drying them well.

Add all the milk to the large container, followed by the filmjölk from the previous batch, as culture. Stir very well until completely mixed. Remove a portion of the newly cultured milk, and fill the small container. Add lids to both containers. Label both containers with time and date of preparation.

Leave containers of new filmjölk in a cool place, 55 to 65 degrees, until set (approximately 24 hours). Store in refrigerator, at about 40 degrees.

Hatted Kit

by Monica Spiller

Makes 1 cup curds, 4 cups whey

Hatted kit, or heated curd, is a delightful Scottish milk dish (see page 196).

> 4 cups (1 quart) fresh filmjölk, at 70 degrees
> 2 cups (½ quart) whole milk, at 102 degrees (pasteurized,
>   nonhomogenized, organic)
> Honey
> Nutmeg

Half-fill a large bowl with filmjölk and warm it slightly to room temperature, 70 degrees. Warm the whole milk until it begins to steam (102 degrees), and pour it into the filmjölk; stir briefly. Cover the bowl with a plate and leave undisturbed at room temperature (about 70 degrees), until set (12 hours).

Drape a cheesecloth over a sieve, set over a bowl. Spoon off the solid curds floating above the liquid whey, and drain them through the cheesecloth. Gather together the corners of the cheesecloth and squeeze as much whey as possible from the curds. Press more of the whey from the curds by setting the curds in the cheesecloth, inside a small clean basket, and weighting the curds for 12 hours, at approximately 40 degrees.

Serve the curds with honey and nutmeg to taste, or spread on bread.

WHEY

Whey from curd and cheese making was not wasted, but was sold in the streets and drunk as a delicious and satisfying beverage, especially in summer.

The Scottish word for whey is "whig," and the parliamentary "whigs" were originally whey drinkers from Scotland, who happened to be in opposition to the Tories.

Yellow Split Pea Soup (Gule Ærter)

by Monica Spiller

Serves 2 to 4

The Danes eat their Gule Ærter every week, the Swedes feel obliged to eat it on Thursday nights, and the Norwegians are likely to include it in their wedding feasts. A selection of regional vegetables also is included in this pea soup, some with a long history in northern Europe such as leeks, onions, carrots, and celeriac. Thyme is usually thought of as an herb from the Mediterranean but varieties of thyme grow wild in northern Europe, and so this is likely to be a very ancient flavoring for pea soup; the combination is perfect. Serve with Dark Barley-Rye Bread (page 208).

1 cup (½ pound) dried yellow split peas	3 medium carrots
6 cups (1½ quarts) water	1 medium celeriac
1 large leek	1 small bunch thyme
4 two-inch-diameter onions	Salt and pepper

Remove any debris or damaged split peas. Wash and drain the peas and add them to a large casserole (suitable for oven and stovetop), together with the water. Cover and allow the split peas to soak for 6 to 12 hours. Bake the peas in the same water, covered, at 250 degrees for 3 hours. Trim top and bottom off leek. Split lengthwise and wash between layers. Cut into 1-inch lengths. Peel the onions and cut into thin round slices. Trim top and bottom from carrots. Soak for a few minutes, then scrub. Cut into small cubes. Trim the uneven rootlets from the celeriac. Wash and drain. Cut into small cubes. Wash the thyme, if necessary. Tie it into a small muslin bag, so that it can be removed before the soup is served.

Bring baked split peas to the oven top, and remove lid. Add the prepared vegetables and thyme, and bring to simmering point. Allow the vegetables to cook in the uncovered pot for 15 to 20 minutes; the shorter cooking time will allow their color and shape still to be seen when serving. A longer cooking time will evaporate excess water and make a thick, smooth soup. Stir frequently with a wooden spoon, and add more water if necessary. Season to taste with salt and pepper. Remove thyme before serving.

Green Split Pea Soup

by Monica Spiller

Serves 2 to 4

Green split peas seem to be preferred over yellow split peas in the British Isles, where they often are combined with spearmint. There are several mint varieties that have grown well in northern Europe, probably since neolithic times. Mint and leeks are included in this split pea soup, which can be completely homegrown and homemade in Scotland. The combination is warming and appetizing. Serve with fresh Oatcakes (page 202).

> ¾ cup (½ pound) dried green split peas
> 6 cups (1½ quarts) water
> 1 large leek
> 1 bunch mint
> Salt

Sort through the peas and remove any debris or damaged peas. Wash and drain the peas, and add them to a large casserole (suitable for oven and stovetop), together with the water. Cover and allow the peas to soak for 6 to 12 hours. Bake the peas in the same water, covered, at 250 degrees for 3 hours.

Trim top and bottom off leek. Split lengthwise and wash between layers. Cut into 1-inch lengths. Add the leek to the baked peas and bring to a simmer on the stove top. Cook, uncovered, for 15 to 20 minutes. Stir frequently with a wooden spoon and add more water if soup becomes too thick. Wash and drain the mint. Remove the stems, and finely chop the mint. Add the mint and season to taste with salt. Serve as a hot soup.

Kale Soup *(Pan Kail)*

by Monica Spiller

Serves 2 to 4

To appreciate this soup at its best, choose a kale that has been grown in cold wintry conditions. Thickening with oatmeal and including some cultured milk (see recipe for Filmjölk, *page 213) makes this an extra-satisfying winter soup.*

When purple kale is used in this recipe the broth takes on a beautiful pink-purple color and the kale pieces become green.

> 1 bunch winter kale
> 3 cups water
> 6 tablespoons oatmeal
> 1 cup fresh or cultured milk
> Salt
> White pepper

Wash the kale, strip the leaves from the stems, and discard the stems. Bring the water to a full rolling boil and add the kale leaves piece by piece, using a wooden spoon. Boil the kale for 1 to 2 minutes. Remove pot from stove. Lift kale out of the water and into a fine sieve above the pot. Press the juices from the kale, catching them in the pan. Chop the cooked kale into fine pieces and set aside. Return the pot of water to the stove top, and bring to boil again. Sprinkle in the oatmeal and stir well. Add the chopped kale, and continue to boil for 1 to 2 minutes more. Add milk gradually, stirring constantly. Remove from stove. Add salt and a generous amount of white pepper to taste. Stir well, and serve with oatcakes (page 202).

Variation: To make **Muslin Kail** (**Mixed Kale and Vegetable Soup**), prepare 1 medium-size leek by cutting off the tough leafy tops and the roots. Cut in half lengthwise, separate the layers, and wash away any mud. Slice into ½-inch lengths. Add the leek to the boiling water and boil until tender and translucent before adding the prepared kale. Proceed with the directions above.

Nettle Soup

by Monica Spiller

Serves 2

Nettle soup appears in both Scottish and Norwegian recipe books as a healthful and cleansing dish that is much recommended at the end of the winter. The nettles to use are the real stinging nettles that appear early in the spring; select only the top four or five leaves from the youngest plants. Nettles collected in the fall are said to be harmful. It is more comfortable to wear protective gloves when picking the stinging nettles. Curiously, when the leaves are soaked in water, they no longer sting. The flavor of nettles in this soup is surprisingly delicate, delicious, and reminiscent of parsley, so that the task of collecting and preparing the nettles seems to be worthwhile after all.

> 1 cup (loosely packed) spring stinging nettle leaves,
>   washed and drained
> 2 small spring onions
> 2 cups water
> Salt
> 3 tablespoons oatmeal
> ½ cup Filmjölk (page 213)

Select the topmost tender leaves from stinging nettles picked in early spring. Wash, drain, and finely chop the nettle leaves. Peel and slice the onions into small rings. Boil the onions in the water, together with salt to taste, until the onions are tender and translucent. Sprinkle the oatmeal into the boiling mixture and stir well. Then stir in the chopped nettles. Gently boil for a minute or two, to allow the oatmeal to thicken the soup mixture. Add the filmjölk and stir in well. Bring the soup back to a boil for a minute, and then serve it.

Laver Jelly
by Monica Spiller

Makes ¼ cup

Serve laver jelly spread over Oatcakes (page 202) as the Scots do, or use it as a seafood sandwich filling. The following laver jelly was made with Californian Porphyra perforata, and so the end result may differ from the Scottish version. Nevertheless, it gives one a sense of a different cooking style, and the realization that it would be easy to prepare over a fire that would be burning almost constantly in a Scottish crofter's cottage.

> 1 cup (½ ounce) cleaned and dried laver (*Porphyra perforata*)
>   or equivalent amount of clean fresh laver
> 2 to 4 cups water

Place cleaned and dried laver in a stainless steel or ceramic double boiler, and cover with water. Cover the cooking pot and boil the laver in the water, over the double boiler, for three hours or more. During this time the blade part of the seaweed will disintegrate, and the ribs will become small, tough, translucent pieces. Remove the laver ribs by passing the boiled laver and liquid through a sieve and collecting the liquid in a wide stainless steel or ceramic cooking pot. Boil the sieved liquid in the uncovered pan, stirring constantly, as the laver concentrates (10 to 20 minutes). Evaporate the water off until the laver is concentrated enough to gel when cool. Allow the green laver jelly to cool and set in a freshly washed and dried bowl or jar. Store, covered, in the refrigerator, and use within one week.

Red Fruit Jelly (Rødgrøt)

by Monica Spiller

Serves 2 to 4

The Norwegians claim red fruit jelly (rødgrøt) as their national dessert. It is similarly made in Denmark and is a delightful finish to many of their dinners. The following recipe is based on an old recommendation for a jelly made from carrageenan and water, when milk can not be tolerated. Modern recipes for rødgrøt call for the use of potato starch, or cornflour or arrowroot starch, all of which are exotic to northern Europe. The Scandinavians use fresh berries, wild and cultivated, such as red currants, raspberries, strawberries, lingonberries, and rosehips for a red jelly. They also use blackberries, loganberries, and wild blueberries to produce a fruit jelly that is dark purple instead. After washing and sorting the fruit, they briefly boil it with a small amount of water until the fruit is soft. The fruit is then sieved free from the larger seeds and tougher skins and the collected juice and pulp is thickened by cooking it with a thickener. The summer harvest of berries is also made into fruit juice concentrate, and stored away for winter use, so that a fruit jelly dessert can be made year-round.

The fruit jelly in this recipe has a slight seafood flavor. Ideally the gelling carbohydrates, which can also be described as "water-soluble dietary fiber," would be extracted from the seaweed and dried to crystals or flakes by freeze drying. After this processing the gelling carbohydrates no longer impart a flavor of the sea. Fruit jellies made this way are delicious served with a Scandinavian cool-cultured milk such as viili (page 212).

The following proportion of carrageenan gives a very firmly set jelly.

> 1½ pounds red fruit, such as strawberries, red currants, raspberries, or lingonberries
>
> 3 cups water
>
> ¼ cup (1 ounce) cleaned, cut, and dried carrageenan
>
> 1 to 2 tablespoons honey

Make a red fruit juice by simmering the red fruit with the water in a wide stainless steel saucepan until the fruit softens and disintegrates (about 20 minutes). Strain the juice free from seeds and fruit skins. Set the juice aside.

Prepare the dried carrageenan by soaking it for 30 minutes in enough cold water to cover. Drain off the soaking water from the carrageenan. In a stainless steel or ceramic saucepan, combine the soaked carrageenan and the red fruit juice. Gradually bring the mixture to a full boil over medium heat, stirring frequently. As the temperature rises and the mixture thickens, stir more frequently. Boil for two or three minutes, stirring well. Remove from the heat, add the honey, and stir well.

While still very hot, strain through a sieve into a dessert mold. Allow to cool, then refrigerate to chill and set the jelly. To unmold, dip the mold in hot water, unmold, and serve with a cool-cultured milk.

Blancmange

by Monica Spiller

Serves 2 to 4

Cleaned, naturally bleached dry carrageenan can be bought at specialty natural food stores or at microbrewer suppliers. The following recipe allows you to experience the texture and very delicate seafood flavor produced when carrageenan seaweed is used to thicken milk into a jelly.

This dish was originally made without any added flavoring and was relished. In its savory form, the taste is reminiscent of clam chowder. When trading began with tropical regions, vanilla beans were imported and used together with a sweetener to make this into a dessert blancmange. This is a recipe to try only as a curiosity, since the natural carrageenan retains a slight sea taste.

> 2 tablespoons (½ ounce) cleaned, cut, and dried carrageenan
> 4 cups (1 quart) milk
> 4 teaspoons vanilla extract
> 2 tablespoons honey

Prepare the dried carrageenan by soaking it in enough water to cover for 30 minutes. Drain the carrageenan completely. Add the carrageenan to the milk in a double boiler pan and stir well. Cover the pan and heat over boiling water for one hour. Stir in the vanilla extract and honey. While still very hot, strain through a sieve into a blancmange mold. Allow to cool, then refrigerate to chill and set the blancmange. To unmold, first dip the mold in hot water. Serve with Red Fruit Jelly (page 220) or Strawberry Honey Jam (page 224).

Jams and Marmalades

by Monica Spiller

A lovely way to preserve the fruits of summer for the cold winter months is to concentrate them as a jam or marmalade. Before cane sugar was imported into northern Europe, there was a good supply of honey available, and the art of concentrating fruits in honey must have been well established. The fruited honey jams would have been immensely welcome in winter as a concentrated flavoring with breads and cultured milks.

Blueberry Honey Jam

Blueberries are a wild berry of cool climates, and they can be found all over northern Europe, where they are harvested both in the wild and from cultivated bushes. Making them into a jam with honey accentuates their flavor and is a way of preserving the fruit.

Blueberry Honey Jam can be made in the same way as Strawberry Honey Jam (next page), using one pound of blueberries instead of strawberries.

Strawberry Honey Jam

by Monica Spiller

Makes 1 cup

Once there were only wild strawberries in northern Europe, to be gathered during a very short season. Even today, cultivated strawberries are precious as a delightfully flavorful fruit. Making them into a jam, especially with a local honey, makes it possible to carry the wonderful flavor into another season. The following strawberry jam is intended as a sampler. Reference should be made to experts on jam-making to properly prepare and seal the jam jars if the jam is to be kept for several months.

> **3 cups (1 pound) fresh strawberries**
> **½ cup water**
> **¾ cup (½ pound) honey**

Remove stems and caps from the strawberries, discard any damaged fruit. Wash and drain the strawberries. In a wide, acid-resistant (stainless steel or glass) saucepan, combine strawberries and water. Place a heat distributor under the saucepan, and using moderate heat, bring the strawberries and water to a steady boil. Allow the boiling to continue, stirring well with a wooden spoon at intervals to prevent sticking, until the strawberries soften (about 20 minutes).

Add the honey, and stir very well from this point until the jam is finished. Continue boiling until the desired consistency is achieved, as follows. For a well-set texture, a drop of the hot jam added to a glass of cold water will momentarily float on the water surface and leave a trail as it sinks. For a stiff-textured jam, boil until a drop of the hot jam forms a coherent blob that immediately sinks in a glass of cold water, leaving no trail on the surface. Alternatively, allow a drop of the jam to cool on a plate, and if it gels firmly enough for your needs, then the jam is finished.

Add the hot jam to warm, clean, dry jars. Allow to cool to room temperature before covering with a clean, dry lid. Store refrigerated. Use within a week.

Cranberry Honey Jelly

by Monica Spiller

Makes 1 cup

The lingonberry of Scandinavia is a wild native cranberry with a flavor similar to the cultivated American cranberry. The flavor of cranberries is refreshingly tart and lends itself to the extreme sweetness of honey to produce a delicious flavor combination. The following recipe is for a jelly, meaning that the cranberry seeds and skins are sieved free from the juice before it is mixed with honey. The same method can be applied to other berry fruit with bothersome seeds or skins to produce a pleasing jelly.

> 2 cups (½ pound) fresh cranberries
> 2 cups water
> ¾ cup (½ pound) honey

Remove any extraneous plant pieces or debris from the cranberries and discard any unsound fruit. Wash and drain the cranberries. In a wide, acid-resistant (stainless steel or glass) saucepan, combine the cranberries and water. Place a heat distributor under the saucepan, and using moderate heat, bring the cranberries and water to a steady boil. Allow the boiling to continue, stirring well with a wooden spoon at intervals to prevent sticking, until the cranberries collapse (about 20 minutes).

Strain the cranberries and liquid through a sieve into a bowl, so that the cranberry skins and seeds are removed. Rinse the saucepan well. Return the strained cranberry juice to the rinsed saucepan. Add the honey, and stir very well from this point until the jelly is finished. Continue boiling until the desired consistency is achieved, as follows. For a well-set texture, a drop of the hot jelly added to a glass of cold water will momentarily float on the water surface and leave a trail as it sinks. For a stiff-textured jelly, boil until a drop of the hot jelly forms a coherent blob that immediately sinks in a glass of cold water, leaving no trail on the surface. Alternatively, allow a drop of the jelly to cool on a plate, and if it gels firmly enough for your needs, then the jelly is finished.

Add the hot jelly to warm, clean, dry jars. Allow to cool to room temperature before covering with a clean, dry lid. Store refrigerated. Use within a week.

Orange Honey Marmalade

by Monica Spiller

Makes 3½ cups

Marmalade in the Scottish sense is made only from citrus fruits, especially the rather bitter Seville orange. When the orange was first imported into Scotland in the Middle Ages, the skill of jam making with honey must already have been well developed and offered a way to enjoy all of the precious orange, including the peel, as well as a way of preserving it.

By using a wide saucepan and small recipe amounts, this marmalade can be made quickly and easily for immediate use as a breakfast spread, as a delicious dessert sauce, or as an orange flavoring for breads and cakes.

> 3 to 4 (1½ pounds) whole oranges
> 4 cups water
> 2 cups (1¼ pounds) honey

Wash and dry the oranges. Trim off any damaged peel and discard. In such a way that the juice is saved, cut the oranges into segments and then the segments into slices. The dimensions of the sliced peel will determine the chunkiness of the finished marmalade. In a wide, acid-resistant (stainless steel or glass) saucepan, combine the orange juice, orange pieces, and water. Place a heat distributor under the saucepan, and using moderate heat, bring the oranges and water to a steady boil. Allow the boiling to continue, stirring well with a wooden spoon at intervals to prevent sticking, until the volume has reduced by half (30 to 60 minutes).

Add the honey, and stir very well from this point until the marmalade is finished. Continue boiling until the desired consistency is achieved (10 to 20 minutes), as follows. For a well-set texture, a drop of the hot marmalade added to a glass of cold water will momentarily float on the water surface and leave a trail as it sinks. For a stiff-textured jam, boil until a drop of the hot jam forms a coherent blob that immediately sinks in a glass of cold water, leaving no trail on the surface. Alternatively, allow a drop of the marmalade to cool on a plate, and if it gels firmly enough for your needs, then the marmalade is finished.

Add the hot marmalade to warm, clean, dry jars. Allow to cool to room temperature before covering with a clean, dry lid. Store refrigerated. Use within a week.

Ãpple Cake

by Monica Spiller

Serves 4

An apple cake made with apples and bread crumbs and sweetened with honey echoes the northern European pattern of combining bread and fruit— apples in Scandinavia and summer berries in Britain—to make delectable desserts. Originally these cakes would have been made with wild fruit. The addition of nutmeg, orange, and lemon was most likely a medieval embellishment.

> 5 small (1½ pounds) cooking apples
> ½ cup water
> 1 teaspoon orange honey marmalade (page 226)
> ½ teaspoon freshly grated nutmeg
> ½ medium lemon for zest
> 3 tablespoons honey
> 1 cup dry whole wheat bread crumbs

Peel and core the apples. Slice the apples into a saucepan (stainless steel or glass), and add the water. Simmer the apples and water until they form a purée. Continue to simmer the purée, stirring constantly, until it thickens and is reduced to 1½ cups or less. Remove from the heat. To the apple purée add the marmalade, nutmeg, lemon zest, and honey, according to taste, using the amounts given as a guide.

Preheat oven to 350 degrees. Form the cake in a soufflé dish by pressing a generous layer of bread crumbs in the bottom, followed by a layer of the prepared purée. Continue forming the cake with alternate thin layers of bread crumbs and layers of purée. Press and spread each layer with the back of a spoon. Finish with a thin layer of bread crumbs.

Bake the cake until it is lightly browned and fairly well set, about 30 to 40 minutes.

Allow to cool. Refrigerate 24 hours before serving to allow flavor and texture to mellow. Serve as a pudding, or turn out from soufflé dish and serve as a soft cake.

A NOTE ON EDINBURGH'S FLORENTINE APPLE PIE

by Monica Spiller

Apples with honey must be an ancient combination and is delightful. Spicing the apples with cinnamon and citrus fruit marmalade probably dates from medieval times when trade routes opened and the import of exotic fruits and spices became possible.

Apple Flory of Edinburgh is an example of how the plain apple pie was transformed by the spice and fruit that became much more readily available through trade during the Middle Ages.

Edinburgh's Florentine Apple Pie (Apple Flory) has a filling of apples simmered with honey and flavored with cinnamon, grated lemon rind, and orange marmalade.

9 ≈

RUSSIA AND
EASTERN EUROPE

As our journey takes us to Russia and neighboring countries, we'll find many of the same basic foods that we discovered in northern Europe. Buckwheat assumes a greater role as a "grain," and among the vegetables there is greater emphasis on cabbages and beets.

The early Slavs augmented their own harvests of wheat, buckwheat, barley, cabbage, and beets with nature's bounty of honey, nuts, wild mushrooms, and greens. As in the Mediterranean and northern Europe, they were hearty bread eaters. Even today in a Slavic home, hardly a meal goes by without including some type of bread. In ancient times it was baked in clay ovens in the yard, even in winter. In Russia, a guest is always greeted with food and at the very least offered bread and salt, the traditional sign of hospitality and happiness.

On our journey we have already encountered many foods—such as rye, wheat, kale, and cultured milks—that are now part of Russian cooking, so we'll just briefly touch on beets, cabbage, buckwheat, and hard red wheat.

CABBAGE AND BEETS

While trekking through northern Europe, we have already encountered cabbage and some of the other *Cruciferae* (page 191) that bring

the protective factors of this family of vegetables to Russia and neigh-boring countries.

Beet is a plant that gives us both edible green (actually red) leaves, which taste like Swiss chard, and an edible root, which ranges in color from white to orange to the classic "beet red." In Roman times, beets were probably grown mostly for their leaves, while now the most commonly used part of the plant is the root, so much so that in the British Isles it is called "beetroot." Beets are so closely linked today to many Russian dishes that we have chosen to place them in this chapter.

BUCKWHEAT

Buckwheat is not a grain in the botanical sense, but rather a fruit from a plant somewhat related to rhubarb; while we eat the stem of rhubarb, we eat the seed of buckwheat. Nutritionally, buckwheat is so similar to a grain that most cookbooks include buckwheat recipes in the grain section. Is it a Russian or a Chinese "grain"? The reason for this dilemma is that buckwheat originated near Lake Baikal, on the border between Siberia and Manchuria, but historically it became associated much more with Russian than with Chinese cuisine.

Outside of its native region, buckwheat did not become well known in Europe until the Middle Ages. Because the invading Saracens brought buckwheat to southern Europe, the Italians called it *grano Saraceno*. It was brought to the Americas by Dutch settlers, probably in the 1600s. Wherever it was grown, buckwheat had the reputation of being a tough plant, resistant to adverse conditions, which may have been one reason for its popularity in Russia. Today Russian immigrants to the United States frequently prepare their kasha with buckwheat, but the term "kasha" is used also to refer to other cooked grains such as oats or rice.

Buckwheat can be raw (white) or toasted (brown) and has many nutrients similar to those of wheat and rye. This makes buckwheat a tier one food on any of the pyramids. Its protein content is about 7 grams in a two-ounce serving, the same as whole rye. Its protein contains no gluten, which makes it great for people allergic to the gluten in wheat and rye. The fiber content of buckwheat is excellent, about 12 percent. This grain has become popular in North America only in recent years as people looked for variety in their choice of grains.

HARD RED WHEAT: A GIFT FROM THE UKRAINE AND RUSSIA TO THE WORLD

The Ukraine is at the center of one of the best regions in the world for growing wheat and was a major exporter of this crop until the Russian Revolution. The hard red wheats that grow well there are among the most desired of wheats, by modern standards, for refined bread flour. This wonderful wheat-growing region includes eastern Europe to the west and the steppes of Russia to the east. In the parts of this region with severely cold winters, the hard red spring wheat is planted in the spring. But in the more southerly parts, hard red winter wheat, which can be planted in the fall, is grown. These two types of hard red wheat have been grown in vast amounts on the North American continent for only about the last 120 years, and both were introduced from Russia.

Hard red spring wheat was introduced from a ship docked in Glasgow, which had come from the port of Gdansk with a cargo of Russian wheat. It was sent to one David Fife in Canada, packaged in a Scottish tam-o'-shanter hat, so the story goes. Some of the seed grew well initially as a spring-sown wheat in Canada, and from this by selection and some hybridization, came the modern varieties of hard red spring wheat that are grown in the northerly plains of North America.

The Mennonites who came from Russia to Kansas in 1874 introduced their hard red winter wheat known as Turkey Red, and this was the forerunner of the modern hard red winter wheats that are grown with great success in the central plains of continental North America.

These hard red wheats have set the standard for bread wheat on the American continent, as well as in Britain and in other parts of Europe, to which this wheat has been exported in large amounts. These bread wheats have a good reputation for breadmaking because they have such strong gluten, the wheat protein that makes good bread leavening successful. This strong gluten requires a lot of energetic kneading to give a well-expanded loaf, and so special mixers have been developed, the latest of which is the home bread machine (see recipe starting on page 235).

HERBS AND SPICES OF RUSSIA AND EASTERN EUROPE

by Cornelia Carlson

In the frigid regions of Russia and eastern Europe, where winter comes early and spring arrives late, fiery horseradish warms many a meal, giving a snap to the region's hearty soups, potato salads, stuffed cabbage leaves, pickled mushrooms, and the cranberry or beet relishes on Jewish Passover tables.

Horseradish's searing qualities come from *allyl isothiocyanate*. In whole roots, this molecule is sequestered in a bland precursor, called *sinigrin*. When the root is chopped, an enzyme is liberated that cleaves sinigrin into an inert sugar and the pungent allyl isothiocyanate. It is this pungency that has made horseradish a folk remedy for centuries, mostly for its irritant properties—as a diuretic, a rubifacient (bringing the blood to the surface like a mustard plaster)—or as an antiseptic. These actions are real, but scientists are even more intrigued with this spice's ability to inhibit a wide range of chemically-induced cancers. Whether horseradish's herbal relatives—watercress, wasabi, arugula, and mustard—share this property requires further study, but they certainly share its delightful piquancy.

You don't need a therapeutic excuse to enjoy horseradish. As with chiles, the "pain" it inflicts is pure pleasure. It adds a great zing to deviled eggs; those made with nonfat yogurt and horseradish are even better than those made with mayonnaise. It is also superlative with beet, bean, barley, or potato salads; with mushrooms baked in nonfat "sour cream"; and with almost any form of its *Cruciferae* relatives such as cauliflower, turnips, kohlrabi, and cabbage. Whenever you want to give a lift to a bland dressing, think of adding a pinch of horseradish. Note that horseradish's ferocity is tamed somewhat by extended heating, so you may need to add an extra amount to give cooked dishes the expected kick.

You can buy horseradish in several forms. The dried powder is unpleasant and acrid; don't buy it. The prepared horseradish you'll find in the deli cold-case is hot and good. But for a really dynamite sauce, buy the whole root in the produce section and make your own (page 245).

EXPLORING THE RUSSIAN KITCHEN

The history of Russian cooking can be traced back to 700 B.C. Scythian and Mongolian foot soldiers, pushed out of Central Asia by the Chinese, brought many food influences along with their pillage and destruction. They taught the Slavs to ferment milk, to make various kinds of cultured milks such as yogurts, and to preserve cabbage with salt as sauerkraut. The latter became a mainstay in the Russian diet throughout the long winters when fresh vegetables were not available. *Shchi*, the soup, even more popular in Russia than borscht, is made of either cabbage or sauerkraut or both. Shchi may well have been the first frozen food, for ancient Russians setting out on long journeys in the winter packed big lumps of frozen shchi to be melted and eaten along the way.

The Tartars, nomadic Mongols who traveled across Asia, introduced the Russians to tea and that ornate brewing pot, the samovar. *Samovar* translates to "self-cooker," and that's how the water is boiled. Hot water is brewed over charcoal in the samovar, then tea leaves are added to steep until the correct flavor and color have been obtained.

In 200 A.D., the Goths emigrated to Russia, bringing with them ancient Scandinavian food traditions, most especially fruit soup, which the ancient Slavs made from apples, pears, cherries, or plums. All are cold-resistant fruits from trees that can flourish after the harsh northern winters.

By and large, the ancient food ways of the Russian people were extremely simple and nourishing. Borscht, *shchi*, and barley soups; buckwheat, beets, cabbage, and mushrooms, along with bread, remained their mainstays.

Let's now visit the Russian kitchen and sample some kasha, beet dishes, and other body-warming foods.

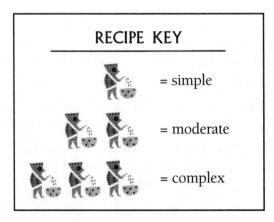

RECIPE KEY

= simple

= moderate

= complex

Dark Russian Hard Red-Wheat Bread

(for use with a modern bread machine)

by Monica Spiller

Makes one 1-pound loaf

HARD RED-WHEAT BARM BREAD STARTER

(see Tips for Barm Breadmaking, page 127)

Refresh a barm starter with whole hard red-wheat flour, sprouted wheat flour, barley malt extract syrup, and water, using the proportions given below. Keep the refreshed barm starter at 55 to 60 degrees, and repeat the refreshment two or three times at 12-hour intervals. Six to twelve hours after the last refreshment, the refreshed barm starter can be used for the Russian bread dough on page 236, using a bread machine.

If you are not baking daily, refrigerate (at approximately 40 degrees) a portion of the refreshed barm ready for the next barm breadmaking session. The barm starter can be kept refrigerated for up to 4 weeks and still be useful for making bread.

Ingredients for 2 cups (500 grams) hard red-wheat barm starter:

1 cup (250 grams) barm starter

⅔ cup (109 grams) whole hard red-wheat flour

½ teaspoon (1 gram) sprouted wheat flour

1 teaspoon (10 grams) wheat or barley malt extract syrup

⅔ cup (141 grams) water (at approximately 40 degrees)

recipe continues next page

RUSSIAN BREAD DOUGH

(using a modern bread machine)

Central to the design of a modern bread machine is a good kneading system in a bowl that can be used as a baking pan later in the process. Doughs made with strong gluten flours also require a rest time to equilibrate the doughs after they have been so vigorously kneaded, and the bread-machine timing system allows for this. Not all varieties of hard red wheat give strong gluten flour, and in some rainy years the gluten level in the hard red-wheat crop may be low. If the whole wheat flour that is to be used in a bread machine is weak, then a small amount of vital wheat gluten flour (1 tablespoon) can be substituted for some of the whole wheat flour in the dough ingredients. (Vital wheat gluten flour is obtained from whole wheat flour by removing the bran and germ, washing out the starch, and then drying it again to make a flour.) This additional gluten hardly reduces the amounts of bran and germ in the recipe, and it ensures that an open-textured loaf will be produced. Since flours contain varying amounts of moisture, it may be necessary to experiment with the amount of water used in the recipe. The dough should be just firm enough to stay in a ball during the vigorous machine kneading, producing a loaf with a well-rounded top and an open texture.

> 1½ cups (250 grams) whole hard red-wheat flour, optionally including 1 tablespoon (10 grams) vital wheat gluten
>
> 1 teaspoon (2½ grams) sprouted wheat flour
>
> 1 tablespoon (25 grams) wheat or barley malt extract syrup
>
> 1 cup (250 grams) hard red-wheat barm (6 to 12 hours since last refreshed, at 55 to 60 degrees)
>
> 1 teaspoon (5 grams) caraway seeds (optional)
>
> ½ teaspoon (1½ grams) finely ground salt
>
> ¼ cup (63 grams) water (at approximately 86 degrees)

To the bread machine pan, add the ingredients in the order given. Follow the bread machine manufacturer's instructions for automatic baking, omitting any step that involves baker's yeast.

BAKING A ROUND LOAF

To bake a round loaf in a regular kitchen oven, using a ceramic baking cloche and base (see equipment supply list in Sources):

Prepare the dough in the bread machine, using the dough setting. Lightly flour the base of the ceramic cloche. With wet hands, form the dough into a ball and dip it in flour so that it is lightly coated with whole hard red-wheat flour. Position the dough ball in the center of the base of the cloche, and cover with cloche. Keep in a warm place (approximately 86 degrees) for 45 minutes for the final rise.

Preheat oven to 425 degrees. Immediately before baking, slash a design of two sets of parallel cuts, $1/4$-inch deep, at an angle on the top of the loaf, and replace the cloche cover.

Bake the loaf inside the cloche for 25 minutes. Remove the cloche cover and continue baking for another 5 minutes, until the top crust is nicely browned. Cool loaf on wooden rack.

Traditional Kasha

by Jody Main

Serves 4

Roasting whole raw buckwheat produces kasha, which has an intense nut-like, toasty flavor that is often an acquired taste. Once roasted, it is best stored in the refrigerator to prevent the oils from becoming rancid. Kasha is traditionally coated with beaten egg before cooking in water. This egg coating keeps the kasha kernels separate and firm, preventing them from becoming mushy during cooking. Here the egg white alone serves the same purpose. Try topping kasha with a medley of sautéed mushrooms for a satisfying and hearty winter meal.

> 1 cup kasha (toasted buckwheat)
> 1 egg white
> 2 cups boiling water or vegetable stock

Toss the kasha with a lightly beaten egg white in a heavy skillet. Stir over medium heat until kernels are dry, about 3 minutes. Add the boiling water and return to a boil. Cover, reduce heat to low, and simmer gently for about 20 minutes or until tender. Fluff with fork and serve immediately.

Kasha *Varnishkes*

by Jody Main

Serves 6 to 8

This traditional Russian dish combines toasted, fluffy buckwheat groats with tender noodles and onions in a savory meal to be enjoyed on any winter night. The noodles help to soften the toasty kasha taste.

> 1 cup dry vermicelli (broken into small pieces)
> Boiling salted water
> 2 onions, thinly sliced
> 1 tablespoon vegetable oil
> 1 recipe cooked kasha (recipe above)

Preheat the oven to 350 degrees. Cook the noodles in boiling water until tender. Drain. Sauté the onions in the oil for a few minutes or until golden. Combine the noodles, onions, and kasha and pour into a lightly oiled casserole dish. Bake, uncovered, for 15 minutes or until piping hot.

Buckwheat Groats

by Jody Main

Serves 4

Whole raw buckwheat groats are creamy white to pale green in color and have a mild and delicate flavor. Whole raw buckwheat should be sealed and stored in a cool, dry place. This is the basic recipe for cooking buckwheat groats. Moist, tender, and delicious, buckwheat groats are wonderful served as a side dish either plain or with the addition of herbs and spices. They make a nice bed for steamed or roasted vegetables as well as a wonderfully rich and robust hot cereal served with yogurt and honey.

> 2 cups water
> 1 cup whole raw buckwheat groats

Bring the water to a boil. Rinse the groats in a colander and add to boiling water. Return to a boil, cover, reduce heat to a simmer, and cook until tender, about 30 minutes.

Buckwheat and Cabbage

by Jody Main

Serves 4 to 6

Tender and nutty buckwheat and sweet cabbage are cooked together for a hearty and savory main course. Serve with plain yogurt or hot applesauce on the side.

> 2 cups water
> 1 cup buckwheat groats, rinsed
> 1 cup shredded cabbage
> 1 onion, sliced thinly
> Plain nonfat yogurt or unsweetened applesauce

Bring the water to a boil. Add the groats, cabbage (reserve about $1/4$ cup), and onion, and return to a boil. Cover, reduce heat to a simmer, and cook until tender, about 30 minutes. Dish onto a hot platter, sprinkle with reserved fresh cabbage, and serve with yogurt or applesauce or both.

Borscht

by Jody Main

Serves 4

This soup is a beautiful rose color and a favorite for many when served cold. With its sweet-tart taste, it is just as wonderful served hot. Borscht makes a good first course because it is not too filling. It also makes a nice luncheon. Serve with pumpernickel bread.

> 2 onions, thinly sliced
> 1 teaspoon vegetable oil
> 4 large beets, shredded (a cheese grater works well)
> Water to cover
> 1 teaspoon vinegar or 1 tablespoon lemon juice
> Plain nonfat yogurt
> 1 cucumber, shredded (optional)

Sauté the onion in the oil on low heat for about 10 minutes. Add the beets and water to cover. Simmer, covered, for 30 minutes. Remove from heat. Purée half the soup in a blender or food processor until creamy. Return to soup pot and simmer for 15 minutes. Remove from heat and add vinegar or lemon juice. At this point the soup may be served hot with a dollop of yogurt and a tablespoon of grated cucumber, or the soup may be refrigerated and served later, chilled.

Beets and Greens with Garlic Yogurt Sauce

by Jody Main

Serves 4

Sweet beets combine well with spicy beet greens and tart Garlic Yogurt Sauce for a satisfying, colorful vegetable dish.

Garlic Yogurt Sauce

> 1 clove garlic
> ⅛ teaspoon salt
> 1 cup plain nonfat yogurt

Beets and Greens

> 1 pound beets with their greens (red, golden, white, or striped beets)
> Water

Pound the garlic with the salt, using a mortar and pestle, to form a thick paste. Combine with yogurt until well blended. Cover and refrigerate several hours for flavors to mellow.

Cut greens from the beets, leaving a 1-inch stem on top. Reserve the greens. Wash the beets; turn into a large saucepan. Cover with water and bring to a boil. Reduce heat, cover, and simmer gently about 1 hour until tender when tested with a sharp knife. While the beets are cooking, wash and coarsely chop beet greens. Steam in a large pan for 5 to 10 minutes until tender; drain well. When the beets are cooked, rub skins under running water to remove them quickly. Dice the beets; combine with beet greens in a warm serving dish. Serve at once, topped with cold Garlic Yogurt Sauce.

Spinach with Yogurt Mint Sauce

by Jody Main

Serves 4

Many traditional Russian dishes combine vegetables and yogurt. This one blends spinach with sweet caramelized onions, pungent garlic, and mint for a wonderful contrast of fresh, light, and rich flavors. Dried mint may be substituted for the fresh.

2 tablespoons finely chopped toasted walnuts

Spinach

1 pound spinach, washed and coarsely chopped
1 small onion, thinly sliced
1 tablespoon walnut or extra-virgin olive oil

Yogurt Mint Sauce

1 cup plain nonfat yogurt
1 clove garlic, crushed
1 tablespoon chopped fresh mint, or 1 teaspoon dried

In a medium-hot, dry skillet, toast 2 heaping tablespoons of raw, halved, or broken walnuts, stirring constantly until golden and fragrant, about 5 minutes. Cool. Chop finely to make about 2 tablespoons.

Steam the spinach for 5 minutes; drain and gently squeeze dry. Sauté the onion in the oil over medium-low heat until golden. Add the spinach and sauté a few minutes.

In a bowl, combine the yogurt, garlic, and mint, blending well. Stir into the spinach and heat through. Turn into a warm serving bowl, sprinkle with the walnuts, and serve immediately.

Kohlrabi with Cabbage and White Beans

by Jody Main

Serves 10 to 12

This country dish is traditionally served over hot noodles. The kohlrabi and cabbage, which are of the same family, combine well to add a tender texture and delicate flavor to the beans. Choose small kohlrabi because they tend to get woody as they get large.

> 1 cup dried white beans (or others)
> Water to cover
> 4 medium-small kohlrabi, peeled and shredded
> ½ head medium cabbage, shredded
> 1 onion, thinly sliced
> 6 cloves garlic, finely chopped
> 1 tablespoon vegetable oil
> Salt (optional)

Soak the beans in tepid water overnight. The next day, rinse and drain the beans well in a colander. Set them aside on the sink to begin to germinate over the day (about 8 hours). This process will decrease the cooking time and make the beans sweeter and more digestible. That afternoon, rinse the beans well and combine with water to cover in a large saucepan. Bring to a boil, cover, reduce heat, and simmer gently until cooked, about 1 hour. Add water as necessary.

In a large skillet, sauté the kohlrabi, cabbage, onion, and garlic in the oil over medium heat until tender, about 15 minutes. Drizzle water into the skillet as necessary to prevent the vegetables from burning and to partially steam them. Add the vegetables to the beans, cover, and simmer gently for 30 minutes. Season to taste and serve over hot noodles.

Braised Cabbage with Walnut Sauce

by Jody Main

Serves 4 to 6

This savory, crunchy cabbage dish is made rich and flavorful with Walnut Sauce. Pomegranate syrup, which is used in many Russian dishes, adds a tart-sweet flavor to balance the richness. Serve with a fruit compote (page 247) as a delightful accompaniment to the crunchy texture of this vegetable dish.

> 1 firm head green cabbage
> 1 tablespoon vegetable oil
> 2 tablespoons pomegranate syrup (page 245)
> Walnut Sauce (see below)

Wash and thinly slice the cabbage. In a large, heavy skillet, sauté the cabbage in the oil for about 4 minutes or until the cabbage turns bright green and is tender. Fold in the pomegranate syrup. Place in a warmed dish and ladle with Walnut Sauce.

Walnut Sauce

> 1 cup shelled walnuts
> 1 large clove garlic
> ¼ cup pomegranate syrup (page 245)
> 1 cup vegetable broth or water
> ½ cup finely chopped onion
> 3 tablespoons finely chopped chervil,
>   fresh mint, or parsley

Pound the walnuts and garlic to a paste using a mortar and pestle. Stir in the pomegranate syrup and broth until well blended. Add the onion and chervil and mix thoroughly, or blend all ingredients together in a food processor. Turn into a small saucepan. Bring to a boil, stirring constantly. Serve immediately.

Pomegranate Syrup

by Jody Main

Makes ½ to ¼ cup

With a delicious sweet-and-sour taste, pomegranate syrup is a wonderful addition to braised, roasted, and grilled vegetables. Pomegranate syrup also is customarily used in refreshing drinks. For a cold, delicious drink, add 1 tablespoon pomegranate syrup to a glass of sparkling water. For a soothing, hot drink, add 1 tablespoon pomegranate syrup to a cup of hot water.

> 6 pomegranates
> 1 to 4 tablespoons honey, or to taste

Wash and cut the pomegranates in half. Extract the juice as you would from oranges. Strain the juice and pour it into a saucepan. Add the honey and bring to a boil, stirring until honey is dissolved. Lower heat and simmer, stirring occasionally, until the syrup thickens and is reduced to about one-third the original amount.

Prepared Horseradish

by Cornelia Carlson

Makes 1 to 2 cups

> 1 (12- to 24-ounce) horseradish root
> 1 to 1½ cups cider or rice wine vinegar
> ¼ to ½ teaspoon salt

Peel the horseradish root and cut into inch-long segments. Put in a blender jar or food processor bowl with the vinegar and salt. Cover. Set the machine under the stove or kitchen vent or take the machine outside. Blend or process until the root is finely chopped.

Warning: Do not lift the lid to sample the fumes. Let the mixture rest a few minutes. While it rests, pour boiling water into one or two half-pint jars and their lids, and let sit for a minute. Slowly lift the lid on the blender or processor, averting your face if the mixture is still fuming. Scrape the horseradish into the jars, seal, and store in the refrigerator. It will keep for several months.

Plums over Kefir

by Jody Main

Serves 4

Kefir is a creamy yogurt-like beverage made of milk cultured with several strains of yeast and bacteria. It is easier to digest than milk and aids in the digestion of other foods by increasing important bacteria in the intestines. Kefir is available plain or flavored and is a good milk alternative for many dishes and baked goods. This creamy drink is delicious for breakfast and also a wonderful end to a meal. Serve with a spoon to allow everyone to mix and eat as they wish. Many will simply drink this plum treat.

> 1 pound fresh plums
> 1 to 4 tablespoons honey
> 2 pints plain kefir

Wash and remove pits from the plums. Coarsely chop the plums and add to a saucepan with the honey to taste. Plums vary in tartness. Begin with a teaspoon of honey and add more as necessary. Bring to a simmer, uncovered. Mash with a fork to help release the juices, being careful not to burn the plums. Plums also vary in juiciness. Once they are at a simmer, if the amount of juice is equal to the amount of fruit, remove from heat. If there is more juice than fruit, simmer very gently, uncovered, for a few minutes until the liquid is reduced to equal the amount of fruit.

Pour the kefir into four glasses. Spoon the plums over the top, dividing equally among the four glasses, and serve with spoons.

Dried Fruit Compote with Kefir Cheese

by Jody Main

Serves 6

Because of their short growing season, Russians have relied a great deal on dried fruits for many months of the year. These nutrient-rich, sweet fruits are chopped and used as toppings for grain and vegetable dishes, or poached until tender to make a naturally sweet, thick sauce. This compote makes a delightful accompaniment for dinner, or a perfect sweet ending to a meal.

> 1 pound assorted dried fruits (prunes, apricots,
>   sun-dried raisins, peaches, pears, apples)
> Water to cover
> Kefir cheese or plain nonfat yogurt

Put the dried fruit in a large saucepan; add water to cover. Bring to boil, reduce heat, cover, and simmer gently for 1 hour, or until the fruit is tender and a thick sauce has developed. Add water if necessary. Serve warm or cold in individual dishes, topped with a dollop of kefir cheese or yogurt.

10 ≈

CENTRAL, EASTERN, AND SOUTHEAST ASIA

For thousands of years, the diets of China, Japan, Southeast Asia, and India have been based on large quantities of grains (most often rice, soybeans or other native beans), very little meat, and vegetables. China, with its colder sections, did not enjoy the more lush vegetation of India and the southern part of the continent, where fruits and vegetables were more widely available. The search by the ancient Chinese for vegetables that could withstand the colder winters of northern China is another example of how ancient peoples knew what fresh vegetables meant for their health.

Today the key foods are rice, soybeans—which make possible the production of many wonderful, highly nourishing foods such as tofu—nuts such as almonds, and vegetables and fruits. We find a heart warming beverage, tea, that has ancient roots in these countries. This fascinating leaf and flower contains some health-giving compounds.

RICE, THE SACRED GRAIN OF ASIA

As is often the case, peasants ate a more healthful diet than wealthy people. For centuries, aristocrats in Japan ate refined white rice, while ordinary citizens ate brown rice, which retains the healthful outer layer. White rice is low in all the B vitamins, including thiamin (also called vitamin B_1), and is lower in fiber than brown rice. The population of Southeast Asia that ate white rice and an otherwise poor diet

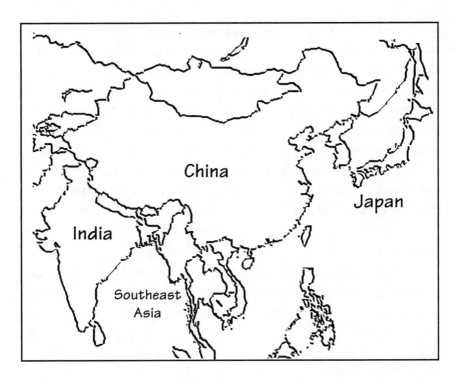

developed beriberi. In the early 1900s, research on the cause of this disease led to the discovery of vitamin B, and signaled the beginning of the vitamin era. A Dutch researcher in that region realized that certain farm animals fed a diet based on white rice were sick and physically unable to live a normal life. By relating this animal disease to the human beriberi, thiamin was discovered in the outer layer of rice, a reminder that the outer layers of grains hold some of the richest parts of the seeds.

Always choose brown rice.

Recently archeologists found jars in China filled with rice that dates back to the seventh millennium B.C. In the central Yangtze Valley, rice was probably grown in 6500 B.C. The most ancient rice found in northern Thailand and North Vietnam appears to be about 3,000 years old. In India and Pakistan, rice was grown about 4,000 years ago.

Even though other foods—including three grains (millet, wheat, and barley) and a bean (soy)—were considered a sacred part of Asian diets, rice held a unique place and was considered the most sacred of all grains by many ancient Asians. We find many myths and rituals about rice: Rice was considered the only plant that had a soul and a feminine spirit. The secrets of its cultivation were "stolen from the gods." Kings would ceremonially plow the first furrow in a rice field, and women were the only ones allowed to go into a rice field at certain times. An entire book could be written about the rituals, myths, and lore of rice. The little we have said here merely reminds us of the high place rice held in the past, and holds now, in the life of Asian populations.

In ancient Japan, reverence for the beauty and bounty of nature ultimately translated into the development of the Shinto religion, which, in essence, is reverence for the fertility of the land. *Ukemochino-kami*, the food goddess, and *Inari*, the rice god, play central and revered roles even today. Thousands of miniature shrines dedicated to Inari, to ensure an abundant rice crop, can still be seen throughout the rural countryside. To this day, the Emperor and Empress of Japan celebrate the ancient national festivals *Niiname Sai* and *Kanname Sai*, dedicated to giving thanks for a plentiful crop. In ancient times, a poor rice harvest could mean near-starvation for millions of Japanese. For centuries in Japan, samurai were paid in rice, and the feudal fiefs fought long and hard to increase their production, for they were ranked in the kingdom according to their yields. *Gohan* (rice) is the Japanese word for "a meal," and for most Japanese, without rice—regardless of what else is on the table—there is no meal.

Rice later journeyed to the western part of Asia and Europe. We find it in the Middle East in the sixth century, and by the year 1000, it was grown throughout that region. Between the years 500 and 1000, we find increasing references to rice in European writings, but early on it was considered a "spice," and in some regions it was taxed as a spice, making it very expensive. It appears to have become a food rather than a spice in Europe in the 1600s, and soon thereafter rice came to America. Early attempts to grow it were not very successful, but rice is now a major crop in Europe and the Americas.

THE GOODNESS OF RICE

Since ancient times, boiled rice has been considered an easy-to-digest grain. Physicians in the sixth century advised people who had overindulged in spiced meats and wine at a banquet the night before to eat rice with goat's milk to settle their stomachs. The protein of rice has no gluten, which makes it useful when there is an allergic reaction to this protein found in wheat and other grains. Its protein content is on the low side—about 4 grams in a two-ounce serving, compared to 8 grams in whole wheat. The wise rice-eaters of Asia always combine rice with beans, very often with the concentrated bean proteins from soybeans, and at other times with Asian beans such as adzukis. Beans also increase the fiber content of a rice-based diet. Although brown rice contains fiber, it is fairly low compared to other whole grains—6 percent as compared to 12 to 14 percent in whole wheat. The outer layers left on brown rice are a good source of B vitamins, as we have already seen, and before the era of synthetic vitamins, brown rice syrup was used as a source of these vitamins. Although rice may not be as high in protein, fiber, and other nutrients as some other grains, when properly complemented with other foods, it is a good source of complex carbohydrates. Rice is a gentle grain that should be a regular part of any good diet.

MILLET, THE MOST ANCIENT OF ANCIENT GRAINS

Millet, or sorghum, has been eaten by humans since the Neolithic era. What better choice for us seekers of the great foods of the ancients than this sadly forgotten grain? Millet is not a common grain on today's tables, but it would be an easy one to bring back; it is cultivated as an animal feed in many countries. In North America, millet is better known as a bird seed.

Millet played a major role in the diet of the northern Chinese, and as far back as 2800 B.C. was considered one of China's sacred crops. Millet was a universal crop in antiquity, grown in just about every Old World region in Roman times. It was considered part of a life-sustaining bread in the Bible: "Take wheat and barley, beans and lentils, millet and spelt, put them in a storage jar and use them to make bread for yourself … "

Millet, like rice, has always been considered an easy-to-digest grain. Like rice, it contains only about half the amount of protein found in wheat, rye, amaranth, or quinoa. Millet should be viewed as a good basic source of complex carbohydrate energy, and should always be combined with high-protein, high-fiber beans or other grains, and some cultured milks or other animal protein.

SOY, THE CHINESE BEAN THAT CONQUERED THE WORLD

Soybeans, mung beans, adzuki beans, and some broad beans do not belong to the same botanical group as the American beans. The soybean, the most important of the Asian beans, is a *Glycine* and the mung and adzuki beans are *Vigna*. The value of these Latin names is to reinforce the concept that certain beans are the gift to us of specific regions of the earth, and there is no doubt that adzuki or mung beans, or certain types of broad beans, have sisters and brothers in other regions. But it is the soybean that is quite unique and has become a major crop in North America and elsewhere.

The soybean appeared as a domesticated plant in the early Chou dynasty in China about 1100 years B.C. But Chinese lore says that soybeans were cultivated much before that time. Details of soybean planting and medicinal properties attributed to the soybean (that we are rediscovering 5,000 years later!) are given in the writings of the Chinese emperor Sheng-nung and other writings dating back as far as 2800 B.C. Processed soybean products were used as far back as 200 B.C. The soybean journeyed to other Asian countries much later, between the years 200 and 700 A.D. It was considered one of the five sacred grains of China, the others being rice, millet, wheat, and barley. Even though soy is not a grain, it was a basic crop that sustained life and was revered as such. It is still considered a sacred food in many Asian countries.

Today, as for centuries, the soybean is used to produce protein concentrates, such as tofu, because of its excellent protein quality. Its oil is extracted for many food uses, commercial lecithin is made from it, and many Asian soybean products are now manufactured in North America and other countries outside of western and southwest Asia. In fact, it is a major commercial agricultural commodity in North America. The soybean is quite different in many ways from other beans. It has more unsaturated oil than common beans (kidney beans have practically no oil!), and its protein is one of the best in the vegetable kingdom, being an almost complete protein that goes well with the rice of Asian diets. Soybeans are seldom eaten as beans in Western countries, even though this is a simple and good use for them. Soy milk powders and prepared drinks are becoming more popular in the Americas, as are various soy products such as tofu.

THE GOOD PROTEINS, OILS, STEROLS, AND PHYTOESTROGENS OF SOY

The oil and protein of the soybean are what made soy a major crop in antiquity and today. The oils are good polyunsaturated oils, well protected—when unrefined—by antioxidants and loaded with plant sterols, the kind that lower blood cholesterol and may protect against colon cancer (page 4). If you buy soy oil, be sure it is not overrefined (true for any oil). Remember that all the other beans we have seen are extremely low in fat, with the exception of chickpeas, which contain a very small amount of good fat, too, about 5 percent.

The soybean's protein is one of the most balanced in the plant kingdom, so much so that it is used to make soy milks and infant formulas for babies who cannot tolerate cow's milk. *Soy protein isolates* are widely used for high-protein drinks. The bean before processing contains about 35 percent protein: What a great combination the ancient Asians found for their low-protein rice!

Many scientists over the years have studied the effects of substituting soy for animal protein in order to lower blood cholesterol. In 1995, Dr. James Anderson of the University of Kentucky published a major article in the *New England Journal of Medicine* on soy and disease prevention. After complex statistical analysis of many studies, he and his colleagues confirmed the theory that consumption of sufficient soy products results in lower blood cholesterol levels.

A group of soy compounds called *phytoestrogens* has come to light recently—compounds, as the name implies, related to estrogens but found in plants (*phyto* means plant). *Lancet*, a major British medical journal, published an article in 1993 by Dr. Herman Adlercrutz and colleagues, who correlated the low mortality from prostate cancer in a group of Japanese men to the higher intake of soy products high in phytoestrogens. Other researchers have found that phytoestrogens inhibit tumor growth, and still others that they help prevent diseases of the coronary arteries of the heart (the arteries that feed the heart muscle). Phytoestrogens protect the heart by altering the composition of lipoproteins that carry cholesterol in the blood, making them less likely to cause harmful deposits that clog the arteries.

Recent studies at the University of Southern California in Los Angeles found that women who consumed soy products regularly had fewer cases of breast cancer than women who did not consume soy products.

TOFU, MISO, TEMPEH, AND SOY SAUCE

TOFU

Tofu is a key product of the soybean and its bland flavor makes it very acceptable to newcomers to soy products. It can be flavored in many ways, used in soup, marinated and baked, or gently sautéed. The Chinese were probably the first to make tofu, about 200 B.C., and it was known in China as "meat without bones." From there it spread to Japan and other countries. In Japan in the Nara period (the eighth century), Japanese, especially those who lived in Kyoto, came to know how to produce and cook tofu. Tofu cooking was developed in the style of *shojin ryori* (vegetarian cooking), mainly in Zen temples. Tofu is not fermented, unlike many other soybean products. *The Tofu Encyclopedia*, a classic cookbook published in 1782 in Japan, introduced 138 variations of tofu dishes and proves how deeply tofu cooking had settled in the Japanese diet.

Tofu is the easiest way to add a large amount of easy-to-digest, high-quality protein—14 grams per 3-ounce serving—to a grain-based diet. It also has some good unsaturated oils, about 4 grams in a serving, but most of the fiber is gone, making it a great concentrated food as long as you don't forget to get your fiber elsewhere.

MISO

Miso is a fermented product of the soybean, and this fermentation makes it flavorful and easy to digest. Since ancient times, soybean paste (miso) has taken deep root in many Asian diets and is now an indispensable ingredient. In ancient Japan, miso was collected as a tax from farmers and enjoyed high popularity throughout Japan. Today miso has many variations; some classics are bean miso (prepared only from soybeans), rice miso (from soybeans and *kome-koji* or malted rice), and wheat miso (from soybeans and *mugi-koji* or malted wheat), and in North America, we find chickpea miso and other variations that can please every palate. Today miso is well-known worldwide.

To prepare miso, the mixture of beans and grain is aged in cedar vats for one to three years, although it can be aged for as long as a decade without spoiling. The addition of different ingredients and length of aging produce different types of miso, which vary greatly in flavor, texture, color, and aroma. Light-colored miso is usually milder in flavor than the heavier brown or reddish varieties. Some are low in salt; others are quite high. Use the high-salt miso in place of salt to season broths and soups, and low-salt miso as a spread for sandwiches.

The most popular way of using miso is miso soup, which has, together with rice, acted as a key food in Japan and other Asian countries from ancient times to the present. In Japan, in the Edo period, miso was prepared as sauce for tofu cooking in the style of "mustard and vinegared miso," "*fuki* (butter-bur) miso," and "*sansho* (*kinome* sprigs) miso."

The protein content of miso, as you might expect, varies with the amount of cereal and soy present. A high-soy product has about 20 percent protein, while a high-cereal product has about 10 percent. The percentage of fat is higher when made with soybeans and low with cereal-soy mixtures.

TEMPEH

Tempeh is another fermented soy product that probably originated in Indonesia. It is produced by fermenting soybeans with a special microorganism that imparts to them a totally different texture and flavor. Tempeh is as deliciously flavorful as tofu is bland, but some people need to learn to appreciate its unusual taste. It shares the same good protein and oils of tofu and can be prepared in the same way. Tempehs are made by blending soy with rice or other grains. This makes it difficult to give exact nutritional data, but a typical serving (3 ounces) of soy tempeh contains 15 to 20 grams of protein, 2 grams of dietary fiber, and only a little more than 7 grams of fat.

SOY SAUCE

Soy sauce (*shoyu*) was mentioned in several classic treatises of Confucius as early as the fifth century B.C. and is one of China's most ancient seasonings. Soy sauce is another fermented product of soybeans and another indispensable item in many Asian diets. It was imported to Japan from China: in the eighth century, 14 kinds of production processes for *shoyu* were recorded in Japan. In the *Heiyokyo*, there was even a record that *shoyu* was on the market. Because an equivalent amount of soybeans produces less *shoyu* than miso, *shoyu* was considered much more valuable in medieval times and used mostly by the upper classes. As the living standards of samurai warriors and ordinary citizens as well as the techniques of *shoyu* production improved, *shoyu* became more and more popular among the general Japanese public.

Its manufacture was a complicated process, starting with a dough-like mixture of soybeans and wheat berries that was allowed to ferment. Salt and water were stirred into this mixture, which was then poured into large, open earthenware urns, which were placed outdoors in the sun for several weeks. Pungently salty, the finished soy sauce had a range of flavor and color, depending on the initial proportion of ingredients used and the length of time it was aged. The best grades of soy sauce take up to six or seven years of aging to reach perfection, and once soy sauce was introduced to Japan, that's how long the Emperor's soy sauce was aged.

SOY AND MUNG BEAN SPROUTS

Mung beans are another important bean in the Asian diet. They originated in India and are part of many Indian dishes. They are known in North America as the "bean sprouts" used in Chinese restaurants.

Sprouts! How could such valuable foods not be a part of the wise Asian diet? The ancient Chinese used to sprout seeds in the cold parts of their vast country in order to have fresh vegetables year-round. Nutritionally, think of sprouts as being somewhere between a bean and a vegetable. In addition, beans become more easily digestible after sprouting. Two popular sprouts are made from soy or mung beans. Great sprouts also can be made from sunflower, wheat, and many other seeds.

SEA VEGETATION ALONG THE ASIAN OCEAN SHORES

Sea vegetation with all its goodness is an important part of the Japanese diet and the diets of other people in Asia living along oceans and seas. We have already encountered them on our journey, when we were in Scotland. Go back and read the stories about these precious foods so overlooked in modern Western nutrition.

FROM KIWIS TO TARO

Kiwis, now becoming popular in North America and grown widely in California and New Zealand, originated in China, and are one of the highest sources of vitamin C. One average-size kiwi has as much vitamin C as ten lemons! As sweet peppers are one of the greatest sources of vitamin C in a vegetable, kiwis are in a fruit.

The Japanese enjoyed *mikan*, the fruit we call tangerines, 2,000 years ago. There is documented history that *mikan* have been used as a tonic for colds for more than 600 years, a tribute to their vitamin C content. The Japanese look upon the bright orange tangerine as a symbol of the sun. It is a winter fruit in Japan and as such reminds them that the sun will return in the spring to warm the earth, the fields, and the people; thus it also symbolizes happiness and good fortune.

In tropical areas of Asia, taro and many other starchy roots have supplied energy for centuries. Taro is of Asian origin and was probably a staple of prehistoric people before rice or other grains were widely cultivated. Taro reached Egypt in Roman times and later was brought to the Americas. Even though it is tropical, the Chinese learned long ago how to grow it in colder parts of their country.

There are too many vegetables and fruits from Asia to be able to talk about them all. Vegetables have been a basic part of the Asian diet, and their protective functions were well understood by ancient people here, as elsewhere, in past millennia.

TEA

Camellia sinensis, the common tea plant, is native to southern China and parts of India, Burma, Thailand, Laos, and Vietnam. It was known as a pleasant and stimulating beverage in China before 2500 B.C. In the centuries that followed, many medicinal properties were attributed to tea. Tea traveled to Japan from China in the sixth century. It eventually became part of all Asian cultures, and rituals developed around tea-drinking ceremonies. Tea reached Europe about 1610, at the same time many other foods were being introduced there from the Americas.

Green teas and black teas contain caffeine and some caffeine-related compounds, but recently their phenolic compounds, such as catechins, have been researched in many laboratories and found to be powerful antioxidants with protective value in heart disease and cancer prevention (page 4). Phenolics are the major component of the tea leaf, about 35 percent of a fresh leaf of Assam tea. Green teas have a higher phenolic content than black teas. Roasted coffee does not seem to be a rich source of these compounds. As for caffeine content, a typical cup of tea is lower than a typical cup of coffee, but both coffee and tea are made in so many ways in various parts of the world that common sense should guide you. Realize the difference between steeping a tea bag for a few seconds and brewing a strong tea in a pot for the duration of your tea-drinking session!

LEARNING FROM CHINESE CUISINE

The eternal Chinese question, "Have you had your rice today?" epitomizes the place of rice in Chinese life. In China, rice is the symbol of life, and the question is an inquiry about how you are today. In legend, if a bowl of rice is upset, bad fortune will come upon the careless hand. Rice is the foundation on which the remainder of the meal has always been built.

The fine art of Chinese cooking had its beginnings about 5,000 years ago. Nuts, seeds, roots, beans, and vegetables such as long beans, mustard greens, snow peas, and Chinese cabbage were added to rice. Such exotic ingredients as lotus root, gingko nuts, dried lily flowers, cloud ear fungi, bitter melon, fuzzy squash, bamboo shoots, and matrimony vines also were added through need and for flavor. Through time these and a myriad of other foods became harmonized into "the eight fundamental flavors."

Eight is a magical number for the Chinese; thus the eight flavors were treasures that possessed the power of protection. Ancient China abounds with place names that invoke this charm, such as the "Hill of the Eight Sanctuaries" close to Beijing. The eight food flavors, which have been refined over the centuries and are still revered today, are listed on the next page.

Hom	Salty (soy sauce)
Tom	Bland (rice)
Teem	Sweet (a natural sweetness like lotus root)
Seen	Sour (pickled mustard greens)
Foo	Bitter (bitter melon)
Lot	Hot (ginger root)
Heong	Fragrant (cooked chard with oil and salt)
Gum	Golden (kumquats)

With rice as their base, the other seven flavors have been incorporated into the daily food of the Chinese for centuries, keeping the people safe in their tradition and protected by the ancient charm. Their cooking methods helped as well. Vegetables were cooked fast and hot in a wok, just until crunchy, retaining their flavor, crispness, and color, as well as their nutrients.

THE WEST MOVES INTO JAPAN

with Tsukiko Hattori

Long ago Japan, surrounded by the sea, was isolated from other countries. This helped develop the unique Japanese style and culture. Later, however, Western cultures began to penetrate Japanese society, and the Japanese accepted them without hesitation. Food was not an exception.

In the fourth century, European people called *wkirishitans* (Christians) propagated Christianity all over Japan and, at the same time, popularized their habit of eating meat. At the end of the fifth century, however, Christians suffered persecution and meat-eating was strictly controlled. Soybean products were a very important source of protein for those Japanese who did not eat meat, and the second most familiar food after rice.

In the sixth century, Buddhism, introduced from the continent, had a major influence on the Japanese diet. The Buddhist philosophy prohibits all kinds of hunting and fishing activities. In the eighth century, whenever there was a drought or flood damage, the law against hunting and fishing was issued by the Emperor. This law did not come about for religious reasons, but rather from a political strategy to keep oxen and horses at work in the fields to promote agricultural production. In the farming-centered community, the concept of an anti-meat diet and that eating four-legged animals is a sin originally came from the Japanese religious view centered on animism, such as ancient Shintoism, before Buddhism was introduced in Japan. In today's Japan, people's taste for food is very much Westernized. This has had many negative effects on the health of the Japanese people, including a rapid increase in heart disease since 1955.

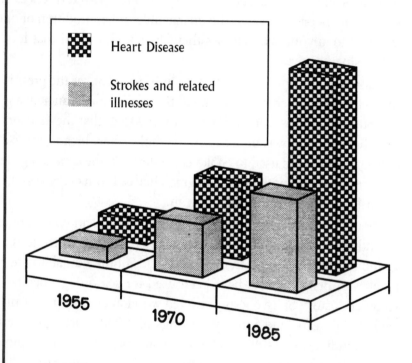

This example for Japan can be repeated for just about every country where the simple, unrefined, ancient diets and foods we have encountered on our journey are being replaced by more refined foods, and animal products are starting to play a major role rather than a supporting one. Think of the food pyramids we have seen on pages 11-12 and follow that basic balance of foods.

FOOD IN INDIAN COOKING AND CULTURE

In ancient India, as we have seen in many other countries around the world, food played a central role in most of their ceremonies, so vital was the production of food. In the northern Punjab, the traditional festival of *Baisakhi* celebrates the wheat harvest with music, dancing, and abundant food. In the southern states, *Pongal*, the three-day rice festival, was celebrated with ox-cart races and foods made from the newly harvested rice. Ancient Sanskrit scripture says *Annam Brahma*, which means "Food is God," and it explains that, like God, food maintains all life and, as such, it must be treated with reverence. This philosophy persists today in the unshakable Indian tradition of offering food to anyone who crosses their threshold, even if that food is only a sip of water.

Cooking as a fine art is a tradition in India, as old as the pre-Aryan Indus Empire, which was thriving at the same time as ancient Egypt and Sumer. There is evidence dating to 2300 B.C. that the *tandoor*, an upright clay oven, was in use to bake whole wheat breads; brass and copper vessels were used to cook vegetables; and the *caru*, a big black cauldron, bubbled with broth and green herbs. From every vessel, the pervasive aroma of spices filled the air.

Spices, in vast array, are indigenous to the Indian continent and to Indian cooking. From the Himalayas in the north to Cape Comorin in the south, from the wheat fields of the Punjab to the rice paddies of Bengal, spices have been used for seasoning since before recorded history. Spice chests of carved wood, incised stone, or tin go back 4,000 years, and Sanskrit writings of 3,000 years ago describe many familiar spices still used today—black pepper, turmeric, ginger, cardamom, coriander, cloves, cumin, cinnamon, mustard, saffron, fenugreek, and garlic. The ancient Sanskrit *Ayurveda*, a book on Hindu medicine, contains a long list of specific spices and their use in combating common ailments, from digestive problems to childbirth to liver complaints to rheumatism. Spices in all their forms have been an integral part of everyday life in India for centuries.

In the north, or wheat country, dry spices were used. Pounded to a powder they kept well in the spice cabinets, each one in a separate container. Each dish was seasoned separately and quite specifically with a blend of seasonings to enhance its natural flavor. Here bread, cooked in the tandoor, served as a utensil and lentils were served with almost every meal. Seasoned and cooked for 9 to 12 hours in a pot set on a clay-baked grate over hot charcoal, the lentils were tenderized in a very mellow, slow-cooked way.

In the south, or rice-growing region, fresh or green spices were most often used. They could not be stored, but were freshly ground with water, coconut milk, or lime juice to make a paste (*masala*) for every dish. These mixtures seasoned sauces and counteracted the dry fluffiness of boiled rice. Unpolished basmati rice is a long-grain rice which, when properly cooked, has a pleasant nutty flavor with each grain separate and individual. Rice comes in many varieties in India and now, as in ancient times, all rice is viewed with great respect. So important is rice to India that today one-fourth of all arable land is given over to its production and over 1,000 varieties are grown.

Vegetables and fruits were abundant in the south because of its more tropical climate, and here, too, lentils and other pulses were a central part of every meal. Banana leaves were used as plates with the seasoned vegetables, lentils, and fruits arranged around the mound of rice. Vegetables were dried in the sun, sliced, and laid out on reed mats; then stored for the sparse times to come. Such abundance of produce from the land may have been one contributing factor leading to the large vegetarian population in the south. Lentils were grown in ancient times in many varieties, shapes, sizes, and colors. In India today there are over 60 varieties to choose from, each with a distinctive flavor and cooking use.

The word "curry" is from the Hindustani word *turcarri*, shortened colloquially to "turri" and Anglicized to "curry." It has always referred to a type of seasoned cooking, never to the powder or paste of mixed seasonings we see today on supermarket shelves. Indian cooks are horrified at the use of premixed powders. In India the seasonings have always been blended specifically, lovingly, and carefully for each dish.

GINGER, THE ANCIENT SPICE OF ASIA

by Cornelia Carlson

> *A meal without ginger on the table, he would not eat.* -Confucius

Confucius may be the first person on record as being addicted to ginger, but the world is now full of ginger lovers. The reason is obvious. No other spice is so versatile, so compatible with foods from breakfast tea to a dessert of wine-poached pears. No wonder virtually all the world's cuisines rely on ginger to season dishes from Chinese ginger beef, Jamaican ginger beer, Japanese pickles, Yemen coffee, Moroccan *B'steeya* (pigeon pie), German *lebkuchen*, Ghanaian peanut soup, to American pumpkin pie.

Ginger has been cultivated so long in India, Southeast Asia, and China that botanists aren't certain in which specific area the plant originated. Ancient documents establish its presence in India and China at least 2,000 to 3,000 years ago, but I suspect that the spice was relished as soon as the first primitive man thrust his digging stick into these flavorful rhizomes (ginger "roots" are actually underground stems called rhizomes).

No matter where ginger was first used, we know that it has long been esteemed for its real or imagined medicinal effects as much as for its flavor. For example, ginger is called *Mahabheshaj* or *Mahaoushdhi* (the great cure or the great medicine) in Sanskrit. Throughout their recorded history, Indians have used it to treat such diverse conditions as elephantiasis, gout, post-partum recovery, and pale skin, as well as to restore amorous feelings and fertility and to cure headaches and colds. For just as long, the Chinese have employed ginger for many of the same folk cures, and even today it is considered a valuable strengthening agent.

Whether these cures are real or imagined, scientists have confirmed other important medicinal properties. Recent experiments have shown that ginger allays nausea and motion sickness just as the Chinese have long claimed. The intact rhizome has strong antioxidant properties, and some compounds isolated from it are even more potent than alpha-tocopherol (vitamin E). Current investigations also indicate that several compounds in ginger have beneficial effects, but more study is needed to confirm these findings.

EXPLORING ASIAN KITCHENS

The variety of Asian cuisines is so great that many volumes have been written full of exciting recipes. Here we've stressed the basic whole foods we have just discovered. Expand your repertoire by modifying recipes from other books, using whole plant foods as the foundation of the meal. The Asian ingredients for the recipes that follow can be found in Asian grocery stores and some natural food stores (see Sources).

We'll begin with a basic rice recipe, then visit Japan, China, Indonesia, and finish with some tantalizing Indian recipes.

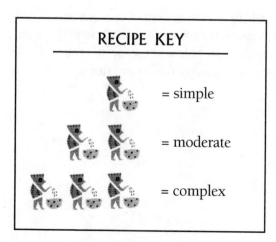

RECIPE KEY	
	= simple
	= moderate
	= complex

Cooked Brown Rice
by Rowena Hubbard

Serves 4

*This simple method of cooking brown rice should be in everyone's repertoire.
It is so easy, yet retains all the nutrients of this staple food of half the world.*

> 1 cup long grain brown rice, washed
> 2 ½ cups water
> Salt

Combine the rice and water in a large saucepan. Add salt to taste, stirring
well. Bring to a brisk boil; turn heat down to simmer, cover, and cook 45
minutes until all liquid is absorbed. Fluff rice with a fork to serve.

Dashi Soup Stock
by Rowena Hubbard

Makes about 2 quarts

*This is the basis of many Japanese dishes. It is almost the cornerstone of
Japanese cooking. Fortunately, it is quick and easy to make.*

> 2 ½ quarts water
> 3-inch square dried kelp, washed
>   under running water

Heat water in a 4- to 6-quart saucepan until it comes to a full rolling boil.
Add dried kelp and return water to a boil. Remove from heat, let stand
about 2 minutes. Remove kelp and use for other dishes or discard. The liquid is now ready to be used as dashi soup stock.

Simmered Daikon Radish

by Tsukiko Hattori

Serves 4

Daikon radish is the long white Japanese radish that is available fresh in many supermarkets. It is very mild in taste with a wonderful crunchy texture. If you can't find it, white turnip is a good substitute.

> 4 pieces daikon radish (1½ to 2 inches thick)
> Water
> 3 tablespoons brown rice
> Simmering Sauce "A" (recipe below)
> One 6-inch piece konbu kelp
> 3½ ounces (scant ½ cup) soybean paste (sakura miso)
> Simmering Sauce "B" (recipe below)

Simmering Sauce A:

> 4 cups Dashi Soup Stock (see previous page)
> 1 teaspoon salt
> 1 teaspoon soy sauce

Simmering Sauce B:

> 4 tablespoons Dashi Soup Stock
> 4 tablespoons honey
> 2 tablespoons sake

Peel the radish slices; make a shallow criss-cross on one side of each slice to speed cooking. Place in a saucepan with plenty of water and the brown rice; bring to a boil. Boil until tender; drain, and rinse with clear water. Return daikon and rice to saucepan; add Simmering Sauce "A" and kelp. Simmer until kelp is tender and daikon is tender all the way through. Combine soybean paste and Simmering Sauce "B" in a saucepan, heat until well blended, stirring with a wooden spoon. Sauce should be smooth and shiny. To serve, spoon daikon into bowls and top with sweetened miso.

Simmered Kelp with Vegetables

by Tsukiko Hattori

Serves 4

These vegetables are crisp and brightly colored in the finished dish. Lightly stir-fried in a little sesame oil, they have a rich, sweet flavor enhanced by the cooking wine and soy.

1¼ ounce sliced konbu kelp
Water
2 small slender carrots
4 dried shiitake mushrooms
Salt
8 fresh string beans, strings removed
2 tablespoons sesame oil

Simmering Sauce

3 cups Dashi Soup Stock (see page 266)
3 tablespoons soy sauce
2 tablespoons sake
2 tablespoons mirin (sweet rice wine used in cooking)
1 tablespoon honey

Soak the kelp in water to soften; cut into bite-size lengths. Scrub the carrots; shred finely. Soak dried shiitake mushrooms in water. When softened, cut off and discard hard stem and slice mushroom thinly. Lightly salt a saucepan of water and bring to a boil. Add the string beans; cook until they are just blanched and turn bright green. Drain and rinse under cold water; cut diagonally into bite-size pieces. Heat the sesame oil in a saucepan. Add the carrots, shiitake, and kelp in that order and stir-fry a minute or two. Add the Simmering Sauce and continue to stir-fry until liquid is reduced to ¼ of the original amount. Stir in cooked string beans just before serving.

Simmered Soybeans With Vegetables

by Tsukiko Hattori

Serves 4

Easy to make, this is an interesting way to cook whole soybeans. They absorb the flavors of the simmering sauce as they cook with the vegetables.

> 2 cups dried soybeans
> ½ large carrot
> ½ long burdock root
> 1 piece konbu kelp (6-inch square)
> Simmering Sauce (recipe below)
> 5 tablespoons soy sauce

Simmering Sauce

> 3 cups Dashi Soup Stock (see page 266)
> 2 tablespoons honey
> 3 tablespoons mirin
> 2 tablespoons sake
> Pinch of salt

Soak the soybeans in water overnight. Boil in the soaking liquid until soft. Rinse in cold water and drain on a bamboo mat or in a colander. Cut the carrot and burdock root into small pieces, about the same size as the soybeans; boil lightly until tender. Soak the kelp in water to soften and cut into thick strips.

In a saucepan, combine the Simmering Sauce ingredients, soybeans, carrot, burdock root, and kelp. Simmer over moderate heat until liquid is reduced by half. Add the soy sauce a little at a time to desired flavor.

Simmered Shiitake Mushrooms with Vegetables

by Tsukiko Hattori

Serves 4

Tofu, green beans, and woodsy-flavored shiitake mushrooms make a very satisfying entrée when served with steamed brown rice. Simmering the mushrooms in soup stock.flavored with sweet cooking wine and soy sauce gives them a slightly sweet-salty taste that enhances their flavor.

> 8 dried shiitake mushrooms
> 2 cups Dashi Soup Stock (see page 266)
> 1 tablespoon sake
> 2 tablespoons mirin (sweet rice wine used in cooking)
> 2 tablespoons soy sauce
> 8 small squares soft tofu (about 4 ounces)
> Simmering Sauce "A" (recipe below)
> 5 green string beans
> Simmering Sauce "B" (recipe below)
> 4 sansho leaf sprigs for garnish or green onion slivers

Simmering Sauce "A"

> 4 cups Dashi Soup Stock
> 4 tablespoons honey
> 3 tablespoons mirin
> 2 tablespoons light soy sauce
> 1 tablespoon sake
> ⅓ teaspoon salt

Simmering Sauce "B"

> 1 cup Dashi Soup Stock
> ½ teaspoon salt
> 1 teaspoon light soy sauce
> 1 tablespoon mirin

Soften the dried shiitake mushrooms in water; cut off and discard hard stems. In a small saucepan, put the shiitake, Dashi Soup Stock, and sake. Simmer over medium heat for 2 to 3 minutes and remove scum. Add mirin and continue to simmer for 3 to 4 minutes until sweetened. Add the soy sauce and simmer over low heat until liquid is reduced by half. Set aside.

Cube tofu. Put Simmering Sauce "A" in a medium-sized saucepan and bring to boil. Add tofu pieces and cover. Simmer over low heat 20 to 30 minutes. Remove scum. Set aside.

Remove strings from beans and boil in lightly salted water 2 to 3 minutes to retain color. Rinse in cold water and drain. Heat Simmering Sauce "B" in a small saucepan. Add the beans and bring quickly to a boil. Drain on a bamboo mat or in a colander, reserving liquid, and let stand to cool. Soak the beans in the cold leftover liquid to absorb flavor.

Place all ingredients into a bowl and pour in tofu with its cooking sauce. Garnish with sansho leaf sprigs or green onion slivers.

Miso Soup with Sticky Rice

by Rowena Hubbard

Serves 4

So-called "sticky" (glutinous or sweet) rice is used in both Japan and China. Round and pearly in appearance, it sticks together when cooked, unlike regular rice. In Japan it is the base rice for sushi, and in China it is used for special ceremonial dishes, especially a snack dish called joong, which is eaten during the Dragon Boat Festival. This Japanese recipe teams it with vegetables and miso. If you prefer a mellower flavor, use miso fermented from barley, rice, or the miso termed "Hawaiian style," which is milder than red miso. Be sure not to boil the miso. Boiling destroys the enzymes.

> 3-inch piece of wahame*
> 5 cups water
> ½ cup sticky rice, washed
> 1 slice fresh ginger (about ¼ inch thick)
> 1 small carrot, cut into ¼-inch dice
> 4 string beans, cut into ¼-inch pieces
> 2 tablespoons miso
> 2 tablespoons water
> 1 large green onion, sliced thinly
> Soy sauce

Combine the wahame, water, rice, and ginger in a large saucepan. Bring to a boil; turn heat down and simmer 15 minutes. Add the carrots and beans and cook 5 minutes longer. Stir miso into 2 tablespoons water. Remove soup from heat. Stir in miso mixture, green onions, and soy sauce to taste.

---

*Wahame is a type of seaweed that is available in natural food stores or from suppliers (see Sources).

Tofu with Vegetables

by Tsukiko Hattori

Serves 4

Bright, crunchy, and full of flavor, these vegetables can be prepared early in the day, refrigerated, and served later at room temperature.

> 11 ounces *konnyaku* (yam jelly)
> ¼ large carrot
> Water
> 4 small shiitake mushrooms
> Small handful of snow peas
> Simmering Sauce "A" (recipe below)
> 2 tablespoons sesame seed
> ½ of a 14-ounce block soft tofu
> Sauce "B" (recipe below)
> 1 tablespoon or more Dashi Soup Stock (see page 266) or water

Simmering Sauce "A"

> 1 cup Dashi Soup Stock
> 1½ tablespoons soy sauce
> 1½ tablespoons honey

Sauce "B"

> 1 tablespoon honey
> 1 tablespoon mirin
> Salt

Slice *konnyaku* into thick matchsticks and stir-fry in a small frying pan without oil. Thinly slice carrot; boil in water until just crisp-tender. Soak dried shiitake in water until soft. Cut off and discard hard stems; shred mushrooms finely. Simmer these ingredients in Simmering Sauce "A" until the liquid is reduced by half. Drain and let stand to cool.

String the snow peas and cut into julienne strips. Blanch in boiling water just until they turn bright green. Rinse in cold water and drain. Carefully toast the sesame seeds until golden; place in a mortar and pestle. Add tofu and grind well. Add Sauce "B" and grind again. Taste and correct seasoning, adjusting smoothness with a little more dashi or water if needed. Mix the tofu mixture into the vegetable mixture. Spoon into a small bowl to serve.

Stir-Fried Bean Sprouts with White Kikurage

by Tsukiko Hattori

Serves 4

Little advance preparation is needed for this fast bean sprout dish. It's truly a good example of ancient fast food.

¾ pound fresh bean sprouts
1 ounce dried kikurage (white cloud ear mushroom)
1 tablespoon vegetable oil

2 cups vegetable broth
1 tablespoon sake
Dash of salt

Wash the bean sprouts and drain well in a colander. Soften the kikurage in lukewarm water; remove and discard stems. Heat the oil in a saucepan and stir-fry the bean sprouts. When the oil is absorbed, add the vegetable broth. Add the kikurage and simmer. When the sprouts and kikurage are softened, add the sake and salt. Continue to simmer 2 to 3 minutes until liquid is absorbed. Correct seasoning and remove from heat. Serve at once.

Yuba Soup

by Tsukiko Hattori

Serves 4

A quick soup for a cold day. It would be good served in a small bowl as a first course to a stir-fry vegetable dish.

2 ounces yuba (half-cooked soy milk skin)
Nori seaweed, a little for flavor
3½ ounces shimeji mushrooms

1 ounce bamboo shoots
5 cups vegetable broth
1 tablespoon sake
1 teaspoon salt

Soak the yuba in water and soften. Thinly cut nori seaweed with scissors. Remove and discard stems from shimeji mushrooms and separate into bite-size bunches. Thinly slice bamboo shoots. Turn vegetable broth into a saucepan. Add the shimeji and bring to a boil. Season with sake and salt to taste, then add the yuba, bamboo shoots, and nori. Bring back to a boil and remove from heat. Serve at once.

Eggplant and Tofu Stir-fry

by Rowena Hubbard

Serves 4

The eggplant originated in Asia as a globe-like, white vegetable that looks very much like an egg with a beautiful stem on it. Today, there are many varieties of this beautiful vegetable. For this recipe try to find the dainty, long, purple Asian variety. Serve this wholesome stir-fry over brown rice.

> 1 pound long Asian eggplant, or 1 large, regular eggplant
> 1 teaspoon salt
> ½ of a 14-ounce block extra-firm tofu
> 2 tablespoons light soy sauce
> 2 tablespoons sweet rice wine (such as mirin) or sweet sherry
> ½ teaspoon grated fresh ginger
> 2 tablespoons peanut oil
> 2 cloves garlic, minced
> 8 green onions, slivered lengthwise and cut into 1½-inch pieces
> 1 teaspoon toasted sesame oil

Cut the eggplant into sticks about 1½ inches long and ½ inch wide, leaving skin on. Place in a colander and toss with the salt. Allow to stand about 30 minutes, then rinse salt off and dry on paper towels. Meanwhile, cut the tofu into bite-size pieces. Combine the soy sauce, rice wine, and ginger in a small bowl; toss tofu cubes with this mixture and marinate 30 minutes.

Heat the peanut oil in a wok or large frying pan, stir in the garlic, and cook a minute or two. Add the eggplant and toss until lightly browned. Add all but a few green onions, tossing to coat with oil. Fold in the tofu and all its marinade and the sesame oil. Cover and allow to steam 3 to 4 minutes, until eggplant is tender and cooked through and tofu is hot. Serve at once. Garnish with remaining green onion slivers.

Stir-Fried Tofu with Snow Peas and Hoisin

by Rowena Hubbard

Serves 4

Snow peas are Chinese in origin, but were first thought to be cultivated in Europe. Delicate and sweet, they differ from regular peas in that they do not develop an inner casing, so that the entire pod is edible. They add a sweet crunch to this dish, which is flavored with the rich, piquant tones of one of the classic sauces of ancient China. Hoisin sauce is a thick, red sauce made of soybeans, garlic, salt, and chile.

> ½ of a 14-ounce block firm tofu
>
> 3 tablespoons sweet rice wine (such as mirin)
>
> 1 tablespoon soy sauce
>
> 1 teaspoon grated fresh ginger
>
> 3 tablespoons peanut oil
>
> 1 medium green pepper, cut in ½-inch squares
>
> 8 large fresh mushrooms, sliced
>
> 6 water chestnuts, diced
>
> 1 cup snow peas, strings removed
>
> 1½ tablespoons hoisin sauce
>
> ¼ cup toasted almonds

Cut the tofu into ½-inch cubes and place in a small bowl. Add 1 tablespoon of the rice wine, the soy sauce, and the ginger. Toss well to combine and marinate about 30 minutes while preparing the vegetables.

Heat the oil in a wok or large skillet. Stir-fry the green pepper and mushrooms until crisp-tender; add the water chestnuts and snow peas and cook about 2 minutes longer. Stir in the tofu. Combine the hoisin sauce with remaining 2 tablespoons rice wine; stir into the tofu-vegetable mixture until heated through. Add the almonds and toss well. Serve at once.

Clear Mushroom Soup with Tofu and Scallions

by Rowena Hubbard

Serves 6 to 8

This is an elegant, intensely flavored mushroom soup, which is perfect served in small bowls as a first course. It awakens the taste buds for the remainder of the meal, and is light enough so that it is not too filling. It is just the sort of soup that might have been found on the Emperor's table.

- 15 small dried shiitake mushrooms
- 2 quarts water
- 3 tablespoons sweet cooking rice wine (such as mirin)
- 3 tablespoons light soy sauce
- 1/3 cup finely sliced scallions
- 1/2 of a 14-ounce block soft tofu

Combine the mushrooms, water, rice wine, and soy sauce in a saucepan. Bring to a boil; turn heat down to simmer, cover, and cook gently for 2 hours for flavor to develop. Remove from heat and remove the mushrooms to a plate with a slotted spoon. Cool the mushrooms and cut into 1/8-inch strips. Return them to the broth with the scallions and tofu. Heat just to boiling, adjust soy seasoning, and serve.

Stir-Fried Tempeh with Chinese Cabbage

by Rowena Hubbard

Serves 4

Tempeh has been a staple food in Indonesia for hundreds of years. It is a complete protein containing all the essential amino acids; it also is a good source of iron, vitamin E, lecithin, and fiber. Today it is available in many different grain mixtures, which always have soybeans as their base. Tempeh has a rich, nutty flavor and the texture holds up very well to quick sautéing, making it a delicious chewy addition to stir-fried dishes.

> 8 ounces soybean tempeh
> 1 cup water
> 3 tablespoons soy sauce
> 1 clove garlic, minced
> 2 tablespoons light sesame oil
> 1 medium onion, chopped
> 1 tablespoon grated fresh ginger
> 4 cups chopped Chinese cabbage
> 1 tablespoon sweet cooking rice wine (such as mirin)
> 1 tablespoon rice flour
> 2 teaspoons dark toasted sesame oil
> 2 tablespoons toasted sesame seeds

Cut the tempeh into ½-inch cubes. Combine the water, 1 tablespoon of the soy sauce, and the garlic in a small saucepan; add the tempeh and simmer for 10 minutes. Drain and reserve liquid. Sauté the tempeh in the light sesame oil in a very large skillet until it is golden brown on all sides. Remove and reserve. Sauté the onion and ginger in the pan until the onion is translucent. Add the cabbage and quickly stir-fry until wilted. Add the reserved liquid and tempeh, rice wine, remaining 2 tablespoons soy sauce, and rice flour (blended into a little cold water), to the pan, cooking until just thickened. Stir in the dark sesame oil and sprinkle with toasted sesame seeds to serve.

Shanghai Tempeh on Rice Stick Noodles

by Rowena Hubbard

Serves 6

Although soybeans were not used in this fermented form in China, tempeh takes readily to Chinese seasonings and absorbs their flavors beautifully while adding a chewy, meaty texture to this dish.

8 ounces tempeh (soybean or soybean and rice)

Vegetables

¼ cup light sesame oil
1 large onion, sliced
2 cloves garlic, chopped
1 red bell pepper, thinly sliced
1 cup thinly sliced celery
4 ounces mushrooms, sliced
1 tablespoon grated fresh ginger
½ cup fresh peas, blanched
Rice stick noodles, deep-fried and drained

Marinade

2 tablespoons sweet cooking rice wine (such as mirin)
2 tablespoons water
1 tablespoon rice flour
1 tablespoon soy sauce
1 teaspoon dark toasted sesame oil
1 teaspoon honey

Stir-Fry Sauce

2 tablespoons soy sauce
2 tablespoons sweet cooking rice wine (such as mirin)
1 tablespoon rice flour
1 cup vegetable stock
1 teaspoon dark toasted sesame oil

Steam tempeh for 10 minutes, or boil for 20 minutes. Cool; cut into small cubes. Toss with combined marinade ingredients and set aside for at least 30 minutes while preparing the vegetables and stir-fry sauce.

When ready to cook, heat the light sesame oil in a wok or large skillet. Stir-fry the onions and garlic until lightly browned. Add the red pepper, celery, mushrooms, and ginger and stir-fry until vegetables are crisp-tender. Add the tempeh and all of its marinade and stir-fry until tempeh is hot. Mix together the ingredients for the stir-fry sauce and add it and the peas to the wok, stirring until the peas are hot and the sauce is thickened slightly. Serve at once on crisp rice stick noodles.

Quick Fried Tempeh Sticks with Spicy Dipping Sauce

by Rowena Hubbard

Serves 4

Crispy little sticks of tempeh are a wonderful snack or appetizer when dipped in a hot sweet-and-sour sauce.

> 8 ounces tempeh
> Peanut oil
> Salt

Spicy Dipping Sauce

> 2 tablespoons light soy sauce
> 1 teaspoon dark sesame oil
> 2 to 3 teaspoons seasoned rice vinegar
> 1 to 2 teaspoons sweet rice wine (such as mirin)
> A few drops hot chile oil

Cut the tempeh into sticks about 1 inch long by ½ inch wide and ¼ inch thick. Place on a plate, cover with plastic wrap, and heat in microwave for 5 to 7 minutes to pre-cook. Meanwhile, prepare Spicy Dipping Sauce by whisking all ingredients together well. Heat about ⅛ inch oil in a sauté pan over medium heat. When hot, add the tempeh pieces and fry, stirring well for 3 to 5 minutes, until they turn golden brown. Remove them and drain well on paper towels. Continue frying until all the sticks are done. Sprinkle with a little salt and serve hot with Spicy Dipping Sauce.

Indonesian Vegetable Soup with Tempeh

by Rowena Hubbard

Serves 3 to 4

Any of our familiar strong-flavored vegetables—such as cauliflower, cabbage, or broccoli—work here. The traditional vegetable in this soup is Chinese broccoli, but if you can't find it, any of the others will do. Use any variety of tempeh you like; it is the texture that will be most noticeable in this soup.

> 4 ounces tempeh, cut into small cubes
> 1 cup water
> 4 cups chopped Chinese broccoli, small cauliflower florets, chopped cabbage, or broccoli florets
> 1 tablespoon vegetable oil
> 1 small onion, chopped
> 2 cloves garlic, minced
> 2 teaspoons ground cumin
> 1 teaspoon ground coriander
> 1 teaspoon salt
> ½ teaspoon turmeric
> ⅛ teaspoon cayenne pepper
> 1 small stalk lemon grass, cut in 1½-inch lengths
> 1 slice fresh ginger, ⅛ inch thick
> 1 quart vegetable broth
> ¼ cup minced fresh cilantro, lightly packed
> 2 tablespoons coconut milk (optional)

Combine the tempeh and water in a small saucepan. Heat to boiling; turn the heat down and simmer the tempeh for 15 minutes. Meanwhile, chop the Chinese broccoli into coarse pieces. Heat the oil in a large soup pot; sauté the onion and garlic until soft and lightly browned. Stir in the cumin, coriander, salt, turmeric, and cayenne; sauté one minute. Add the lemon grass, ginger, vegetable stock, and Chinese broccoli. Simmer about 20 minutes. Add the tempeh, with all of its cooking liquid, and the cilantro. Continue cooking 5 more minutes. Stir in the coconut milk, if using, just before serving.

Savory Chickpeas Bombay

by Rowena Hubbard

Serves 4

These tasty, savory chickpeas are often served as snacks.

> 1 pound dried chickpeas
> Water
> ½ teaspoon turmeric
> 1 teaspoon ground cumin
> ¼ teaspoon chile powder
> 2 tablespoons lemon juice

Soak the chickpeas overnight; drain well. In a large pot, cover chickpeas with at least 3 inches of water. Stir in the turmeric and ½ teaspoon of the cumin. Cook the chickpeas about 1 hour until soft and tender. Drain; turn into a large bowl. While still hot, sprinkle with the remaining ½ teaspoon cumin, chile powder, and lemon juice. Cover and cool at room temperature until ready to serve.

Golden Dhal (Lentils)

by Rowena Hubbard

Serves 4

Most Indian meals are served with lentils of some sort. There are over sixty varieties of lentils in India, but very few are available here, even in Indian groceries. Best known, and easiest to find, are brown or red lentils. Classically, there are three ways to cook them. First, they may be fried with the spices and seasonings, then cooked very slowly with just enough water to make them tender. The second way is to cook them at a very low simmer until tender, and then season them; or third, they can be cooked in water and spices, then folded together with green herbs. This recipe follows the first cooking method.

> 1 cup red lentils
>
> 2 tablespoons vegetable oil
>
> 1 large onion, thinly sliced and diced
>
> 3 cloves garlic, finely chopped
>
> 1 teaspoon grated fresh ginger
>
> 1 teaspoon Garam Masala (page 287)
>
> ½ teaspoon turmeric
>
> 1 teaspoon salt
>
> 3 cups water

Wash and drain the lentils. Heat the oil in a saucepan; fry the onion and garlic until golden. Add the lentils, ginger, garam masala, and turmeric and sauté slowly until the lentils have absorbed the oil. Add the salt and water, cover, and cook over low heat until lentils are tender and all liquid is absorbed, about 25 minutes.

Lentil Curry

by Lorna Sass

Serves 4

Lentils have provided sustenance to mankind since the days of Esau's pottage. In addition to their excellent nutritional profile, lentils cook quickly and don't require pre-soaking—a great boon to today's cook. Because of their strong, earthy flavor, lentils stand up nicely to assertive curry seasonings. For a special treat, try this with French Le Puy lentils, which are very flavorful and hold their shape beautifully. Serve this curry over steamed basmati rice accompanied by your favorite chutney.

> 4 cups water
> 1½ cups brown or green lentils, picked over and rinsed
> ½ cup dried, unsweetened, shredded coconut
> 2 teaspoons minced garlic
> 2 cups coarsely chopped onion
> 2 large carrots, halved lengthwise and sliced
> 1 tablespoon mild curry powder
> 1 teaspoon whole fennel seed
> ½ teaspoon ground cinnamon
> Salt

Bring the water to a boil in the pressure cooker as you add all of the remaining ingredients except the salt. (Note: Owners of jiggle-top cookers must add 1 tablespoon oil to control foaming action. Be alert for any hissing sounds.) Lock the lid in place. Over high heat bring to high pressure and cook for 9 minutes. Allow the pressure to come down naturally or use a quick-release method. Remove the lid, tilting it away from you to allow any excess steam to escape. Stir well and add salt to taste. This mixture will thicken on standing; thin with water as needed.

For a lower-fat version, you may omit the coconut and substitute ¼ cup sun-dried raisins and ¼ cup additional lentils.

Mixed Vegetables (Aviyal)

by Rowena Hubbard

Serves 4

This dish from northwest India can use any combination of vegetables, so it's a wonderful dish to make when the refrigerator vegetable bins need a little tidying. Foods from this region use yogurt and elegant seasoning, which is spicy but not hot. Termed Moghul *cuisine, it relies heavily on whole wheat flour* chapatis *(small, flat, pancake-type breads) as the basic carbohydrate.*

1 pound thin carrots
1 pound green peas, in their shells
1 pound string beans
1 clove garlic
2 teaspoons grated fresh ginger
¾ cup water
2 tablespoons vegetable or light olive oil
3 medium onions, sliced
2 teaspoons chopped mint leaves
½ cup plain nonfat yogurt
2 teaspoons cumin
1 teaspoon turmeric
Salt and freshly ground black pepper

Dice the carrots; shell and wash peas; clean and slice the beans. Combine them in a saucepan of boiling water; cover, remove from heat, and set aside. Pound the garlic and ginger together using a mortar and pestle; blend with the ¾ cup of water. Heat the oil in a large skillet; sauté the onions until golden brown. Add bruised mint, fry a minute longer. Add the yogurt, cumin, and turmeric; cook slowly for 5 minutes. Add the garlic-ginger water and salt and pepper to taste. Cook until the liquid has evaporated. Add the carrots, peas, beans, and about 1 cup of the vegetable liquid. Cover and cook very slowly until vegetables are tender. Check frequently to make sure there is always a little liquid in the pan.

Fresh Spinach with Spicy Yogurt Dressing

by Rowena Hubbard

Serves 6

Quick, easy, and delicious, this can be served hot or cold. The use of dry mustard and oil simulates mustard oil, the favorite cooking oil of the Bengal region, which can be hard to find.

1 large bunch fresh spinach	½ teaspoon hot dry mustard
2 tablespoons water	½ teaspoon Garam Masala
1 tablespoon vegetable or light	(page 287)
olive oil	½ teaspoon salt
1½ teaspoons ground cumin	1 cup plain nonfat yogurt

Wash and stem the spinach. Place the leaves and water in a very large frying pan. Cover pan and turn heat to high. When steam begins to escape, turn heat very low and cook 2 minutes longer until leaves are wilted. Drain well; chop. Wipe frying pan dry, add oil, and heat. Add cumin, mustard, garam masala, and salt and fry them, stirring constantly, until frothy. Remove from heat, stir in yogurt and toss with spinach. Serve warm or cold.

Onion and Coriander Salad

by Rowena Hubbard

Serves 4

There are always many accompaniments to Indian dinners, including salads, sambals (hot and fiery salads), lentil wafers, fresh chutneys, fruits, raitas (see page 288), coconut mixtures, and nuts. This very simple salad would be good served as part of a picnic lunch or an elaborate dinner.

1 medium-size sweet onion	1 cup roughly chopped
(Maui or Vidalia)	coriander leaves
2 tablespoons fresh lemon juice	Salt

Peel the onion; slice in half and then into paper-thin slices. Toss with the remaining ingredients, cover, and chill for at least an hour before serving.

Garam Masala

by Rowena Hubbard

Masalas are ground-spice mixtures that are the key to Indian cooking. They vary widely and are often freshly ground for a particular dish. The traditional Indian cook uses a grinding stone as well as a mortar and pestle to make the masala. Two versions are given here, one using the pre-ground spices you can purchase easily, the other the whole seed form. If you are using ground spices make sure that they are fresh. If you are using seeds, a blender or a small food processor does a fine job. If you have trouble, the motor in an electric coffee grinder is more powerful and may grind them finer. Always store garam masala in a tightly sealed jar, away from heat and light. All spices lose flavor over time, so it's best to make this in small quantities to be used up quickly.

QUICK GARAM MASALA

Makes about 2 tablespoons

2 teaspoons ground cardamom
2 teaspoons ground cinnamon
1 teaspoon ground cumin

1 teaspoon ground coriander
1 teaspoon fine black pepper
¼ teaspoon ground nutmeg

Combine all spices and toast in a dry frying pan, stirring constantly, until fragrant and toasty. Store in an airtight container.

WHOLE SPICE GARAM MASALA

Makes about 2 tablespoons

1 tablespoon cardamom seed
1-inch piece of cinnamon stick
1 teaspoon cumin seed

1 teaspoon whole cloves
1 teaspoon black peppercorns
About ¼ whole nutmeg

Combine all spices in a small food processor or coffee grinder and grind to a fine powder. Turn into a frying pan and toast until fragrant. Store in an airtight container.

Cucumber Raita

by Rowena Hubbard

Serves 4

Refreshing as an addition to any Indian dinner, this also makes a wonderful dressing for tomato salads or a tasty sauce spooned over Baked Falafel (page 159) in pita bread.

> 1 large English cucumber
> 2 teaspoons salt
> 1 cup plain nonfat yogurt
> ¼ cup finely minced scallions
> ½ teaspoon grated lemon peel
> 2 teaspoons fresh lemon juice

Wash the cucumber, slice thinly, then dice. Place in a colander and toss with the salt; allow to stand 30 minutes. Rinse and drain well. Toss with all remaining ingredients. Cover and chill about 1 hour for flavors to blend.

Indian Cheese (*Panir*)

by Rowena Hubbard

Serves 4

Panir is a simple-to-make nonfat cheese used as a condiment in East Indian cooking. Make it the day before you wish to use it if you like a firm texture.

> 1 quart nonfat milk
> 2 tablespoons lemon juice

Bring the milk to a rolling boil until it begins to rise in the pan. Remove from heat, stir in the lemon juice, and allow to stand 5 minutes. Line a sieve with eight thicknesses of fine cheesecloth. Pour the milk mixture into the sieve and allow to stand 30 minutes. Press cheesecloth to wring out any excess moisture. Twist cheesecloth closed, place on a plate, and cover with a weight. Refrigerate for at least 2 hours, or overnight.

11 ≋

EQUATORIAL AFRICA

We have already visited Africa, when we stopped in the Mediterranean region (Chapter 7). But our journey wouldn't be complete if we did not make at least a quick stop in equatorial Africa, where we will find teff, the fabulous grain of Ethiopia; okra, a unique vegetable and one of the most delightful sources of a special type of soluble fiber; and many starchy roots. There is much more to be found in this area, but our goal is to seek out foods that should become a more important part of the diet in industrialized societies (here teff and okra), that have an important historical correlation to modern nutrition (starchy roots and the new fiber era), or that must be preserved in their native countries (teff).

TEFF, THE ETHIOPIAN GRAIN

Ethiopia, settled sometime before 500 B.C., is a land of contrasts. Most of it sits on a plateau 7,000 to 10,000 feet above sea level, with the Simyen mountains rising above to 15,000 feet and river gorges cutting deeply into the land, as deep as the Grand Canyon in Arizona. Ancient Ethiopians scorned personal safety in their fight to keep their land intact, while maintaining their grand nobility of character, tenderness, dignity, and good manners. Teff, appropriately enough, is a grain of the highlands. While some people consider teff a kind of millet, they do not appear to be related. The botanical name of teff is

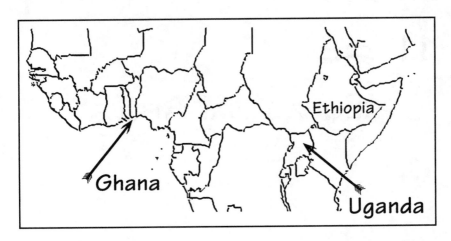

Eragrostis teff and related varieties of *Eragrostis*, while the common millet that we found in Asia (page 251) is *Sorghum vulgaris*. In his doctoral dissertation on teff, Muluseta Assefa tells us that even the long literary tradition of Ethiopia does not provide clues as to teff's ancient cultivation, but we know that it has been grown in Ethiopia for millennia. It was only as late as 1927 that expeditions to the northern highlands of Ethiopia discovered cultivated teff. It has recently traveled all the way to North America, finding a home in Colorado, where some pioneering farmers are now introducing teff to the North American market. In its native land, teff currently finds little support; other grains such as wheat—much easier to harvest and less labor intensive than teff—have become more popular.

Teff is a small grain, so tiny that Rebecca Wood, in "Teff: Ethiopia's Wonder Grain" (*East West* magazine, August 1988) tells us that 150 grains of teff weigh as much as 1 kernel of wheat. Its high protein content, about 10 percent, was enough to make it the grain of choice for the tough inhabitants of the Ethiopian highlands. Teff's iron content is higher than that of all other common cereal grains, which may explain the low frequency of anemia in Ethiopians who still consume teff. Its calcium content is also somewhat higher than other common grains. Although grains should not be considered our primary source of calcium—they do not compare with the calcium content of milk products or dark green leaves—a cereal high in calcium can be a valuable addition to other higher-calcium foods.

Teff, high in protein, iron, and calcium, should be consumed more widely. You'll find a grain-based diet to be most successful if you eat a variety of grains.

EXPLORING TEFF IN ETHIOPIAN CUISINE

Basic to Ethiopian cuisine is *injera*, a flat, pancake-like bread cooked over a wood fire on a heated flat stone, or in more modern times, on a griddle. Made of teff and water, the mixture is left for three days to ferment, so that small bubbles rise to the surface when it is cooked, almost like pancakes. A thin, soft bread with a slightly sour flavor, *injera* is used to line the large basket or tray used as the common, central container for the meal. The foods of the day are poured out onto the *injera*. Then, each person tears off pieces of the bread with their right hand and uses it as a scoop for the saucy *wats*, the traditional stews of the country. *Injera* is to Ethiopian cooking what rice is to Asian cooking, or whole wheat breads are to the Mediterranean region. *Injera* is the backbone of an Ethiopian meal.

The Coptic church has been the dominant religious group in Ethiopia since the fourth century A.D. and, as such, is responsible for many of the food customs. There are numerous meatless days on which lentils, beans, chickpeas, and peanuts form the basis of the traditional stew (*wat*). The wat stew is always seasoned with *berbere*, a fiery ground-spice mixture, while the *alecha* stew, often made of almost the same ingredients, has none of these blazing seasonings and is much milder than the wat.

OKRA

Okra (*Hibiscus esculentus*) originated in the tropics of the Old World and is known by different names: In India it's called *bhindi*, and North

American cookbooks often call it *gumbo*. It's part of African and Asian cooking. On our journey we find okra in the tropical countries of Africa. Its fruit is mucilaginous, and this mucilage gives it a unique texture and flavor after cooking. While okra supplies many protective factors typical of dark green vegetables, it is this mucilage that makes it special; this is a soluble fiber with the potential to lower blood cholesterol. Okra seeds also have been used to make oil and a coffee substitute.

STARCHY ROOTS OF AFRICA

Many starchy roots are among the staples of equatorial African countries and are the equivalent of the American potato. In a diet based on these foods, such as those in tropical African countries from Uganda to Ghana, fiber intake is high and diseases of the digestive system are rare. Two British physicians, Doctors Hugh Trowell and Denis Burkitt, who practiced in Uganda in the 1950s and 1960s as medical missionaries, developed the fiber hypothesis. They were treating both the native Ugandans, who ate this high-fiber diet, and the English people living there. Among the natives the frequency of diseases of the digestive system, including colon cancer, diverticular disease, and heart disease, was low. Trowell and Burkitt started the "fiber era," and their discovery, not yet appreciated by many scientists for its full impact, was among the greatest of the twentieth century. Although less glamorous than discoveries in genetics or other fields of medicine, many researchers feel these physicians should have received a Nobel Prize in medicine for the impact of these discoveries.

HONEY

A book on ancient foods would not be complete without a brief mention of honey. Honey could have been described in other chapters of this book, but we chose to discuss it here because in Ethiopia the ancient methods of beekeeping are still used. Hives are fashioned of tall cylinders of straw, bound by leather. A fragrant incense is burned in the top to attract the bees. Once they have gathered in the hive, it is strung by a leather strap to a tree. Honey might be harvested in a year, depending on the weather. This rich, natural sweetener was eaten in slabs between folds of bread, used to sweeten the ancient drink called *tej* (rather like mead, a fermented honey wine of Europe), and held under the tongue while drinking coffee to sweeten the beverage.

Natural, unrefined sweeteners—honey, maple syrup, unrefined brown sugars, cane sugar syrups such as molasses, and concentrated grape or other fruit juices boiled down to a syrupy consistency—are delightful sources of sugars and contain traces of other nutrients that are absent from highly refined white sugar. Best of all, they have more flavor than purified sugars, and add variety to the diet.

A MAN FROM GHANA

A fit young man from Ghana, now a taxi driver in Washington, D.C., likes to tell his impressions of black America compared to black Ghana as he drives people to the Dulles Airport, a long drive from downtown Washington. He recalls how he hardly ever saw overweight people in his native country and how in the United States, while he finds many very fit blacks, he also finds many of them quite overweight. When asked about the Ghana diet, he talks about roots, vegetables, grains, and other plant foods with only modest intake of meats and related products. Until recently, little of what we have called refined foods was part of the daily diet in Ghana, but as in many other African countries, Western diets are slowly beginning to penetrate!

BERBERE, THE ETHIOPIAN NOT-SO-NATIVE SPICE

by Cornelia Carlson

Berbere, although not based on ancient, native plants, is so much a part of the cuisine of Ethiopia that it must be included in our African journey.

When Ethiopian women make *berbere*, an incendiary mixture of spices, it is always a communal affair, whether they live in a village in southern Harare, suburban Silicon Valley, or the 10th Arrondissement of Paris. Together they share the labor of toasting spices, crushing garlic, and grinding endless pounds of chiles, while they catch up on what's happening in each other's lives. *Berbere* marks the cuisine of Ethiopia, just as soy and curry mark those of China and India. It is used to flavor virtually all meats, poultry, and fish, and often to season vegetables, stews, chickpeas and lentils, breads, and breakfast barley porridge.

While recipes for this ferocious melange vary by geographic region, family preference, and to some extent by season and what is available, chiles are the constant and dominant element. To their heat are added the spicy counterpoints that make this blend a taste sensation: the fresh bite of ginger; the sweetness of cinnamon, nutmeg, and cloves; the camphorous touch of cardamom; ajwain's medicinal sting; sulfurous onions; bitter rue; licorice-flavored basil; and fenugreek's odd blend of maple, celery, and toast. *Berbere*, as we know it, can't be more than about 475 years old, since chiles didn't exist in Ethiopia prior to that time. But I suspect that another version must have preceded it, with black pepper or the equally hot West African Melegueta pepper (*Aframomum melegueta*) producing its heat. Certainly the other spices found in this melange were available to Ethiopians hundreds of years earlier, and most probably arrived thousands of years ago along offshoots of the maritime spice trade from the Orient to Egypt, Greece, and Rome.

Whether Ethiopian cooks recognize it or not, *berbere* could be a pharmacologist's "cure-all." And in an area where doctors are remote and drugs are scarce, this spice blend may have a secondary therapeutic function. In it are chiles with vitamin C, carotenoids, and capsaicin with its multifarious benefits (pages 26–27); garlic and onions to ward off colds and lower blood pressure; ginger with its ability to stimulate appetite, aid digestion (page 264), and inhibit cancer; cloves and ajwain's antiseptic/antioxidant molecules (eugenol and thymol); and fenugreek with its soothing mucilage and trigonelline, a precursor of niacin.

You don't have to believe in herbal cures to like *berbere*, but you'd better like hot foods. If you do, try the simplified recipe on page 306. It is flexible, so include ingredients to suit your taste. The common spices are sold in every supermarket or natural food store.

Note that rue is an optional herb. *Use it with caution.* Although records indicate that humans have eaten rue for more than 2,000 years, it can cause rashes. More seriously, an overdose of the concentrated oil extracted from the herb can cause hallucinations, abortions, and death. Certainly pregnant women should not sample rue. Keep in mind that a small amount of most spices and herbs will deliver plenty of flavor with little risk, whereas a massive dose of a few may not be healthy.

EXPLORING THE CUISINES OF EQUATORIAL AFRICA

Let's discover the delights of okra, with its unique taste and texture, of teff breads, starchy roots, and equatorial spices. The ways of cooking in Ethiopia and other African countries haven't changed much for centuries. Let's hope that the West will bring in the good things of modern life and not the negative parts of their refined, high-meat diets!

Teff Bread

by Jody Main

Serves 4

This flat bread is very easy and quick to make. It is crisp around the edges and chewy in the center. Serve warm teff bread with stews and other dishes that have rich sauces. The bread is torn and used to scoop up the stew and sauce for a chewy delicious bite. Teff flour comes in two varieties: whole grain ivory teff flour and whole grain dark teff flour. The ivory flour is more wheat-like with a sweet nutty flavor, and the dark has a more robust, toasty flavor. Use the one that will be most complementary to the meal.

> 1 cup teff flour, plus extra for flouring the pastry board
> ½ cup water
> Salt

Blend 1 cup teff flour, water, and salt to taste together to make a stiff dough. Knead well. Cut the dough into 4 pieces. Sprinkle teff flour on a pastry board. Roll one piece of dough into a ball in the palm of your hand. Sprinkle with teff flour and pat into a pancake. Set onto the floured board and press into a 6-inch circle. Place in a dry skillet over medium-low heat and cook 5 minutes on each side.

Ethiopian Teff Bread (Injera)

by Rowena Hubbard

Serves 2 to 4 (Makes four 12-inch rounds)

Injera is Ethiopia's oldest and best-loved bread. It makes a perfect foil for the fiery berbere *seasoning ubiquitous to Ethiopian cuisine. Even today, it is made pancake-fashion over open fires in the more remote villages.*

Traditionally, the teff flour and water are mixed and set aside to catch the wild yeast and ferment for about three to four days. This adaptation allows the mixture to be ready for cooking in about 20 minutes, depending on the temperature in the house. If it is a warm day, you can mix the dough and set it outside in the sun for about 10 minutes before cooking.

The wild yeast and slow fermentation of the old Ethiopian way produces a slightly sour taste to the bread. This recipe doesn't have that little tang, but you can achieve it by adding 1 tablespoon of plain nonfat yogurt to the dough when mixing the base ingredients if you like. I like the plain version just as well as the slightly sour one.

> 1 cup teff flour*
> 1½ cups hot tap water
> ¼ teaspoon granular yeast
> Dash salt
> 1 teaspoon vegetable oil

Combine all the ingredients except the oil in a medium bowl. Cover and set in a warm place for about 20 minutes (10 minutes if placing in the sun), until small fermentation bubbles begin to form on the surface. Meanwhile, place a 12-inch, nonstick skillet over medium heat. Put the oil on a paper towel and rub the surface of the skillet. Using a half-cup measure pour batter in a circle, starting at the outside edges and moving in toward the center. Add a little more if needed and tilt pan to coat bottom. Cover and cook about 1 to 2 minutes, just until the top is set. Uncover and cook a few seconds longer until the edges begin to curl up and away from the pan and the bottom is just beginning to brown. Slide out onto paper towels, and continue cooking the breads, rubbing the oiled paper over the surface of the pan before each addition of batter.

---

*See Sources for ordering teff and teff flour.

Collard Greens and Teff Loaf

by Leslie Cerier

Serves 6

Serve this with a salad for a wonderful meal.

>1 tablespoon olive oil
>1 large onion, sliced (1½ cups)
>5 cloves garlic, sliced
>1 sweet potato, peeled and sliced (3 cups)
>5 collard leaves, sliced
>1 cup teff
>1 cup brown lentils, rinsed
>5 cups water
>½ teaspoon ground cardamom
>Salt

Heat the oil in a heavy-bottomed stock pot. Sauté the onion and garlic in the oil for 5 minutes; then add the sweet potato. Sauté for 5 minutes. Add the collards and sauté for another 2 to 3 minutes. Add the teff and sauté for a minute. Stir in the lentils, water, and cardamom. Bring to a boil; simmer about 45 minutes until all water is absorbed. Add salt to taste. Pour into a loaf pan. Allow to stand one hour; slice and serve.

Variations: Use diced carrots or zucchini in place of the sweet potato. For a faster version, substitute red lentils for the brown and simmer 20 minutes instead of 45 minutes.

Vegetable Stew (Shiro Wat)

by Rowena Hubbard

Serves 6 to 8

The yam used in this recipe is the tuber known as name *or* igname, *not the vegetable we call "yam" in the United States. The* igname *tuber can grow to 100 pounds or more, and the raw flesh is crisp and mucilaginous. Cooked it is quite potato-like with a bland flavor.* Igname *and the plantain can be found in most Latin American grocery stores. When choosing an* igname, *prick the skin with your fingernail to make sure it is juicy and slippery. If the flesh is dry, don't buy it.*

2 cups peeled and chunked *igname*

2 cups chunked carrot

Boiling water

1½ cups green beans, trimmed

1 large green pepper

¾ cup freshly ground peanut butter

1½ cups boiling water

2 tablespoons olive oil

1 large onion, chopped

2 large cloves garlic, minced

2½ teaspoons *Berbere* without onion and garlic (page 306)

1 large semi-ripe plantain, sliced ½-inch thick

¼ cup fresh lemon juice

Salt

Cook the *igname* and carrot in boiling water to cover for approximately 30 minutes, until soft. Meanwhile, cut the green beans into 1-inch lengths; seed the green pepper and cut into 1-inch chunks. Combine the peanut butter and 1½ cups boiling water in a bowl, stirring well to combine. Heat the oil in a large sauté pan. Sauté the onion and garlic until the onion is translucent. Stir in the berbere and cook 2 to 3 minutes. Drain the igname and carrot, reserving the cooking water. Stir the peanut butter mixture into the onions and cook 3 to 4 minutes. Stir in the *igname*, carrots, green beans, green pepper, and sliced plantain. Cook, stirring occasionally, until plantain is soft. Add 1 cup reserved vegetable water as needed; the sauce will thicken as it cooks. When vegetables are soft, stir in the lemon juice and season with salt to taste. Serve at once.

Lentil Salad
(Yemiser Selatta)

by Rowena Hubbard

Serves 6 to 8

The heat of the chiles penetrates into the lentils, so if you are not used to their heat, start by using only a very small amount. This salad is traditionally served with injera bread (page 296), which helps to tame the chile.

> 1¼ cups dried lentils
> Boiling water
> 3 tablespoons fresh lemon juice
> 2 tablespoons olive oil
> ¾ cup slivered shallots
> 2 fresh green chiles (3 inches long) stemmed, seeded, and chopped
> Salt and freshly ground pepper

Wash and pick over the lentils. Cook in triple their quantity of boiling water at a simmer for 25 minutes, until they are tender but still firm. Drain and rinse in a colander under cold water. Combine all remaining ingredients in a large bowl, adding salt and pepper to taste. Gently fold in the lentils. Cover and refrigerate for at least 30 minutes for flavors to blend. They can be marinated longer, but the chile heat will continue to penetrate the lentils.

Mashamba Pumpkin and Ground Nuts

by Rowena Hubbard

Serves 6

Mashamba *pumpkin is not available in the United States, but Kabocha squash has a firm, meaty texture that works very well in this simple, classic dish of West Africa.*

1 medium Kabocha squash, about 3 pounds
   (3 cups cooked squash)
½ cup freshly ground peanut butter
1 tablespoon grated fresh ginger
¼ cup water

Preheat oven to 350 degrees. Pierce holes in the squash with a very sharp, long-blade knife. Bake for 50 to 60 minutes, until the squash is tender. Cool, cut open, and remove the seeds (you can save them to toast later). Scrape out the cooked squash to make about 3 cups. Combine the squash with all other ingredients in the bowl of a food processor, and blend well. Serve warm.

Note: This can be made in advance, placed in a casserole, covered, and refrigerated overnight. When ready to use, cook about 5 minutes in the microwave till heated through.

Spinach and Groundnut Sauté

by Rowena Hubbard

Serves 2 to 4

This very simple, tasty recipe for spinach comes together quickly and easily at the last minute.

> 2 tablespoons olive oil
> ½ cup finely chopped onion
> ½ cup raw peanuts
> 1 large bunch fresh spinach, washed well and chopped
>   (4 cups chopped)

Heat the oil in a very large sauté pan. Stir in the onion and cook until translucent. Meanwhile, whirl the peanuts in a food processor until finely chopped. Stir the ground peanuts into the onion and cook, stirring constantly, until onions and peanuts are well browned. Add the spinach and stir constantly until the spinach is wilted and coated with the onions and peanuts. Serve at once.

Black-Eyed Pea Fritters (Akara)

by Rowena Hubbard

Serves 4 to 6

The black-eyed peas in this recipe are not pre-cooked, just soaked overnight. They are soft and do not have the usual raw legume flavor. The deep-fat frying cooks them to a nice texture. You can make the fritters ahead, put them on a pie plate, and then heat them in a 250-degree oven for about 30 minutes before serving. They would be excellent with a dipping sauce as an appetizer. In West Africa, they are most often served one or two to a plate as a vegetable, providing a nice contrast in texture to a stew.

1½ cups raw black-eyed peas
Boiling water
¼ large onion, chopped
1 tablespoon grated fresh ginger
1½ teaspoons salt
⅛ to ¼ teaspoon cayenne pepper
½ to ¾ cup water
Vegetable oil for frying

Cover the peas with the boiling water by at least 2 inches; cover the pot, and soak overnight. Drain off the liquid and rub the peas between your hands to rub off the skins. Rinse again. Add to the bowl of a food processor with the onion, ginger, salt, cayenne, and ½ cup water. Process to a smooth paste, adding a little more water as needed, but don't exceed ¾ cup water total. Heat the vegetable oil to 375 degrees in a deep-fryer or deep saucepan. Drop the batter by teaspoonfuls into the oil, cooking a few at a time for about 5 minutes each until golden on all sides. Remove with a slotted spoon and drain on paper towels.

Spiced Okra
by Rowena Hubbard

Serves 4

Okra is called okro or "ladyfingers" in Africa and is used in soups and stews in all West African countries. Quick cooking keeps the okra firmer in this recipe. If you like the more traditional soft gelatinous texture, cook it a little longer. Spiced okra is most often served as a relish with dishes such as Shiro Wat (page 299) and Fufu Dumplings (page 305).

> 1 cup water
> 1/4 cup minced onion
> 1 small clove garlic, minced
> 1/4 teaspoon cayenne pepper
> Salt and freshly ground black pepper
> 1/3 pound fresh okra, cut into 1-inch long pieces (1 1/2 cups)

Combine the water, onion, garlic, cayenne pepper, and salt and black pepper to taste in a saucepan. Bring to a boil. Add the okra and cook about 15 minutes until almost all liquid is absorbed. Turn the okra into a colander and run under cold water to stop cooking. Chill before serving.

Cassava (Gari)
by Rowena Hubbard

Makes 2 cups

Cassava is a staple in the diets of many African nations. When the root is ground to a granular powder it is known as gari or farinhe de mandioca, or more familiarly to us as "tapioca." It is a superb and nutritious thickening agent for soups and stews, and in the larger granular form it is used much as rice and couscous are used in other areas.

> 1 cup large tapioca granules
> Salt to taste
> Cold water to cover

Place the tapioca in a small bowl, add the salt and cold water to cover, and allow to stand until all water is absorbed. It should swell to about double its original size (in about 30 minutes). Fluff with a fork and serve with any hot dish that has a sauce.

Fufu Dumplings

by Rowena Hubbard

Serves 6 to 8

These dumplings are made with the African yam, igname, which is available here in some specialty markets. When cooked, African yam has a potato-like flavor, but its texture is coarser and drier than potato. These dumplings are used in soups and as side vegetables all over West Africa.

> **2 pounds** *igname*
> **Boiling salted water**

Peel the *igname,* cutting off the skin and the underlayer. Cut into large pieces and drop into the boiling salted water. Cook 40 to 45 minutes until tender. Drain; purée in a food processor until the mixture forms a compact, slightly sticky paste.

To form the balls, place a bowl of cold water beside a large dinner plate. Sprinkle a little water on the plate; moisten your hands, and using about ¼ cup yam paste, form it into a dumpling by rolling it across the plate until it becomes a smooth, firm, slightly translucent ball. Arrange the dumplings on a plate as you finish them and serve at once.

Berbere

by Cornelia Carlson

Makes about 1¼ cups (about 2½ cups if using onions)

This recipe calls for ground chiles, which will save you time and tears. If you have the inclination, you can substitute the more traditional whole chiles, using an equal weight. For the mildest mix, use California chiles; New Mexican are hotter; for a real kick, substitute some hontaka, tepin, or arbol for part of the tamer chiles. Include at least three of the sweet spices (cinnamon, cloves, nutmeg, cardamom), and if possible, the basil, and either fenugreek or ajwain, or their suggested substitutes.

If you are cooking for a horde and will use the whole batch on the same day, add the garlic and onions. If you plan to store it longer, be sure to leave them out of the mix and add some directly to the dishes as you cook them. Without them it will last for at least a year in the refrigerator, ready to flavor mild soups, beans, grains, or blanched vegetables as well as traditional Ethiopian foods. Add it to taste, starting with a very small scoop.

Middle Eastern and Indian grocery stores usually stock fenugreek and ajwain. If you can't find them locally, check the suppliers listed in the Sources section. Rue and sacred basil are herbs you'll have to grow at home. See cautions regarding rue (page 295).

> ¼ pound (about 1 cup) ground chiles
> ¼ cup minced fresh ginger
> 1½ tablespoons ground cinnamon
> ½ teaspoon ground cloves
> 1 teaspoon freshly ground nutmeg
> 1½ tablespoons ground cardamom
> ¼ cup minced fresh sacred basil (or sweet basil)
> 1 teaspoon ground fenugreek seed (or cumin seed)
> 1 to 2 tablespoons crushed ajwain seed (or minced fresh thyme)
> ¼ teaspoon minced fresh rue (optional)
> Boiling water
> 1 to 2 tablespoons vegetable oil

If using immediately add:

> Peeled cloves of garlic from 1 large head
> 2 medium onions, peeled and chopped

Put the spices and herbs in a food processor. Add garlic and onions if serving the berbere within the day. Pulse to mix. Fill two clean half-pint (1-cup) jars with boiling water and pour more water into their lids to sterilize them. (You'll need two more jars if you are adding the garlic and onion.) Stick a clean spoon in one jar. Slowly add boiling water to the spice mixture with the motor running, until it becomes a stiff paste. Turn off motor. Drain the jars and lids, and scrape the paste into them with the spoon. Pack down to eliminate air bubbles. Spread a film of vegetable oil over the top of each. Screw the lids on tightly, and refrigerate immediately.

Note: Be sure not to add the garlic and onions if you plan to store the berbere more than 1 day. The combination of the other ingredients with the garlic and onions can lead to the development of undesirable toxic by-products if improperly stored.

Teff and Sweet Potato Pie

by Leslie Cerier

Serves 6

Using cooked teff as a pie crust, this dish is a creative adaptation of the way that Ethiopians eat their foods, with flat bread as the traditional bottom layer for stews and sauces.

Pie Crust

>⅔ cup teff
>2 cups water
>Pinch salt
>2 tablespoons honey
>1 teaspoon vegetable oil

Pie Filling

>2½ cups baked, mashed sweet potato (about 1¼ pounds)
>1 tablespoon honey, or to taste
>1 teaspoon cinnamon
>¼ teaspoon nutmeg
>¼ teaspoon allspice
>¼ teaspoon cloves

To make pie crust, combine the teff, water, salt, and honey in a small saucepan. Simmer 15 to 20 minutes until all water is absorbed. Oil a 9-inch pie plate with the oil. Pour the cooked teff into the pie plate, spreading it out like a pie crust with a spatula.

For pie filling, combine all ingredients in the bowl of a food processor and blend. Taste and adjust seasonings. Pour into the teff crust. Serve warm or chilled.

Variations: You can substitute pumpkin or winter squash for the sweet potato. For a creative touch, you may cook the teff with some sun-dried raisins, dates, or other dried fruits.

12 ≈

PUTTING TOGETHER THE FOODS AND FLAVORS OF THE WORLD

On our journey we have found great health-giving foods that at one time were available in only certain regions of the world. Over the centuries crops and foods began to travel from one continent to another—Chinese and Indian teas became a sophisticated European beverage, and the South American tomato became an intrinsic part of the Italian diet. In today's world of jet travel and rapid communication we can creatively fuse ancient foods for truly *universal* dishes and combined health benefits.

Have fun with new combinations of color, taste, and texture. Remember that all the recipes in this book are here to inspire you to create your own original dishes, simple or complex, fast or time-consuming, but all based on some of the healthiest foods we have inherited from our ancestors.

Tuscan White Bean Soup with Potatoes and Pasta

by Deborah Madison

Serves 4 to 6

This is a cold-weather soup I thoroughly enjoyed in rustic and chilly conditions in the mountain area of Carrara, Italy. It's utterly reviving when you need warmth and encouragement. If you take the time to cook your beans you'll have a delicious stock to use for the soup.

1 cup cannellini or other white beans, sorted and soaked 4 hours

10 cups water

3 cloves garlic

3 sage leaves

Salt and freshly ground pepper

3 medium red or white potatoes, diced in ½-inch cubes

2 celery stalks, diced in small pieces

1 small onion, diced

1 leek, white part only, sliced in rounds

8 sage leaves, finely chopped (or 1½ teaspoons dried)

2 teaspoons minced fresh rosemary (or 1 teaspoon dried)

3 garlic cloves, pounded to a paste with 1 teaspoon salt

2 tablespoons extra-virgin olive oil plus extra to finish

1 tablespoon tomato paste

1 cup dried small pasta shapes

Chopped parsley or sage leaves

Parmesan cheese

Drain the beans, put them in a pot with the water, and boil hard for 5 minutes. Remove any scum that floats to the surface, then add the 3 cloves garlic and the 3 sage leaves. Simmer, partially covered, until the beans are partially tender, about 45 minutes. Season with 2 teaspoons salt.

Meanwhile, wash and cut all the vegetables. I prefer them finely cut but you can make them larger and chunky if you like. In a wide soup pot, heat the oil and fry the tomato paste, stirring it around, for about a minute. Then add the potatoes, celery, onion, leek, sage, rosemary, and smashed garlic. Cook for 3 to 4 minutes, stirring frequently to expose the vegetables to the direct heat, then add 8 cups of the bean broth and the beans, and simmer until the beans are fully tender, another 20 to 30 minutes.

While they're simmering, boil the pasta in any remaining broth or water until it's *al dente*; drain and rinse to stop the cooking. When ready to eat, taste the soup for salt and season it with freshly ground pepper. Add the cooked pasta just long enough for it to heat through, then ladle the soup into soup bowls. Garnish each with fresh parsley or a pretty sage leaf and serve with a little extra-virgin olive oil—preferably Tuscan—drizzled over the top and a little freshly grated Parmesan cheese.

White Bean and Polenta Soup with Cabbage and Cumin (Jota)

by Deborah Madison

Serves 4 to 6

Jota is a warm, thick, nourishing pottage, which might have been cooked in hard times in the past, using perhaps a stored cabbage, beans and cornmeal from the pantry, a piece of pancetta for flavoring, and olive oil for the cooking. Untypically it is seasoned with cumin, which is unusual for Italian food. If you cook the cabbage separately it will remain bright and fresh.

Beans

1¼ cups dried navy beans, soaked 6 hours or overnight

10 cups water

Aromatics

1 small diced onion

2 bay leaves

1 carrot, finely diced

3 cloves garlic, peeled and chopped

Soup

2 tablespoons extra-virgin olive oil plus extra to finish

2 garlic cloves, sliced

2 teaspoons cumin seeds

1 tablespoon flour

½ cup polenta (coarse, stone-ground cornmeal)

Salt and pepper

1 small savoy or smooth green cabbage

1 bay leaf

Chopped parsley

Drain the beans and cover with the water. Boil hard for 5 minutes and remove any scum; lower the heat, add the aromatics, and simmer until the beans are partially tender, about 45 minutes. Add 1½ teaspoons salt and continue cooking until the beans are tender. When done, remove and discard the bay leaves. Set beans and broth aside.

In a soup pot, heat the oil with the sliced garlic. Remove the garlic when golden, then add 1½ teaspoons of the cumin seeds and flour and cook until the flour is lightly browned. Whisk in the bean broth and add the beans. Slowly whisk in the polenta, then simmer a half hour. Stir frequently to keep the polenta from sinking to the bottom and sticking. If the mixture becomes too thick, add more water or vegetable stock. Taste for salt and season with pepper.

Remove the outer leaves of the cabbage and cut the cabbage into wedges, one or two for each bowl. Put them in a wide skillet with the remaining ½ teaspoon of the cumin seeds and the bay leaf. Add about a half cup of the bean broth or water, a pinch of salt, and cook uncovered until bright green and tender, about 7 minutes.

To serve, ladle the soup into soup plates and place a wedge of cabbage into each. Add a pinch or two of finely chopped parsley to each bowl, drizzle lightly with fruity olive oil, and serve.

Winter Squash *Chakchuka* with Peppers and Tomatoes

by Deborah Madison

Serves 4

Sun-dried tomatoes replace meat in this fall stew. If tomatoes aren't in season, fry 2 tablespoons tomato paste in the oil instead.

> 1 piece of winter squash (about 1¼ pounds)
> 3 tablespoons olive oil
> 4 sun-dried tomatoes, cut in narrow strips
> 2 onions, diced
> 3 ripe tomatoes, peeled and diced (or 2 tablespoons tomato paste)
> 2 red peppers, roasted, peeled, and cut into short strips
> 2 to 3 teaspoons *Harissa* (page 179)
> ¼ teaspoon red pepper flakes
> Salt
> Chopped parsley

Peel the squash, remove seeds, and dice into 1-inch cubes. Heat the oil with the sun-dried tomato strips. (If substituting tomato paste for the fresh tomatoes, fry it in the oil for a minute at the same time.) Cook gently for several minutes, then add the onions and squash and sauté over high heat until lightly colored. Add the fresh tomatoes, peppers, *harissa*, and red pepper flakes. Season with salt, mix together and sauté 3 or 4 minutes, then add a cup of water. Lower the heat, cover the pan, and simmer until the squash is tender. Add more water if needed while it's cooking. Taste for salt and garnish with parsley.

Optional garnish: Tunisian dishes, especially couscous, are frequently topped with 1 or 2 fried green chiles. Though I don't think it's traditional here, I think the chile would taste good with all these sweet vegetables. Choose 4 New Mexican or Anaheim chiles and sauté them in hot oil until the skins blister in places and they begin to wilt. Serve one with each portion.

Potato and Chickpea Stew (Chakchuka)

by Deborah Madison

Serves 4

The combination of potatoes and chickpeas makes this dish filling but not heavy. Many Tunisian stews use a small amount of dried meat for flavoring. I find a few sun-dried tomatoes, sautéed with the onions, give this dish a similar depth of flavor.

> 3 tablespoons olive oil
> 1 large onion, finely diced
> Pinch saffron threads
> 4 sun-dried tomatoes, cut in thin strips
> 1 heaping tablespoon tomato paste
> 2 heaping teaspoons *Harissa* (page 179)
> 1 pound red potatoes, peeled and quartered lengthwise
> 1 cup cooked chickpeas
> Salt, pepper, and red pepper flakes
> 1½ cups water or chickpea broth
> Chopped parsley

Heat the oil in a casserole or cast-iron skillet. Add the onion, saffron, and sun-dried tomatoes and fry for about a minute. Add the tomato paste and *harissa* and cook briskly, stirring frequently, a few minutes more. Add the potatoes and fry, letting them color a bit, about 4 minutes, then add the chickpeas, 1 teaspoon salt, a few twists of pepper, and pinch of red pepper flakes. Pour in 1 cup of water or chickpea broth, cover, and simmer gently 15 to 20 minutes. Raise the lid and add another ½ cup water and continue cooking until the potatoes are tender when pierced with a knife. Taste for salt and pepper, garnish with parsley, and serve.

Barley Yogurt Soup with Caramelized Onions and Burdock Root

by Jody Main

Serves 10 to 12

This hearty soup is enriched and lightly sweetened by the caramelized onions. Burdock adds a depth of flavor and earthiness that can be obtained only from this root that grows deep within the earth. Enjoy it with fresh sliced oranges on the side.

> 2 onions, thinly sliced
> 1 tablespoon vegetable oil
> Water
> 1 cup barley
> 1 (6-inch) piece burdock root
> 1 tablespoon vinegar or lemon juice
> 2 tablespoons chopped fresh tarragon (or 1 teaspoon dried, crushed tarragon)
> 1 cup plain nonfat yogurt

Sauté the onions in the oil and ¼ cup water in a large skillet over medium-low heat for 20 to 30 minutes, stirring frequently. Add an additional ¼ cup water as necessary as the liquid evaporates. The idea is to bring out the sugars of the onions without burning them. This process will make them melt-in-your-mouth soft and very sweet.

While the onions are cooking, bring 12 cups of water and the barley to a boil in a large soup pot. Reduce heat, cover, and simmer gently for 1½ hours.

While the onions and barley are cooking, scrub clean and thinly slice the burdock root. Do not peel. Lay the burdock slices in a small skillet with the vinegar and ¼ cup water. Cover and simmer gently for 15 minutes. Add the caramelized onions, burdock, and tarragon to the barley pot. Simmer for 30 minutes. Remove from heat. Stir in the yogurt and serve.

Wild Mushroom and Barley Soup with Horseradish

by Jody Main

Serves 10 to 12

This creamy, hearty soup is enlivened by a bit of fresh horseradish. Shiitake mushrooms give it an earthy, rich flavor. The longer the barley cooks, the thicker the broth. This soup is wonderful served with a light salad of wild greens drizzled with a little Pomegranate Syrup (page 245).

> 10 cups water
> 1 cup hulled barley, rinsed
> 4 onions, quartered
> 1 pound fresh shiitake mushrooms (or ¼ pound dried)
> 4 carrots, chopped
> 4 celery stalks, chopped
> 1-inch piece of fresh horseradish, grated (or 1 tablespoon
>   prepared horseradish)
> Salt (optional)

In a large soup pot, bring the water, barley, onions, and mushrooms to a boil. Reduce heat, cover, and simmer for one hour. Add the carrots, celery, and horseradish and simmer for an hour more. Season to taste.

Barley Soup with Pink Beans and Corn (Papozoi)

by Deborah Madison

Serves 4

Papozoi is a hearty Italian soup that brings grains and legumes together in one bowl. Each enhances the other, providing an amiable contrast of textures. Native dried roasted corn, called chicos, would be ideal here, but it's not commonly available, except in the Southwest. Fresh or frozen corn will do in a pinch. Normally this soup would have a piece of pancetta for flavor or be made with a light meat broth. Instead, I added a vibrant accent of fresh green parsley sauce.

Soup Ingredients

- 1 cup borlotti or pink beans, sorted and soaked 4 hours or overnight
- 1 cup barley, soaked for an hour or more
- 10 cups water or vegetable stock
- 1 tablespoon extra-virgin olive oil
- 1 large garlic clove, finely minced or pounded to a purée
- Salt and pepper
- 2 cups corn kernels

Parsley Sauce

- 1 clove garlic
- Salt and freshly ground pepper
- 1/3 cup chopped parsley
- 1 1/2 tablespoons extra-virgin olive oil
- 1 tablespoon freshly grated Parmesan cheese (optional)

Drain the beans and the barley and put them in a soup pot with the stock or water, oil, and garlic. Bring to a boil, skim off any foam that rises to the surface, then simmer, partially covered, for 30 minutes. Add salt to taste, a twist of pepper, and the corn. Cook until the corn is tender. Meanwhile, make the sauce. Pound the garlic in a mortar with a few pinches of salt and a few grindings of pepper until smooth. Add the oil and the parsley and pound another minute or so, bruising the parsley to bring out its aroma. If you like, you can work in a tablespoon of cheese as well. Serve the soup and stir a bit of the sauce into each bowl.

Fava Beans in Thick Soup

by Tsukiko Hattori

Serves 4

A simple soup to take advantage of the wonderful flavor of the beans.

1⅓ pounds fresh, in-shell fava beans
Salt
Water
1 quart Dashi Soup Stock
  (page 266)

1 tablespoon rice flour or potato
  starch
½ teaspoon light-colored soy sauce
4 sansho leaf sprigs for garnish,
  or any garden-fresh herb

Shell the beans and rub them lightly with salt. Boil in hot water to cover until the beans turn a fresh green color. Strain and peel skins off of beans. Bring the dashi soup stock to boil in a medium saucepan. Add salt to taste. Blend the rice or potato starch with a little cold water, and stir into dashi until slightly thickened. Gently stir in cooked fava beans and add soy sauce to flavor. Pour into soup bowls and garnish each with a sansho sprig.

Stir-Fried Fava Beans with Pickles

by Tsukiko Hattori

Serves 4

Karashina is a quickly cooked vegetable that brings a whole new flavor dimension to fava beans. Serve this and Tofu with Vegetables (page 275) over steamed brown rice for a colorful and satisfying meal.

> 1½ pounds fresh fava beans
> 3½ ounces pickled *karashina* (leaf mustard)
> 2 tablespoons vegetable oil
> ⅔ cup vegetable broth

Pod the fava beans. Rinse the pickled leaf mustard in water to remove excess salt. Squeeze out water and chop. Heat the oil in a saucepan. Stir-fry the fava beans lightly and add broth. When the fava beans have softened, add the karashina and stir-fry lightly. Taste for salt; if more is needed, use pickling liquid to adjust and remove from heat.

Teff and Chickpea Stew

by Leslie Cerier

Serves 6

1 made this one day when my five-year-old had a friend visiting. These two kindergartners enjoyed it so much that they had seconds. Adults love it too.

> 1 onion, sliced (1 cup)
> 5 cloves garlic, minced
> 1 tablespoon cumin seed
> 1 tablespoon vegetable or extra-virgin olive oil
> 2 cups sliced celery
> 2 cups sliced broccoli
> 4½ cups sliced plum tomatoes
> 2 cups drained, cooked chickpeas
> ⅓ cup teff
> 2 cups water
> ½ cup chopped fresh cilantro
> ½ teaspoon salt

Sauté the onion, garlic, and cumin seed in the oil in a large, heavy saucepan for about 3 to 5 minutes, until onion is translucent. Stir in the celery, broccoli, and tomatoes. Simmer about 5 minutes until the tomatoes are juicy and the broccoli and celery are bright green. Stir in the chickpeas and teff. Add the water and simmer about 20 minutes until the teff is cooked. Stir in the cilantro and salt.

Punjabi Peas and Tomatoes with Panir

by Rowena Hubbard

Serves 4

This mellow spiced dish is typical of northwestern India. It is excellent served with fluffy brown rice.

> Panir (page 288)
> 1 pound fresh peas
> 2 tablespoons vegetable oil
> 1 medium onion, finely chopped
> 1 large clove garlic, chopped
> 1 teaspoon grated fresh ginger
> 1 teaspoon ground coriander
> ½ teaspoon ground cumin
> ½ teaspoon ground turmeric
> ¼ to ½ teaspoon ground chile
> 2 firm ripe tomatoes, chopped
> Salt
> ½ teaspoon Garam Masala (page 287)
> 2 tablespoons chopped fresh cilantro

Cut the panir cheese into small cubes; shell the peas. Heat the oil in a large sauté pan. Brown the cheese on all sides; remove and reserve. Sauté the onion, garlic, and ginger in the pan, stirring constantly over low heat until golden. Add the coriander, cumin, turmeric, and chile and stir a minute longer until they are fragrant. Add the tomatoes, a little salt to taste, and ¼ teaspoon of the garam masala. Cook until the tomatoes are soft. If the mixture is too dry add a little hot water. Add the peas and cook until almost tender. Add the cheese cubes, 1 tablespoon of the cilantro, and simmer, covered, until the peas are cooked, about 10 minutes. Sprinkle with the remaining ¼ teaspoon of the garam masala and the remaining 1 tablespoon cilantro. Serve at once.

Okra Soup with Black-Eyed Peas and Tomatoes

by Rowena Hubbard

Serves 6 to 8

Hearty and savory, this soup combines the beans, vegetables, and roots of West Africa with the tomatoes and chiles of the Incas and Aztecs. Tomatoes and chiles have become an indigenous part of West African cooking since their introduction there many hundreds of years ago. The black-eyed peas do not need pre-soaking.

3 onions, chopped

3 large cloves garlic, chopped

¼ cup peanut oil

1 teaspoon turmeric

2 chopped green chiles, or ¼ teaspoon red chile flakes

½ cup dried black-eyed peas

6 cups cold water

3 cups chopped fresh tomatoes with their juice

1 pound fresh okra

1 cup diced cassava (yucca) root*

4 cups coarsely chopped collard greens

Salt and freshly ground pepper

Sauté the onion and garlic in the oil in a large soup pot, until the onion is translucent. Stir in turmeric and chiles and fry lightly. Stir in black-eyed peas until lightly coated with oil. Add the water and bring to a boil. Cover, turn heat down, and cook on a brisk simmer for 1 hour. Add the tomatoes, okra, cassava, and collards. Continue to cook 30 minutes longer, adding an additional cup of water if needed. Taste and season with salt and pepper. Serve at once.

*Cassava is available in Mexican, South American, African, and Carribbean food stores.

Couscous with Greens

by Lorna Sass

Serves 3 to 4

On a recent trip to Tunisia, I tasted dozens of varieties of couscous. Using the spices popular in that part of the world, I have created this version using calcium-rich kale, an inexpensive green that deserves much more popularity in American kitchens. Traditionally, couscous is steamed over boiling water. In this quick version, it is steeped in the liquid used to cook the kale.

I pound kale
I tablespoon olive oil
I tablespoon minced garlic
I cup thinly sliced leeks, or coarsely chopped onions
2¼ cups water
2 tablespoons tomato paste
½ teaspoon *Harissa* (page 179), or pinch of crushed red
   pepper flakes
I teaspoon salt
I teaspoon sweet paprika
½ teaspoon whole caraway seed
1½ cups whole wheat couscous
2 teaspoons ground coriander seed
I cup loosely packed, chopped fresh dill

Trim off the kale stems; coarsely chop the leaves. Set aside. Heat the oil in a pressure cooker. Sauté garlic and leeks for 1 minute. Stir in the water (stand back to avoid sputtering oil), tomato paste, *harissa*, salt, paprika, and caraway seed. Add the kale and lock the lid in place. Over high heat bring to high pressure. Reduce the heat just enough to maintain high pressure and cook for 1 minute. Release the pressure with the quick-release method. Remove the lid, tilting it away from you to allow any excess steam to escape. Quickly stir in the couscous and coriander. Nest, but do not lock, the lid in place and allow to steep in the residual steam until the couscous is soft and has absorbed all of the liquid, about 5 to 7 minutes. Stir in the dill just before serving.

Rice Gruel with Sweet Potato

by Tsukiko Hattori

Serves 4

This is a sturdy, stick-to-the-ribs dish that warms the body as it soothes the spirit.

> ½ to ¼ pound sweet potato
> 1 cup brown rice
> 5 cups water
> Salt

Seasoning Sauce

> 2 cups Dashi Soup Stock (page 266)
> Pinch salt
> 3 tablespoons soy sauce
> 3 tablespoons mirin (sweet, cooking rice wine)
> 1 to 2 tablespoons rice flour or potato starch
> ½ cup cold water

Cut the sweet potato into half moons about ¾ inch thick. Soak in slightly salty water to remove bitterness. Meanwhile, wash the rice and add to the 5 cups of water in a large, heavy pot. Cover and cook over high heat until rice is just tender. Add the sweet potato pieces; turn heat down to simmer. With lid ajar, cook very slowly until rice is extremely soft.

Combine all the Seasoning Sauce ingredients, except the rice flour and cold water, in a saucepan. Bring to a boil; add the rice flour dissolved in ½ cup cold water to make a thick sauce.

When the rice gruel is cooked, stir lightly and pour into bowls. Spoon thickened sauce over the top to serve.

Wild and Brown Rice with Herbs

by Rowena Hubbard

Serves 4

Mixing brown and wild rice makes for a richly flavored, chewy dish that is hearty and filling. If you wish to enrich the mixture it can be drizzled with a tablespoon of olive oil before serving.

> ½ cup California wild rice
> ½ cup California long grain brown rice
> 4 cups water
> Pinch salt
> 4 to 5 sprigs fresh thyme (or marjoram, summer savory, dill, or parsley)
> 1 whole clove garlic, peeled and chopped

Combine all the ingredients in a large pot. Bring the mixture to a boil; turn heat down to simmer, place cover on pot slightly ajar, and cook 35 to 40 minutes until all liquid is absorbed and the rice is tender but chewy.

Tepary Bean Fritters with Salsa

by Deborah Madison

Serves 4

Tepary beans are native to the Sonoran desert. Irrigated only by flash floods, tepary beans are small, sometimes wrinkled, and colored white or shades of brown. They can take a long time to cook so start them well in advance. Tepary beans can be purchased through Native Seed/Search (see the Sources section).

Beans

> 2 cups white tepary beans, soaked overnight
> ½ onion
> 1 clove garlic
> 1 teaspoon dried epazote, or a fresh sprig

Drain the beans, cover them with fresh water, and simmer with the onion, garlic, and epazote until tender. Season with salt once they're soft. Pour off the cooking water and purée half of them until smooth. Set aside.

Seasoning

 ¼ cup sunflower or safflower oil
 1½ cups finely diced white onion
 1 clove garlic, minced
 2 teaspoons fresh roasted, diced green chile
 ¼ teaspoon turmeric
 2 teaspoons roasted, ground cumin
 ½ teaspoon ground coriander seed
 ½ cup chopped fresh cilantro
 Salt
 ¼ cup semolina or whole wheat flour, if needed
 1 cup toasted sesame or amaranth seeds
 Sunflower or safflower oil for frying
 Green Chile Sauce (page 81) or Cooked Chile Salsa (page 82)

Heat the oil and add the onion, garlic, chile, turmeric, cumin, and corian-der and cook over medium heat, stirring frequently, for 10 minutes. Fold this mixture into the puréed beans along with the cilantro and whole cooked beans. Taste and season with salt. If the mixture is dry and holds a shape easily in your hand without feeling too sticky, leave it as it is. If it's a little moist, stir in the semolina or flour.

Form the beans into 3-inch croquettes. As a change from the usual disks, try shaping them into triangles or squares. Set them in the sesame or ama-ranth seeds and coat both sides. To cook, heat enough oil in a cast-iron or other heavy pan to a depth of about ⅛ inch and fry the croquettes on both sides until brown and crisp. Keep warm in the oven, then serve, two to a plate, with the Green Chile Sauce or Cooked Chile Salsa.

Roasted Rosemary Vegetables

by Rowena Hubbard

Serves 4

Easy and delicious, these roasted potatoes take on a Mediterranean flavor with the resinous scent of rosemary and garlic. Use red potatoes and leave the skins on for best flavor and the most nutrients.

> 8 medium red-skinned potatoes
> 6 large shallots, peeled and sliced
> 3 large cloves garlic, slivered
> 2 to 3 tablespoons olive oil
> Salt
> ⅓ to ½ cup fresh rosemary leaves, stripped from stems

Preheat oven to 350 degrees. Wash and cut the potatoes into quarters. Place in a large glass baking dish. Sprinkle with the shallots and garlic and toss with the olive oil until well coated. Sprinkle with salt and rosemary, tossing again lightly to combine. Bake for 50 to 60 minutes until potatoes are browned. To have all sides browned, stir once during cooking.

Teff-Stuffed Peppers with Sacred Basil and Tomatoes

by Leslie Cerier

Serves 6

Teff cooked in this manner can be stuffed into other vegetables besides peppers. Try it in cabbage, small dumpling squashes, large ripe tomatoes, or zucchini.

> 1 large onion, chopped (1½ cups)
> 5 cloves garlic, minced
> 1 tablespoon vegetable or olive oil
> 1 cup teff
> 3 cups water
> Salt
> 2½ to 3 cups chopped plum tomatoes
> 1 cup tightly packed sacred or regular basil leaves
> Red pepper flakes (optional)
> Freshly ground black pepper (optional)
> 6 green bell peppers, rinsed

Sauté the onions and garlic with the oil in a large saucepan for 5 minutes until light golden brown. Stir in the teff, water, and salt to taste. Bring to a boil, reduce heat, and simmer 15 minutes. Stir in the tomatoes and basil. Simmer 2 minutes. Add the red pepper flakes and black pepper, if desired, and adjust the salt.

Slit each bell pepper lengthwise about ½ inch from the top to about 1 inch from the bottom. Make a crosswise slit at the top about 1 inch wide and another lengthwise slit to form an opening. Gently scoop out the seeds and as much white membrane as you can with your fingers. Do not pierce skin. Spoon the cooked teff and vegetable mixture into the peppers, and close the flap. Serve immediately as an appetizer or a side dish.

Bulgur and Amaranth Pilaf with Olives, Sun-Dried Raisins, and Onions

by Rowena Hubbard

Serves 4

This hearty pilaf combines the great Mediterranean triad of wheat, olives, and sun-dried raisins with the New World grain amaranth. Quick, easy, and delicious, it is perfect served with stir-fried vegetables or a big vegetable salad.

1 tablespoon olive oil
1 medium onion, chopped
2 cloves garlic, minced
¾ cup bulgur
¼ cup amaranth
3 large ripe tomatoes
½ cup sliced pimiento-stuffed olives
⅓ cup sun-dried raisins
1½-inch cinnamon stick
Pinch red pepper flakes
4 teaspoons fruity extra-virgin olive oil

Heat 1 tablespoon olive oil in a large, heavy saucepan. Cook onion until wilted and lightly browned. Add garlic and sauté until golden. Stir in bulgur and amaranth until coated with oil. Chop tomatoes coarsely. Put into a quart measuring cup and add all the juice from the tomatoes with water as needed to make 2¼ cups. Add to bulgur with olives, sun-dried raisins, cinnamon, and pepper flakes. Bring mixture to a boil, cover, and lower heat to a simmer. Cook 25 minutes until all moisture is absorbed. Remove cinnamon stick and serve each portion drizzled with 1 teaspoon of fruity olive oil.

Wild Rice and Papaya Salad

by Cornelia Carlson

Serves 2 to 4

This salad makes an attractive appetizer and serves 8 to 10 if served this way. The fresh herbs help to unite the sweet fruitiness of papaya with the smoky tone of the wild rice. If you don't grow bee balm, you can substitute an equal amount of fresh basil, spearmint, or a combination of the two. Serve it lukewarm or chilled.

> 1 cup wild rice
> ¼ cup minced fresh bee balm
> 2 to 4 teaspoons extra-virgin olive oil
> 1 to 2 tablespoons rice wine vinegar
> 1 teaspoon balsamic vinegar (optional)
> Pinch sugar (optional)
> Pinch salt (optional)
> Pinch freshly ground pepper
> 1 ripe papaya
> Juice of 1 lime
> Whole fresh herb leaves for garnish

Bring a large saucepan of water (about 4 cups) to boil and add the wild rice. Reduce heat so that the water maintains a brisk simmer and cook until the grains are barely tender and just beginning to split. This can take from 20 to 40 minutes, so check frequently, and don't overcook. Drain and rinse briefly with cold water. Drain again. Scoop the rice into a large bowl. Add the remaining ingredients—except for the papaya, lime juice, and whole herb leaves—using the smallest quantity suggested, stirring them gently into the wild rice. Taste for seasoning and add the remainder as needed. Mix, cover, and cool briefly. If you prefer it cold you can store it up to one day in the refrigerator at this point.

Peel the papaya and discard the seeds. Slice the papaya into thin, lengthwise sections and set them on a plate or glass baking dish. Pour the lime juice over the slices and set aside in the refrigerator until ready to serve.

To serve, divide the papaya slices as needed per serving. Fan them out across one side of each plate, and scoop the wild rice into the center. Top each with a few herb leaves.

Dandelion Greens with Avocados

by Jesse Cool

Serves 4 to 6

*Simple, elegant, and innovative, a delightful salad for any time of the year.
When I was a child my grandfather would forage the neighborhood picking
wild dandelion leaves from the adjacent yards. Everyone thought he was
crazy but I thought he was wonderful to give me the gift of eating wild foods.*

> 2 bunches dandelion greens
> Juice of 1 or 2 oranges (or tangerines)
> 2 tablespoons extra-virgin olive oil
> 2 cloves garlic, crushed
> Salt and freshly ground pepper
> 1 ripe avocado, thinly sliced
> 2 hard-cooked eggs, thinly sliced (optional)

Wash dandelion greens, drain, and place in a large bowl. In a small bowl, combine the orange juice, oil, garlic, and salt and pepper to taste. Combine with the dandelion greens and toss. On a large platter, arrange the avocado slices, and eggs if using, around the outer edges. Sprinkle with freshly ground pepper. Pile dressed greens in the center of the plate.

Breakfast Millet with Sun-Dried Raisins and Apricots

by Rowena Hubbard

Serves 4 to 6

Sweet-tart, crunchy, and mellow all describe this hearty breakfast cereal perfectly. It's a nice change from oatmeal on a blustery day. Pan-toasting the millet before cooking gives it wonderful flavor and it only takes a minute. I like the texture a little crunchy, but if you prefer it softer and more like porridge, add an extra ¼ cup water during cooking. The sun-dried raisins make it sweet enough for my taste, but a drizzle of honey over the nonfat yogurt would be delicious.

> 1 tablespoon extra-virgin olive oil
> 1 cup millet
> 2 cups water
> ½ cup sun-dried raisins
> ½ cup dried apricot, snipped into pieces
> 3-inch cinnamon stick
> Plain nonfat yogurt
> Honey (optional)
> ¼ cup chopped walnuts

Heat oil in a heavy saucepan. Stir in millet until it begins to smell toasty and has turned golden. Add water, sun-dried raisins, apricots, and cinnamon stick. Bring mixture to a boil. Cover, turn heat down to simmer and cook 25 minutes, until all liquid is absorbed. Remove cinnamon stick and serve topped with a generous amount of nonfat yogurt, honey to taste, and a sprinkling of chopped walnuts.

EPILOGUE

IN JOY AND SADNESS, WE END OUR JOURNEY

There has been much joy and excitement during our long journey from the land of the Incas to equatorial Africa. We have made many discoveries along the way as we learned the nutrition secrets of the ancients. We have encountered the kinds of foods that kept these people alive and strong and that can keep us healthy and strong in the new millennium.

At the end of our trek, there is some sadness, too. We encountered tragic events, such as the destruction of amaranth in the Aztec civilization. And we have not had enough time to discover all of the great foods of each region—to do so would take decades and thousands of book pages.

Along with Robert Frost, we hope you'll choose the road less traveled; a road surrounded by fields of ancient foods that may make all the difference in your joy of life and in staying healthy. Stay on the path of ancient, real, unrefined whole foods. As time goes by, go beyond this book; discover some new berries or other fruits, some different beans and grains, some vegetables you have never tried before. Make whole plant foods the foundation of your diet. And forgive us if we left out some precious foods!

Sources

ANCIENT GOAT CHEESES

Yerba Santa Dairy
6850 Scotts Valley Road
Lakeport, CA 95453
707-263-8131
Goat cheeses

CULTURES FOR MILK, SOY PRODUCTS, AND BREADMAKING

Alton Spiller Inc.
P.O. Box 696
Los Altos, CA 94023
650-941-8288
barmbaker@aol.com
Dried leavening barm, acidity testing paper, sprouted wheat flour

GEM Cultures
30301 Sherwood Road
Fort Bragg, CA 95437
707-964-2922
gemcult@msn.org
Sourdough starters; tempeh, miso, and other cultured soy products; viili, filmjölk, and kefir starter; sea vegetation and food culturing cookbooks.

Rosell Institute, Inc.
8480 Boulevard St-Laurent
Montreal, Quebec H2P 2M6
Canada
514-381-5631
Cultures for yogurt, kefir, buttermilk, acidophilus milk; insulated yogurt maker

HERB AND SPICE PLANTS AND SEEDS

Companion Plants
7247 N. Coolville Ridge Road
Athens, OH 45701
Herb plants

Frontier Cooperative Herbs
P.O. Box 299
Norway, IA 52318
Herbs and spices

It's About Thyme
P.O. Box 878
Manchaca, TX 78652
Bee balm, epazote, Mexican tarragon

Mo-Hotta-Mo-Betta
P.O. Box 4136
San Luis Obispo, CA 93403
Dried chiles

Native Seed/Search
2509 N. Campbell Avenue, #325
Tucson, AZ 85719
Chile seeds

Pepper Gal
P.O. Box 23006
Fort Lauderdale, FL 33307
Chile seeds

Redwood City Seed Co.
P.O. Box 361
Redwood City, CA 94064
Chile seeds

Seeds of Change
P.O. Box 15700
Santa Fe, NM 87592
505-438-8080
www.seedsofchange.com
*Herb, edible flower, and
vegetable seeds*

Seed Savers Exchange
P.O. Box 70
Decorah, IA 52101
Chile seeds and other herbs

Shepherd's Garden Seeds
6116 Highway 9
Felton, CA 95018
408-335-6945
Herb and edible flower seeds

Sunnybrook Farms Nursery
9448 Mayfield Road
Chesterland, OH 44026
Herb plants

Well-Sweep Herb Farm
205 Mt. Bethel Road
Port Murray, NJ 07865
Bee balm, Mexican tarragon

KITCHEN EQUIPMENT

Kuhn-Rikon Corporation
P.O. Box 1184
Enfield, CT 06083-1184
800-662-5882
Pressure cookers

The Grain & Salt Society
273 Fairway Drive
Asheville, NC 28805
800-TOPSALT (800-867-7258)
www.celtic-seasalt.com
*Small grain mills, sea salt,
whole grains*

Sassafras Enterprises, Inc.
1622 West Carol Avenue
Chicago, IL 60612
312-226-2000
*Unglazed ceramic baking tiles,
bread cloches (domes), baking pots*

Williams-Sonoma
3250 Van Ness Avenue
San Francisco, CA 94109
415-421-7900
www.williams-sonoma.com
Specialty kitchen equipment

MAIL ORDER

Mail Order Catalog
P.O. Box 180
Summertown, TN 38483
800-695-2241
www.healthy-eating.com
*Whole-grain flours, sea vegetables,
baking supplies*

NUTRITION INFORMATION

Sphera Foundation
P.O. Box 338
Los Altos, CA 92023-0338
650-941-7251
nutrition@sphera.org
spiller@sphera.org
www.sphera.org
General nutrition information and videos

OLIVES AND EXTRA-VIRGIN OLIVE OILS

California Olive Oil Council
P.O. Box 7520
Berkeley, CA 94707-0520
888-718-9830
510-528-2271 fax
www.cooc.com
Information on olive oils from California

Manicaretti Italian Foods
5332 College Avenue, Suite 200
Oakland, CA 94618
510-655-0911
www.manicaretti.com
Olive oils and olives from Italy

Santa Barbara Olive Co.
12477 Calle Real
Santa Barbara, CA 93117
805-688-9917, 800-624-4896
805-562-1464 fax
www.sbolive.com
Olives and olive oils

RICE

Kenneth Ralph
Artistic Expressions
10338 Berkshire Road
Bloomington, MN 55437
612-832-0804
Ojibway Indian wild rice

Lundberg Family Farms
P.O. Box 369
Richvale, CA 95974
530-882-4551
Specialty brown rice varieties

SALT

The Grain & Salt Society
(see entry under Kitchen Equipment)

SEA VEGETATION

Maine Coast Sea Vegetables
3 Georges Pond Road
Franklin, ME 04634
207-565-2907
Edible sea vegetation and related food products

San Francisco Herb Co.
250 14th Street
San Francisco, CA 94102
415-861-7174
www.sfherb.com
Edible sea vegetation

TEAS

Silk Road Teas
P.O. Box 287
Lagunitas, CA 94938
415-488-9017
Ancient Chinese teas

UNUSUAL VEGETABLE OILS

Spectrum Naturals
1304 South Point Blvd., Suite 280
Petaluma, CA 94954
707-778-8900
www.spectrumnaturals.com
A wide variety of vegetable oils

VIDEOS

Sphera Foundation
videos@sphera.org
(see entry under Nutrition Information)

WHOLE GRAINS, WHOLE-GRAIN
FLOURS, BEANS, AND BARLEY
MALT SYRUPS

Arrowhead Mills, Inc.
110 South Lawton
Hereford, TX 79045
806-364-0730

Whole grains, whole-grain flours,
and beans

Bob's Red Mill
5209 SE International Way
Milwaukee, OR 97222
505-654-3215
www.bobsredmill.com

Whole grains, whole-grain flours,
and beans

Deer Valley Farms
P.O. Box 173
Guilford, NY 13780

Whole grains, whole-grain flours

Giusto's Specialty Foods
241 East Harris Avenue
South San Francisco, CA 94080
415-873-6566

Whole grains, whole-grain flours

Gold Mine Natural Food Co.
7805 Arjons Drive
San Diego, CA 92126-4368
800-475-3663, 858-537-9830
www.goldminenaturalfood.com

Whole grains, beans, and kitchen
equipment

The Grain and Salt Society
(see entry under Kitchen Equipment)

Kamut Association of North America
295 Distribution Street
San Marcos, CA 92069
619-752-5230

Kamut

King Arthur Flour
Route 5 South
Norwich, VT 05055

Baking supplies, barley malt syrup

Purity Foods
2871 West Jolly Road
Okemos, MI 48864
517-351-9231

Spelt

Quinoa Corporation
P.O. Box 279
Gardena, CA 90248
310-217-8125, 310-217-8140 fax
www.quinoa.net

Quinoa

Shiloh Farms
P.O. Box 97
Sulphur Springs, AR 72768

Whole grains and whole-grain flour

Tadco/Niblack
900 Jefferson Road, Bldg. 5
Rochester, NY 14623

Barley malt syrup

The Teff Company
P.O. Box A
Caldwell, ID 83606
208-454-3330

Teff

Walnut Acres
Penns Creek, PA 17862
717-847-0601

Whole grains and whole-grain flour

References

The following books and articles were great sources of information as we wrote *The Power of Ancient Foods*.

BOOKS

Andrews, Jean. *Peppers: The Domesticated Capsicums*. Austin: University of Texas Press, 1990.

—. *Red Hot Peppers*. New York: Macmillan, 1993.

Apicius. *De Re Coquinaria* (On Cooking). Edited and translated by Joseph Vehling. New York: Dover, 1977.

Assefa, Mulugeta. "Floral Morphogenesis, Temperature Effect on Growth and Development, and Variation in Nutritional Composition and Distribution Among Cultivars in *Eragrostis Tef* (zucc.)" Trotter. Dissertation, University of Wisconsin-Madison, 1978.

Ausubel, Kenny. *Seeds of Change: The Living Treasure*. San Francisco: Harper, 1994.

Bianchim, F.; Corbetta, F.; and Pistoia, M. *The Complete Book of Fruits and Vegetables*. New York: Crown, 1973.

Braun, Thomas. "Ancient Mediterranean Food" in *The Mediterranean Diets in Health and Disease* (G. Spiller, ed.). New York: Van Nostrand Reinhold, 1991.

Brennan, Jennifer. *The Cuisines of Asia*. New York: St. Martin's Press, 1984.

Burkitt, Denis P. and Trowell, Hugh C. *Refined Carbohydrate Foods and Disease: Some Implications of Dietary Fibre*. London: Academic Press, 1975.

Campbell-Pratt, G. *Fermented Foods of the World*. London: Butterworths, 1987.

Coe, Sophie D. *America's First Cuisines*. Austin: University of Texas Press, 1994.

Cost, Bruce. *Ginger East to West—A Cook's Tour With Recipes, Techniques, and Lore*. Berkeley, CA: Aris Books, 1984.

—. *Bruce Cost's Asian Ingredients*. New York: William Morrow, 1988.

David, Elizabeth. *A Book of Mediterranean Food*. Middlesex, England: Penguin Books, 1965.

DeWitt, Dave, and Bosland, Paul A. *The Pepper Garden*. Berkeley, CA: Ten Speed Press, 1991.

DeWitt, Dave, and Gerlach, Nancy. *The Whole Chile Pepper Book*. Toronto: Little, Brown (Canada), 1990.

Dille, Carolyn, and Belsinger, Susan. *The Chile Pepper Book*. Loveland, CO: Interweave Press, 1994.

Field, Carol. *The Italian Baker*. New York: Harper & Row, 1985.

Fitzgerald, C. P. *The Horizon History of China*. New York: American Heritage, 1969.

Foster, Steven. *Herbal Renaissance*. Salt Lake City, UT: Gibbs Smith, 1984.

Frost, Robert. *The Road Not Taken*. New York: Henry Holt, 1971 (first published 1916).

Fussell, Betty. *The Story of Corn*. New York: Alfred A. Knopf, 1992.

Garland, Sarah. *The Complete Book of Herbs and Spices*. New York: Viking, 1979.

Greene, Bert. *The Grains Cookbook*. New York: Workman, 1988.

Hampstead, Marilyn. *The Basil Book*. New York: Pocket Books, 1984.

Ho, Chi-Tang; Lee, Chang Y.; and Huang, Mou-Tuan (eds.). *Phenolic Compounds in Food and Their Effects on Health*. Washington, D.C.: American Chemical Society, 1992.

Jit Singh, Dharm. *Classic Cooking from India*. New York: Houghton Mifflin, 1956.

Katzen, Mollie. *The Enchanted Broccoli Forest*. Berkeley, CA: Ten Speed Press, 1982.

Kremezi, Aglaia. *The Foods of Greece*. New York: Stewart, Tobori and Chang,1993.

La Place, Viana. *Verdura: Vegetables Italian Style*. New York: William Morrow, 1991.

Lappe, Frances Moore. *Diet for a Small Planet: High Protein Meatless Cooking*. New York: Ballantine Books, 1982.

Lathrop, Norma Jean. *Herbs: How to Select, Grow, and Enjoy*. Tucson, AZ: HP Books, 1981.

Madison, Deborah. *The Savory Way*. New York: Bantam Books, 1990.

Madison, Deborah, and Brown, Edward Espe. *The Greens Cookbook*. New York: Bantam Books, 1987.

Moseley, Michael E. *The Incas and Their Ancestors*. New York: Thames and Thomas, 1993 (first published in 1992).

Naj, Amal. *Peppers: A Story of Hot Pursuits*. New York: Alfred A. Knopf, 1992.

National Research Council. *Diet and Health*. Washington, D.C.: National Academy Press, 1980.

National Research Council. *Lost Crops of the Incas*. Washington, D.C.: National Academy Press, 1989.

Owen, Sri. *The Rice Book*. New York: St. Martin's Press, 1993.

Passmore, Jacki. *The Encyclopedia of Asian Food and Cooking*. New York: William Morrow, 1991.

Paul, A. A., and Southgate, D. A. T. *The Composition of Foods*. London: Her Majesty's Stationery Office, 1978.

Popenoe, Paul B. *Date Growing in the Old and New Worlds*, Los Angeles: George Rice & Sons, 1913.

Rama Rau, Santha. *The Cooking of India*. New York: Time-Life Books, Foods of the World, 1969.

Robbins, John. *May All Be Fed: Diet for a New World*. New York: William Morrow, 1992.

Roden, Claudia. *A Book of Middle Eastern Food.* New York: Vintage Books, 1974.

Rose, A. H. (ed.). *Fermented Foods.* London: Academic Press, 1982.

Rosengarten, Frederic. *The Book of Spices.* New York: Jove, 1971.

Sabat, J., and Hook, D. G. "Almonds, walnuts, and serum lipids" in *Handbook of Lipids in Human Nutrition* (G. Spiller, ed.). Boca Raton, FL: CRC Press, 1995.

Sass, Lorna. *Recipes from an Ecological Kitchen.* New York: William Morrow, 1992.

Schafer-Schuchardt, Horst. *L'Oliva: La Grande Storia Di Un Piccolo Frutto.* Italy: Schafer-Schuchardt, 1988.

Schneider, Elizabeth. *Uncommon Fruits and Vegetables,* New York: Harper & Row, 1986.

Solomon, Jay. *Lean Bean Cuisine.* Rocklin, CA: Prima Publishing, 1995.

Spiller, Gene A. *The Methylxanthine Beverages and Foods.* New York: Alan R. Liss, 1985.

—. *The Superpyramid Eating Program.* New York: Times Books, 1993.

Spiller, Gene A. (ed.). *Handbook of Dietary Fiber in Human Nutrition.* Boca Raton, FL: CRC Press, 1986.

—. *The Mediterranean Diets in Health and Disease.* New York: Van Nostrand Reinhold, 1991.

—. *Handbook of Lipids in Human Nutrition.* Boca Raton, FL: CRC Press, 1995.

Spiller, Monica. *The Barm Bakers Book.* Los Altos, CA: Sphaera Publishing, 1992.

Steinberg, Raphael. *Pacific and Southeast Asian Cooking.* New York: Time-Life Books, Foods of the World, 1970.

Tarmahill, Reay. *Food in History.* New York: Crown, 1989.

Toussaint-Samat, Maguelonne. *History of Food.* Cambridge, England: Blackwell, 1992.

Townsend, Richard F. *The Aztecs.* New York: Thames and Hudson, 1993 (first published 1992).

Trowell, Hugh C., and Burkitt, Denis P. *Western Diseases.* Cambridge, MA: Harvard University Press, 1981.

Trowell, Hugh C.; Burkitt, Denis P.; and Heaton, Kenneth. *Dietary Fibre, Fibre-Depleted Foods and Disease.* London: Academic Press, 1985.

van der Post, Laurens. *African Cooking.* New York: Time-Life Books, Foods of the World, 1970.

Vennum, Thomas, Jr. *Wild Rice and the Ojibway People.* St. Paul, MN: Minnesota Historical Society Press, 1988.

Waldron, K.W.; Johnson, I.T.; and Fenwick, G.R. (eds.). *Food and Cancer Prevention: Chemical and Biological Aspects.* Cambridge, England: The Royal Society of Chemistry, 1993.

Weatherford, Jack. *Indian Givers.* New York: Fawcett Columbine, 1988.

Wills, Wirt H. *Early Prehistoric Agriculture in the American Southwest.* Santa Fe, NM: School of American Research Press, 1988.

Wood, Rebecca. *Quinoa the Supergrain, Ancient Food for Today.* Japan Publications, 1989.

EGYPTIAN BREAD REFERENCES

Faridi, Hamed. "Flat Breads" in *Wheat Chemistry and Technology*, (Y. Pomeranz, ed.). American Association of Cereal Chemists, St. Paul, MN: 1988.

Roden, Claudia. *Mediterranean Cookery*. New York: Alfred A. Knopf, 1987.

NORTHERN COUNTRIES REFERENCES

Brown, Dale. *The Cooking of Scandinavia*. New York: Time-Life Books, Foods of the World, 1968.

Hartley, Dorothy. *Food in England*. London: Macdonald & Janes, 1954.

McNeill, F. Marion. *The Scots Kitchen: Its Lore and Recipes*. London: Collins, 1989 (first published 1929).

Renfrew, Jane. *Food and Cooking in Prehistoric Britain: History and Recipes*. England: Historic Buildings and Monuments Commission, 1985.

Slebsager, Astrid. *Cooking with the Danes*. Copenhagen: Host & Sons Forlag, 1978.

Nilson, Bee. *The Penguin Cookery Book*. Middlesex, England: Penguin Books, 1952.

Waaland, J. Robert. *Common Seaweeds of the Pacific Coast*. Seattle, WA: Pacific Search Press, 1977.

White, James and Elizabeth. *Good Food from Denmark and Norway*. London: Frederick Muller, 1959.

Wilson, C. Anne. *Food and Drink in Britain*. Chicago: Academy Chicago Publishers, 1991 (first published 1973).

RAISIN BREAD AND OLIVE BREAD REFERENCES

Dick, J. W and Matsuo, R. R. "Durum Wheat and Pasta Products" in *Wheat Chemistry and Technology* (Y. Pomeranz, ed.). St. Paul, MN: American Association of Cereal Chemists, 1988.

Roden, Claudia. *The Good Food of Italy: Region by Region*. New York: Alfred A. Knopf, 1991.

Romer, Elizabeth. *Italian Pizza and Savoury Breads*. London: Grafton Books, 1990 (first published 1987).

RUSSIAN BREAD REFERENCES

Chamberlain, Lesley. *The Food and Cooking of Eastern Europe*. London: Penguin Books, 1989.

Papashvily, Helen and George. *Russian Cooking*. New York: Time-Life Books, Foods of the World, 1969.

Wechsberg, Joseph. *The Cooking of Vienna's Empire*. New York: Time-Life Books, Foods of the World, 1968.

ARTICLES AND SCIENTIFIC PAPERS

Anderson, J. W.; Johnstone, B. M.; and Cook-Newell, M. E. "Meta-analysis of the effects of soy protein intake on serum lipids." *The New England Journal of Medicine* 333 (5): 276-314, 1995.

Caragay, A. B. "Cancer-preventive foods and ingredients." *Food Technology*, April: 65-68, 1992.

Chili Pepper (bimonthly magazine). Out West Publishing, P.O. Box 80780, Albuquerque, NM 87198.

Doll, R. "The geographical distribution of cancer." *British Journal of Cancer* 211-8, 1969.

Grundy, S. M. "Monounsaturated fatty acids, plasma cholesterol, and coronary heart disease." *American Journal of Clinical Nutrition* 45 (5 Suppl.): 1168-1175, 1987.

Hertog, M. G. L.; Hollman, P. C. H.; and Katan, M. B. "Content of potentially anticarcinogenic flavonoids of 28 vegetables and 9 fruits commonly consumed in the Netherlands." *Journal of Agricultural and Food Chemistry* 40: 2379-2383, 1992.

Jenkins, D. J. A., and Wong, G. S., et al. "Leguminous seeds in the management of hyperlipidemia." *American Journal of Clinical Nutrition* 38: 567-573, 1983.

Kastellot, H., and Da Men, Huang, et al. "Serum lipids in the People's Republic of China." *Arteriosclerosis* 5: 427-433, 1985.

National Institute of Health. "Lowering blood cholesterol to prevent heart disease." Consensus Development Conference Statement. Volume 5, number 7, 1985.

Peto, R., and Doll, R., et al. "Can dietary beta-carotene materially reduce human cancer rates?" *Nature* 290: 201-208, 1981.

Spiller, G. A. "Beyond dietary fiber," *American Journal of Clinical Nutrition* 54 (4): 615-617, 1991

—. "Health effects of Mediterranean diets and monounsaturated fats." *Cereal Food World* 36: 812, 1991

Spiller, G. A.; Jenkins D. J. A.; Cragen L. N., et al. "Effect of a diet high in monounsaturated fat from almonds on plasma cholesterol and lipoproteins." *Journal of the American College of Nutrition* 11(2): 126-130, 1992.

Trevisan, M.; Krogh, V.; and Freudenheim, J. et al. "Consumption of olive oil, butter, and vegetable oils and coronary heart disease risk factors." The Research Group ATS-RF2 of the Italian National Research Council. *Journal of the American Medical Association* 263 (5): 688-692, 1990.

Watson, R. R., and Leonard, T. K. "Selenium and vitamins A, E, and C: Nutrients with cancer prevention properties." *Journal of the American Dietetic Association* 86: 505-510, 1986.

Willet, C. W. "The search for the causes of breast and colon cancer." *Nature* 338:389, 1989.

Recipe Index

Subject Index

BOOK PUBLISHING COMPANY

since 1974—books that educate, inspire, and empower

To find your favorite vegetarian products online, visit:
www.healthy-eating.com

Authentic Chinese Cuisine
for the Contemporary
Kitchen
Bryanna Clark Grogan
1-57067-101-X $12.95

Japanese Cooking:
Contemporary & Traditional
Miyoko Nishimoto Schinner
1-57067-072-2 $12.95

Nonna's Italian Kitchen
*Delicious Home-Style Vegan
Cuisine*
Bryanna Clark Grogan
1-57067-055-2 $14.95

From the Tables of Lebanon
*Dalal A. Holmin &
Maher A. Abbas, MD*
1-57067-040-4 $12.95

From a Traditional Greek
Kitchen: *Vegetarian Cuisine*
Aphrodite Polemis
0-913990-93-0 $12.95

Flavors of the Southwest
Vegetarian Style
Robert Oser
1-57067-049-8 $12.95

Purchase these vegetarian cookbooks from your local bookstore or natural foods
store, or you can buy them directly from:

Book Publishing Company
P.O. Box 99 • Summertown, TN 38483 • 1-800-695-2241

Please include $3.95 per book for shipping and handling.